Elements of Information Systems

The AAT Series

Paper 5	ACCOUNTING	P.G. Cassidy
Paper 6	ELEMENTS OF INFORMATION SYSTEMS	L. Seymour-Smith
Paper 7	BUSINESS LAW	D. Palfreman
Paper 8	ECONOMICS AND STATISTICS	A.C. Shafto
Paper 9	FINANCIAL ACCOUNTING	P.G. Cassidy
Paper 11	ANALYSIS AND DESIGN OF INFORMATION SYSTEMS	L. Seymour-Smith

ELEMENTS OF INFORMATION SYSTEMS

A Study Text for AAT

Leonard Seymour-Smith

Stanley Thornes (Publishers) Ltd

First published in 1990 by:
Stanley Thornes (Publishers) Ltd
Old Station Drive
Leckhampton
CHELTENHAM GL53 0DN
England

British Library Cataloguing in Publication Data

Seymour-Smith, Leonard.
    Elements of information systems: a study text for AAT.
    1. Accounting. Applications of computer systems
    I. Title
    657.0285
    ISBN 0–7487–0405–1

Typeset in Century Schoolbook and Optima by Tech-Set, Gateshead, Tyne & Wear.
Printed and bound in Great Britain at The Bath Press, Avon.

Contents

	Preface	vi
1	The concept of information	1
2	Information processing	13
3	Computer hardware 1	25
4	Computer hardware 2	39
5	Files and their storage	51
6	The storage media	65
7	Communications and networks	73
8	Software	83
9	Flowcharting, decision tables and programming	95
10	Organisation and control 1	111
11	Organisation and control 2	123
12	Organisation and control 3	135
13	Organisation and control 4	147
14	Twenty questions and answers	155
15	Abbreviations used in this book	161
16	Bibliography	163
	Index	165

Preface

The syllabus of *Elements of Information Systems* is designed so that, provided you have put the necessary effort in, you will develop an understanding of:
- the role of information technology (IT) in business – with special reference to accounting
- the ways in which the necessary information is captured, stored, processed and transmitted.

One very important aspect is that in the examination you *must* be able to explain and use the relevant terminology, so you would be very well advised to pay special attention to this! It would also be useful to read newspapers and journals, and extract relevant articles and reports on the latest kind of IT development. These will usually be found in the business sections of newspapers, and, of course, in professional journals.

This subject is especially important from the practical aspect. IT is rapidly becoming a significant part of the accountant's working life and your study of EIS will give you a valuable background to system developments in the office.

The syllabus contains the following topics.

Information   (weighting 20%)
- the nature of data and information
- the role of information in business
- general characteristics of information
- methods of information processing, from manual to batch, on-line and interactive methods
- general concepts of files, structure, content and organisation

Hardware   (weighting 30%)
- input equipment for batch, on-line and other data capture methods
- the central processor unit, structure and function
- file hardware, and implications for processing methods
- output equipment in both hard and soft form
- data transmission, modems, multiplexors and local area networks

Software   (weighting 30%)
- using and acquiring packages
- computer language and utilities
- problem definition and flowcharting
- programming principles and good practice

Organisation and control   (weighting 20%)
- procedures for data vet and validations
- staff tasks in a data processing department
- security and controls
- standards and documentation

Note that EIS is the basis for studying *Analysis and Design of Information Systems* (ADIS) which is a subject in the final stage of AAT. Questions will not be set on the analysis and the design of information systems in the EIS paper.

CHAPTER 1
The concept of information

Introduction

We begin by pointing out that there are two terms which must not be confused: *data* and *information*. Data (strictly speaking a plural word, though generally regarded as singular, so that we usually say 'data is') is really day-to-day items – the *raw material* or figures, which do not in themselves allow any effective decisions to be made. The data is *processed* and this results in *information*.

It is information derived from the basic data which provides the management of an organisation with the foundation upon which to make their decisions. So we have:

INPUT OF DATA ⟶ PROCESSING OF DATA ⟶ MANAGEMENT INFORMATION

We have used the term *management information* here but the same principle applies to all data, for whatever purpose it may be used. We *input* data by reading a train timetable, and then we can make a decision about our plans for travelling from point A to point B. Our *processing* would involve such important calculations as how long the journey takes and so on. However, we are concerned here with information for management use.

The role of information in business

The term *business* denotes a very broad range of organisations including public and private sector units. The former are government controlled and their specific objectives may relate to economic, political and/or social concerns, yet they have to operate within given budget limits. This means that such bodies need sufficient information concerning their operations and their environment to enable them to work within these constraints. Those controlling public sector bodies need up-to-date information to determine whether they are acting within ministerial guidelines.

The private sector body is similar in its approach to information, except that it has different objectives. The private firm is concerned with maintaining its profitability and thereby raising the value of its shares. However, there are likely to be other goals, such as diversification of product, establishing overseas markets and so forth. Irrespective of this difference, the need for data to input and produce decision-making information is vital.

Functional activity areas in business

Let us consider the typical manufacturing organisation in order to look at the kind of areas which would have to be covered by adequate information.

Production
- levels of output (by product and by shift)
- operating statements
- manpower utilisation (man-hours)

- machine capacity required (forecast)
- reject levels (i.e. wastage and scrap arising from production)

There is also *production control,* an extremely important element. Production planning determines what is to be manufactured, over what period of time and how this is to be carried out. Production control makes sure that the production plans are properly implemented. This requires information as to:

- the quantity of raw materials required per period of production
- the quantity of machine time, tools and other equipment required
- man-hours needed per shift
- progress made with each job, and any explanations for delays.

Clearly, there is much more to it than this, but here we have a general idea of the size of the information-provision task.

Marketing
- customer orders (by product and sales region)
- levels of stock
- survey results (marketing and opinion research, etc.)
- sales representative performance
- costing of stockholding, transport

Personnel
- total number of employees, by grade and category
- job descriptions
- hours (worked, absent, overtime, unpunctuality)
- recruitment and training and development needs

Purchasing (or acquisition)
- price, quality and delivery quotations from suppliers
- order progress (checking orders placed, delivery, orders overdue)
- goods received (monitoring correct delivery – quantity, type, quality)
- supplier invoices – monitoring for accuracy prior to payment
- up-to-date supplier prices, supplier performance in relation to future orders

Financial
Under this broad heading, we have to be careful to distinguish between these financial activities:

- financial management, with the objective of maximising the effective usage of company funds
- financial accounting, which is the more general recording of company activities in financial terms
- management (cost) accounting, which is really founded on the management's need to obtain information for decision-making (related to undertaking the organisation's activities at acceptable cost) and for the monitoring of discrepancies.

If we take these activities as falling under the *financial* heading, then we find we have:

- annual (statutory) accounts
- budgets
- capital project appraisal
- statutory returns (e.g. VAT)
- standard costing.

Inventory control
This is clearly linked to *warehouse control* which is concerned mostly with methods of operating the warehouse, or *stores,* and is for the purpose of monitoring and deciding about items held in store. The stock items are held at the optimum level at which demand may be satisfied from the

store supply, the latter being from an external supplier (in the case of raw materials) or from the firm's own output (in the case of finished goods). For this activity information is needed to cover:

- capital tied up in stocks
- deterioration and wastage
- stock levels
- costs of storage, re-ordering
- issues from stock.

Clearly, we have not provided a complete list of the firm's activities or, therefore, its information needs. We do now have a good idea of the wide-ranging requirements which an information system has to meet if the firm is to be successful – or even continue to exist!

Note that this need for information results in the need for a way of processing data rapidly and accurately. Today this is provided for by computerisation.

The management information system (MIS)

Before we begin this area of our study, we must explain the term *system*. This is important because we shall be using it many times from now on! A system is

a collection of components or elements which interact in an organised manner in order to achieve a pre-determined objective.

In other words a tree, a motor vehicle and a human being are each examples of systems, the last two being complex versions! A system can be very basic and simple, or it can be highly involved.

Sometimes the *components* of a system are in themselves systems or, more accurately, *sub-systems*. If you examine our definition carefully, you will see that the system has

- a reason for existing
- organisation so that the components work together
- different parts.

So, what is a management information system? A straightforward definition is

an approach to the collection, processing and communication of data in the format which is appropriate to assist those responsible for the use of resources.

From what we have already said, it may be reasonably inferred that each team of managers within a given organisation may well have their own individual, specialised MIS. However, contemporary computer systems allow the introduction of the *Integrated Management Information System* (IMIS).

The IMIS consists of sub-systems developed and coordinated so that each separate sub-system may relate to the others. There is centralisation, which means simply that the electronic data processing (EDP) unit acts as the headquarters of the IMIS and so one set of data may be associated with another set, or sets, for processing. One way of doing this is to use the network of budgets in the organisation as the foundation.

The MIS (integrated in some way or not) consists of a grouping of disciplines, techniques, methods and procedures, use of which permits the collection, analysis and distribution of material to help management. The advanced form of MIS, integrated and using IT, would incorporate:

- special techniques such as simulation and modelling, and critical path analysis approaches (CPA), to apply to management problems
- means of processing and distributing very large quantities of data, such as a linkage of a large mainframe with several processors to microcomputers
- sub-systems for dealing with necessary routines such as sales invoicing or stock analysis.

We must not forget that when we talk about the MIS we refer to a system which deals with both internal and external information. The source of the data may be internal, i.e. generated within the organisation itself. On the other hand, it may stem from outside the firm, as in the case of official statistics of industrial output, the national income and so on. The effective and efficient MIS will incorporate all kinds of facts and figures relating to the organisation and its management.

Expressing the idea of the MIS in categorical terms we usually refer to it as a *complex, deterministic system.* It is complex because it embraces a number of major functions in the organisation (marketing, production, purchasing, warehousing, and all the others which exist). It is deterministic because the output of the MIS – information – is predictable in the sense that it is the outcome of formal, logical rules and procedures by which the processing is carried out. Thus, total sales would be the result of the input of all sales orders accepted during a given period in relation to each product. This obviously does not mean that an exact figure can be forecast beforehand, but only that *some* accumulated total will be made available through the MIS procedures. If the existence of the outcome could *not* be predicted, then the system would have to be classed as *probabilistic,* not *deterministic.* The organisation, in all its complexity, subject to many forces and influences from inside and outside, is in itself a complex, probabilistic system. So is a betting system which guarantees a winner!

Internal and external facts and figures

Let us take a closer look at the nature of the internal and external inputs to the MIS. We shall take as our example the Marketing Department of a large firm. Here we have:

Inputs generated by the firm's activities (documents)
- customer sales orders
- goods returned notes, despatch notes
- details of arrangements for discounts and credit conditions
- reports of sales representatives (regarding customers, expenses incurred, etc.)

Externally presented information (official and other statistics)
- national income and other figures
- population (demographic) statistics – totals, regional location, age-structures, etc.
- statistics from industrial associations and other bodies
- reports resulting from research (marketing, etc.)

Information output by marketing department
- results analysis (by area and by product)
- customer analysis (by industry, region, order size)
- sales cost analysis (by region, representative, product)
- forecasts (stock levels, sales)

The very important thing to bear in mind is that *everybody* who is working for a given organisation, quite irrespective of its type, or the product or services it creates, or its location, *must* have information – but not everybody requires the same frequency of presentation, or the same detail, or the same kinds of facts and figures.

The grading of information

In general, we can say that managers relate the information they get to the facts and figures which they already have, and also to their individual experience. We can grade information in several ways. In broad terms, we can say that managers have to know about the following three major aspects of their task:
- the nature and availability of resources of all kinds (e.g. man-hours available, manpower allocation, capacity of machines, budget data)
- actual resource usage (progress, achievement of objectives, targets, etc.)
- usage rate of resources (output rate per worker, raw materials consumption rate, expenditure or budget rate).

On the other hand, we can consider the *levels* of information. These correspond to the three broad gradings of management: strategic or *top* management, tactical or *middle* or *line* managers, and *operational* or *supervisory* management.

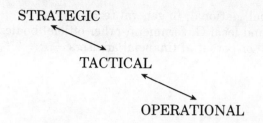

Strategic

This level of information is needed by senior management. These are functional heads, such as the Director of Marketing, or Head of Finance. This information allows them to determine corporate strategies (i.e. the long-term courses of action which are to achieve the corporate objectives some years ahead), and also to maintain strategic control.

This information stems from internal and external sources and is general and wide-ranging in nature. It also relates to a broad span of time and is used for long-term forecasting (a vital requirement for corporate planning activity). Typical information items include:

● market forecasts
● level of capital expenditure necessitated by plans
● government industrial policy.

Tactical

Here, the information is required by line management so that they can carry out the monitoring of their work activities. This means that they must monitor use of resources in order to maintain or improve effectiveness and efficiency.

The information is fundamentally accounting-based and is mainly derived from internal sources. Outline information is provided by their superiors (strategic managers) and this serves as a set of guidelines within which the tactical managers must work.

Typical items are:

● levels of productivity (relationship of output to input)
● manpower availability
● costings.

Operational

Management here consists of supervisors, foremen, heads of clerical sections. The need is for information which permits given activities to be carried out in both workshop and office. Facts relate to the short-term (i.e., what is happening now or will happen tomorrow), and is thus day-to-day, in contrast with the facts and figures for strategic management's use. This information is also, of necessity, very detailed, as opposed to broad and wide-ranging.

Some operational information may be based on weekly periods (as in the case of a wages section), or it may be needed much more frequently (as in the case of Air Traffic Control at Heathrow Airport). Examples are:

● customers' names and addresses (e.g. for deliveries)
● product price lists
● customers' credit status.

Note that, in respect of the three levels, the information needed does differ in the amount of detail. The lower the grading, the greater the detail demanded and also, in the time-span, the lower the grade, the narrower this span is.

A third approach to grading information is in accordance with the user groupings. These may be considered as three groups.

Group A
- the public – international, national, in general terms
- official units – central and local Government, other official bodies
- shareholders and actual or potential financial advisers

Group B
- the Board of Directors
- strategic management
- tactical (line) management, and operational management

Group C
- persons in employment of the organisation, trade unions

Note that Group A is comprised of external recipients of information. However, they can influence the organisation in some way and they have the right to obtain information which is a statutory obligation.

Group B require information, otherwise they are not able to undertake their activities – they constitute management.

Group C may well be provided with *motivational* facts and figures since they are employed by a *participatory management* firm for the making of certain decisions which affect them or their work conditions. There may also be a statutory requirement that certain information must be provided.

Reports

The kind of information provided for managers – as well as the utilisation of this – is hardly likely to be the same for all organisations. Even so, we can produce a standard list of categories of reports produced and received by management.

Regular reports
These are created on a cyclical basis as an automatic procedure. Generally speaking, they are linked to some regular activity, such as wages preparation or stocktaking, or perhaps to the budgetary cycle.

Ad hoc reports
Such reports are special in that they are not listed as part of the regular reporting sequence. They are usually required within a short period of time and may never be wanted again.

On-demand reports
Here, we have an attempt to avoid the regular production of reports when there is no actual need for them. The reports are listed for preparation on a regular basis, but are not actually prepared unless specifically sought. On the other hand, there is simply the facility available for the report to be presented whenever it is wanted (e.g. on 10 January instead of 1 January).

Exception reports
This type of report is presented if an unusual event or *exception* occurs. The philosophy here is that 'good news is no news at all'! If no report is presented, then all is well. In this manner, management attention is drawn to unusual events and/or items.

The chief problem here is the definition of *exception*. When should the report be presented, and subject to what conditions?

Information flows

Information travels or flows in several directions, and it is essential to understand what these are if the MIS is to be effective and efficient.

Vertical flow

This direction is directly upwards, or directly downwards. The simplest way of expressing it is like this.

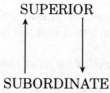

SUPERIOR

SUBORDINATE

Note that the upwards flow is the passing of information to the superior (this is *feedback*).

The downwards flow would comprise of instructions, or the making of suggestions, to the subordinate.

Horizontal flow

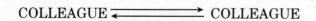

COLLEAGUE ⟵⟶ COLLEAGUE

Here, we have the transfer of information between people of the same grade (in the same section or department or not).

Diagonal flow

This signifies that a given superior's subordinate is giving information to another superior, not his own. On the other hand, a superior could be in direct contact with somebody else's subordinate.

SUPERIOR A   SUPERIOR B

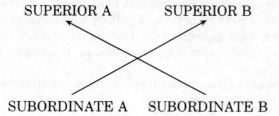

SUBORDINATE A   SUBORDINATE B

This sometimes occurs as a short-cut to save time, and may well be an informal method.

The diagonal flow is generally undertaken when all the parties have agreed to this as a useful approach. If it is not acceptable, then, for instance, there would have to be horizontal flow between B and A, vertical downward flow from Superior A to Subordinate A, vertical upward flow from Subordinate A to Superior A, and then horizontal flow from Superior A to Superior B.

It must also be remembered that these flows are undertaken through channels or *media* and there are very many versions of these, such as: written reports, oral reports, electronic transmission, graphics, facsimile, meetings, videos, etc.

Information handling

Information handling is the term used for collecting, manipulating and transmitting information. It is the basic activity in all office functions.

The handling process

Expressing the process of handling more precisely, we see that there are several specific activities involved:
- input of data – facts and figures are transcribed onto a document which is a report, or a *worksheet*

- validation of data – these facts are then examined for any errors
- presentation of data – in such a way as to give management facts and figures which are of use
- distribution – so that specific persons receive the facts and figures.

By the time the stage of distribution has been reached, the data will have become information.

We still have two further activities (which cannot be undertaken by electronic devices): *productive and creative thinking,* and *administering* or *managing.* The whole range of information available is processed as and when it is received in data form, and then communicated.

Information to be placed in storage is determined by specialists in the functional areas (e.g. marketing) and the extent to which this will be available in general and usable form will depend upon the internal and external environment of the organisation. Thus we have information classified as:

- *short-term* (accessible without difficulty, but which is not useful for more than a given period of time, e.g. current stock levels)
- *long-term* (including archive, historical information for occasional reference).

The key question to be asked is always *who* needs *what* information so that they can provide a maximum contribution to the efficiency and effectiveness of the organisation?

The information environment (IE)

The information environment is really the overall, complete view of how the total organisation (*all* the individuals working in it, their opinions, their views) perceives the firm's objectives, products, performance, attitude, culture. This overall perception has to be linked to the information and communication characteristics of the firm's external environment to be complete, thus becoming the IE.

The complete overall view is often called the *information space* and is subjective – it is collective personal opinion. It is likely to alter as the firm itself alters. The idea of this is that the organisation – whatever kind it may be – has a behaviour pattern or culture which makes it react in accord with its overall view. The information generated by the organisation will be in accordance with the individual's reaction to, and his or her perception of, the degree of uncertainty existing.

You will see that this is so when we now look at the four main categories of information environment. One category will result in the creation of another.

Stable environment
The forces which act in conflict with the organisation are considered to be of a stable kind, more or less. Problems are tackled when they manifest themselves. From this state of affairs the restrictive environment arises.

Restrictive environment
The advantage of possessing longer-term information is acknowledged in order to prevent – or at least reduce the impact of – groups of problems which are now recognised as existing. For this reason, trends, cycles and data analysis are determined and also forecasting is undertaken. This situation may become a competitive environment.

Competitive environment
Other organisations enter the market and competition is heavy. Strategic (corporate) plans must be developed and thus the need for relevant information is perceived. This becomes a dynamic environment.

Dynamic environment
Now there is the essential need to introduce continuous monitoring of the situation. Feedback of information must be given major priority to combat rapidly changing influences.

It will be the task of management to allow or to restrict the reactions of individual members working within the firm, in strict accord with their own (management's) perception of the real position.

Communication implications of information

Clearly, information has to be communicated in some way. A communication network must exist. A message is transmitted and someone, somewhere, has to receive it. Diagramatically, we have this situation.

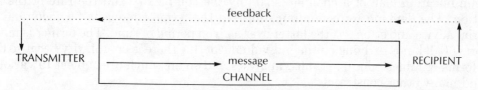

All systems of communication have the objective of comprehension. The transmitter encodes the message in the appropriate format and the recipient decodes it. The channel is the medium through which the message is sent, and feedback acknowledges receipt and seeks any necessary clarification.

The danger is the presence of *noise,* which, as earlier studies of communication will have told you, is anything at all which interferes with comprehension of the message. This can range from actual sounds (e.g. background noises on a telephone line) to use of jargon which the recipient may not understand.

Problems in communicating information

It is very important that we recognise potential problems in the communication of information. Since the facts and figures transmitted form the foundation upon which management decisions have to be made, difficulties must not be allowed to cause a barrier between the transmitter and the recipient. We may classify these problems as *organisational* and *individual.*

Organisational communication problems
- *Organisational levels* These constitute the basic structure of the organisation and there is a definite association between the size of the body – be it a commercial enterprise or a local authority – and the number of hierarchical levels of management. Any information channel would be obliged to follow the course of its transmission which is determined by the procedures currently applying. This could result in delay caused by the structure of the formal (officially established) organisation. So, a message from A to F would have to proceed via B, C, D and E. In such cases the route actually followed could be an *unofficial* or *informal* one, perhaps directly from B to F. However, this avoidance of the official route may not be tolerated.
- *Team, or group, interaction* The standards and *culture* (behaviour pattern) of the group to which the recipient belongs can cause misinterpretation of the message received. In other words, the message could be decoded wrongly because of a faulty perception (remember the information environment?). The words and the manner in which the message is expressed have to conform.
- *Location* A geographical distribution of warehouses, workshops, branches and other work units can, as you would expect, make setting up a communication network very difficult where the distances involved are great.
- *Overall size* The bigger the organisation is, the less easy it is to determine individual responsibility for information provision, precise need and appropriateness, and the objectives of the facts and figures. In the same way, a large organisation may well have a high staff turnover so that the communication approach may well need to be re-determined relatively frequently.

Individual problems

- *Incorrect assumption concerning the recipient* The transmitter may assume, wrongly, that the recipient is aware of specific matters and/or of the meaning of certain terminology.
- *Compatibility* The message has to be compatible with the awareness, intelligence, standing and experience of the recipient.
- *Indifferent presentation* The information provided may be shrouded in complex narrative, and/or be accompanied by too many confusing charts and diagrams.

Loading the channel

The communication load of a channel is simply the complexity and the rate of the input of information. The demand for communication – in the form of requests for facts and figures, managerial advice and so on – is the latter over a given period of time. The former is made up of the reports of all kinds arriving on the individual's desk – there is complexity because there are various forms of tables, charts, graphs, analyses and so on which are subject to various time-scales and many other constraints.

The actual total flow of information is caused because firstly, there is a set of conditions (the organisation's environment, the circumstances in which it exists) which dictate the number of communication channels in existence at a given moment, as well as their capacity and the physical constraints involved (e.g. geographical location). Also, there is the general requirement for information within the organisation, and the perception of this by everyone concerned. The third element giving rise to the information flow is the extent to which the individuals receiving and handling the facts and figures are capable of undertaking this activity effectively.

So we have:

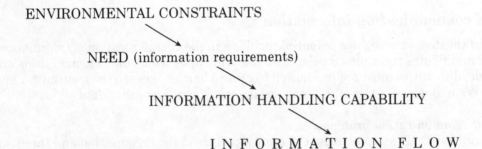

ENVIRONMENTAL CONSTRAINTS

NEED (information requirements)

INFORMATION HANDLING CAPABILITY

INFORMATION FLOW

Once the flow of information is established, we can determine the information load. What is sought is the optimum loading, whereas, in fact, there may often be *overload* or even *underload*.

Information overload

This arises where the source of the information using a channel is actually greater than the channel's capacity. The input of information (inflow) exceeds the actual capacity of the system for processing.

Overload causes tension and stress and, frequently, errors. The processing time has to be extended to cope.

Information underload

The channel's capacity is greater than the inflow of information required. Monotony may well be experienced by individuals in this situation. 'Sitting all day waiting for the telephone to ring' is an illustration of this.

Ways in which organisations attempt to cope with information overload include complete reorganisation of MIS responsibilities and contracting with external agencies (e.g. computer bureaux) to handle the extra work.

Information characteristics

We have looked at a wide variety of facts relating to information, and we can infer that information undertakes three kinds of tasks.

Modification and amendment
It changes misunderstandings, misrepresentations, wrong views, mis-statements.

Education
It educates because it provides the foundation for long-term comprehension in matters such as organisational interrelationships and company perceptions.

Explanation
Information also gives an account of, for example, the objectives of the organisation, or activities undertaken. As a general rule, we would expect information for this purpose to fall within the Groups A, B, and C considered earlier in this chapter.

The important issue here is that all information, for whatever purpose, must accomplish the objective of the communication and must be correctly and appropriately encoded for recipients.

Essential information characteristics

Information which achieves its purpose must possess the following characteristics. It must be provided:
- to the right people
- at the right time
- at the right level of accuracy
- clearly
- through the appropriate channel
- cost-effectively.

In these circumstances, the information communicated will allow situations of all kinds to be controlled, decisions to be made, and analysis of how the organisation's resources are being used. It is also important to be aware that information:
- may be communicated regularly or *ad hoc* and therefore relates to various frequencies
- will always have both external and internal sources
- possesses the ability to provide a basis common to many different users, so the same facts and figures have various organisational uses
- is communicated in different presentational forms, e.g. charts, tables, narrative.

Information value

Unused information has no value, just cost! The actual value of information depends upon the *action* taken following the decision to act, based on the information provided. So, to find out about information's value, in relation to its cost effectiveness, we need to ask:
- exactly *what* information?
- *how* is it used?
- by *whom*?
- *how often* is it needed?
- *how often* is it presented?
- *could* alternative information be used instead?

The key issue is always,
  If the information were not used, would it really matter?
Looking at the potential, we would assess whether it would cost more to provide certain information than the benefits derived would justify. In simple language, we want to know whether the

information would somehow be of use to managers and whether the cost of obtaining it would be greater than the gains.

We have already discussed the fact that managers' needs for information relate to their grading and functions (you will remember the kinds of management within the hierarchy: strategic, tactical, operational), and that this will affect the frequency of the reports presented. Frequent provision of information is costly, and so we have to consider the idea of exception reporting (referred to above). Linked to this is the need for a given level of accuracy and the fact that unnecessary accuracy is also the generator of unnecessary expense.

Summary

In this chapter we have discussed:
- the role of information in business, connected with the various organisational functions (marketing, production, and so on)
- the MIS and the development of the IMIS, the inputs and outputs involved, and the ways in which we are able to grade information, mainly as strategic, tactical, operational
- reports – to and from management – and information flows (vertical, horizontal, diagonal)
- information handling
- the information environment incorporating the information space and the external environmental characteristics of information and communication
- the communication implications for information, including the need for encoding and decoding, and the presence of noise
- communication problems within the organisation
- channel loading (the complexity and rate of input) and the concepts of information overload and information underload
- characteristics of information (must be provided to the right people, at the right time, at the right level of accuracy, clearly, through the appropriate channel, cost-effectively)
- the value of information. If the information were not to be used at all, would it really matter?

Self-test Questions

Try answering these in outline and then check back in the chapter to see how correct you are.

1 Explain the meaning of MIS.
2 Suggest information areas worth establishing in the functions of marketing, production and purchasing.
3 How can we grade organisational information?
4 How does tactical information differ from operational information? Does it matter?
5 What activities constitute information handling?
6 What is the information environment?
7 What organisational problems can arise in communication?
8 What gives rise to the information flow?
9 What are the characteristics of successful information?
10 How can we evaluate information?

CHAPTER 2
Information processing

Introduction

The information we have been looking at in the previous chapter may be processed (actually converted from data into relevant or meaningful information) by various methods, ranging from manual to advanced electronic (computers). At the end of the 1980s, we tended to adopt the term *data processing* to include input, manipulation of the data input and then ultimately output (in information format). However, we also tended to use the term *information processing* for the same activities.

A third term, *knowledge processing,* is now generally adopted as an overall approach. We shall be using *information processing* which has been adopted in your syllabuses, and thus avoid confusion!

What we must do first of all is take a look at the collection of activities which we call the *information processing cycle.*

The information processing cycle

It is important for you to understand that the stages of this cycle, quite irrespective of what the organisation may call it, must exist for all systems concerned with information (data) processing. Again, it does not matter how complicated or how expensive the processing method may be.

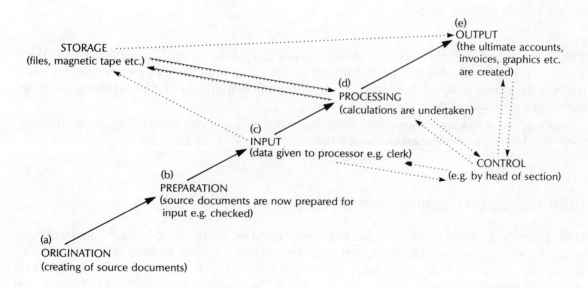

Note that we have five separate activities and two separate overall ones (storage and control). Let us look at each activity in turn.

Origination

This is the start or *conception* of the cycle and it gives rise to *source documents* (i.e. any form, note, chit, card containing messages or facts, such as an order written down on a message pad and received by telephone). These documents are carefully designed to be collated for information processing.

Preparation

The collated source-documents (the facts and figures they contain) are checked for error, incompleteness and so on and also for correct authorisation. This is a vital stage and is often emphasised in importance by the slogan *GIGO:* garbage in: garbage out. This means that if rubbish is input, then the output will also be rubbish!

Input

The data is now put into the hands of the *processor* – either literally or figuratively speaking. If the processing unit is a member of the clerical staff, it is given to that person. If the processing unit is a device, then it is fed into the device in one of a number of ways.

Processing

Information is here derived from the input data. This usually involves:

- *storage* (files) referred to (e.g. to obtain correct addresses of customers for invoicing output)
- *calculations* of various kinds (addition, percentages, etc.)
- *final preparation* (e.g. production of a report in summary form, or perhaps a listing of employees for the ultimate users of the information).

Output

The information is now in the exact format needed by the user, and it is handed to that individual. Note that output includes absolutely everything produced, e.g. invoices, replies to queries, building designs, stocklists, etc.

We must not forget the other two important constituents of our cycle: storage and control.

Storage

This consists of files of many different kinds. In information processing these may be physical manual files, such as the typical ring-binder, cassette tapes and so on. Strictly speaking these are the *file media* – the physical entities holding the facts and the figures. We shall be looking at files in the next chapter.

Control

This is concerned with the accuracy, completeness and relevance of the data input. The three stages of input, processing and output are all subjected to some form of monitoring, i.e. comparing actual results with expected results or *standards* and then taking necessary action to see that errors and omissions are corrected.

Now that we are aware of the nature of the processing cycle, we can go on to look at the different ways in which processing may be carried out.

Information processing methods

One thing we have to recall here is that even the most costly, sophisticated and complex computer systems still require some manual processes at some point or other of their operation! In any case, despite the advances made in personal computers (PCs), some small businesses do not consider such devices necessary and, as a result, they undertake processing in simpler and cheaper ways.

The sections which follow consider alternative approaches to information processing.

Handwritten methods

The completely manual approach is not commonly encountered today. There are usually several aids which help in the creation of manual records, especially in transcription.

A typical supportive device is known as the *3-in-1 system.* One version of this is a sales ledger system comprised of three documents placed and held in position by a special board. The documents have carbon paper placed in between them and thus a single entry posts all three documents at the same time. Where a different customer account is required, the top two pages are removed, new documents for the new account are inserted on the board and the next line of entry is chosen. In this way, the third (bottom) copy is the record list and the other two are used for despatch to the customer and as a sales ledger card respectively. This is sometimes called an *accounting board.* Such simple but helpful devices are sometimes referred to as *pseudo-mechanical.*

Calculators are also in this category; these may be either *pocket* or *desktop.* The earlier device (still encountered in some offices) was the adding machine (mechanical or electrical) which had a basic keyboard of numerical keys (0–9), registers for accumulating totals, and a paper roll on which the figures to be calculated were printed.

Today, calculators are small and sophisticated and they offer a range of calculations (some formulae being programmable by the user), displays of sub-totals, memory facility and so on. A major benefit they offer is absence of noise.

Accounting machines

These really result from a marriage of the typewriter and the adding machine, and they resemble big typewriters with extra keys and large paper carriages. They are known as *electro-mechanical* devices. They cope with basic book-keeping transactions and may be used for such activities as cheque-writing, accounting for sales and payroll. They allow the operator to enter data on a number of sheets of paper simultaneously, perform calculations automatically and also type a descriptive narrative as required. Most machines existing today are also programmable (not strictly in the computer sense!) and, under the control of a *program bar,* carry out various stages automatically without guidance from the operator. They also undertake error-checking.

VRCs

A VRC is a *visible record computer* and is a progression from the electro-mechanical accounting machines. It earns its title of *computer* in that it is controlled by stored instructions.

This machine uses *magnetic strip* or *magnetic stripe* cards, usually of A4 size, and the strip – fastened down one side of the card – is used to recall carried-forward information from one posting to the subsequent posting. On more advanced versions, magnetic disks and/or tapes may be used to act as file storage. Programs may be fed into the VRC from magnetic cards, tape cassettes, punched cards or paper tape.

It is called a *visible record computer* in that records are in completely visible and humanly readable format. When the card is input, any data on it is read by the VRC, so data is recorded in two ways: one in human-recognisable form and the other in machine-recognisable form. In this way, such items as customer number, name and address are all simply read automatically by the machine and there is no need for the operator to enter anything which is already on the card.

When the ledger card is inserted, the machine also automatically adjusts the card's position so that the next vacant line is ready for entry. There is also an *automatic feed* which accepts cards to be read in order for the VRC to produce an analysis.

The punched card or unit record system

Now not far from its hundredth birthday, the punched card processing system was devised by Hollerith in order to cope with data for census purposes. At one time the punched card was the

15

most commonly-encountered way of inputting data to computer systems but today it has become far less popular.

The fundamental principle is that of recording data on cards by punching a pattern of holes on them. Devices then read the patterns and undertake basic processing activity. The same card – and thus the same data – can be used for different applications. If, for example, one card contains details of a sales order item then the card can be used for the processing of the invoice, for inventory control, for sales ledger posting and for analysis of sales.

The standard Hollerith punched card size is 180 mm × 75 mm, with 12 rows and 80 columns, each column representing a single character. Each digit is represented by a hole punched in the appropriate row, whereas a letter of the alphabet is represented by a combination of two holes. Special characters may be represented by three holes.

In our heading we referred to a *unit record system*. The alternative title is derived from the fact that a single card can be the record of one line of an order. Each card is a record or unit.

Data recorded in this way can be processed on various devices, which are electro-mechanical and operate at around 1000 cards per minute. Alternatively the cards may be fed into the computer. The essential components of the punched card system are listed below.

Card punch

This machine converts the source data into hole patterns. The key-punch operator (usually working at a speed of some 10 000 key depressions per hour) keys on to the device's typewriter keyboard and the machine punches appropriate holes. A stack or *hopper* of blank cards is fed into the machine.

Verifier

The operator keys in the data for a second time, and the verifier device indicates any error on the punched card previously prepared by the card punch. The card containing the error is indicated for future modification.

Sorter

This machine sorts out the punched cards into a pre-determined sequence.

Collator

The major uses for this machine are to merge two separate files of cards, to select cards from a file and to match cards.

Other machines are:
- the *reproducer* (copying information from one card to another)
- the *calculator* (undertaking calculations from data punched on cards)
- the *tabulator* (converting card data into printouts).

One season for the decrease in popularity of the punched card system is the amount of storage space required by cards which must be kept to maintain records. This is especially the case where offices are situated in city centres where space is expensive to purchase or rent. Storage space then becomes an important cost-effective factor.

Of course these systems pre-date electronic data processing (EDP) systems for the production of information, and so we now proceed to this major section.

The computer system

The term *computer* really means any device which is able to accept data on an automatic basis, apply a series or sequence of processes to this data and provide results. It is also capable of storing instructions, and also of modifying these if instructed.

The term computer is a broad one, covering devices which are able to manipulate symbols of any kind (coded messages, formulae, equations, numbers, words and so on).

In this section we look at the general working of the computer; in Chapters 3 and 4 we shall be looking at categories of computers and the hardware.

Computer operation

The computer manipulates symbols by means of electronic circuitry. It uses the *binary coding* method of representing symbols, storing both the data which is to be processed and the instructions for the processing, in the same format and in the same memory store.

The binary system means *base two system* because it uses two (and only two) states or conditions: 0 and 1. Our usual human way of counting is not like this because it is a *decimal system,* i.e. it is based upon ten digits: 0, 1, 2, 3, 4, 5, 6, 7, 8, 9 not merely two. The binary digits 0 and 1 are referred to mostly as *bits.*

Electric power has two states: *on* and *off.* So, for the computer, operations are undertaken in terms of *pulse* or *no pulse,* positive or negative. These are translated effectively as 1 and 0.

The character representation used by human beings has to be translated to binary. The conversion is carried out in a number of stages. The actual accuracy and efficiency of the activity depends on the the basic structure of the computer system, which includes the people using it. The computer works in combinations of ones and zeros, irrespective of whether the item is made up of numbers, letters or symbols (e.g. %).

Once the numeric format has been produced from the input of numbers, letters and symbols generally, it will be in a suitable medium and can then be converted through the input unit into electrical impulses (on or off).

So, using a binary coding approach, sets of two-state electronic switches are able to represent numbers, etc. Now, each switch may be either closed (0) or open (1), and so two switches in pairs represent four different symbols. For example,

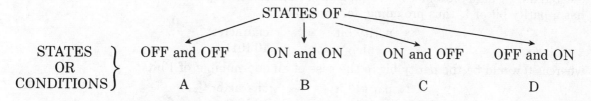

So, a set of switches represents a number of symbols. In general terms,

   n bits (switches) $= 2^n$ symbols.

This indicates that two switches provide four representations, four switches provide 16 (i.e. $2 \times 2 \times 2 \times 2$) and so forth. It follows that a computer able to cope with switches in groups or sets of eight (i.e. 256 representations of symbols) can have no difficulty in dealing with the interpretation and conversion of a wide range.

The sets of on-off switches used as representations of the coded data and the instructions are known as the computer's *registers* and they are restricted in their number. The registers relate to the data or the instructions which are being dealt with at a given moment. They connect with electronic circuitry which is able to cope with any processing required at that time, and also with the *immediate access storage* (IAS) – or the internal computer memory.

What we have established so far is that:
- the *bit* (or **bi**nary digi**t**) is the basic unit for data representation
- the binary coding approach permits bits to be allocated in groups to represent symbols of all kinds.

We now have to look at a few terms, which concern bit combinations used to represent data.
- A *byte* is normally eight bits, representing either a single character or a couple of digits. We know from our comments earlier that eight bits are able to represent 2^8 characters (i.e. 256).
- A *word* is a group of bits representing a number, instruction or one or more characters. Different makes and models of computer have adopted different numbers of bits to a word.
- A *character* is a letter, number or symbol represented by a unique coding of binary digits.
- *Instructions* are groups of bits used to represent an instruction.

The computer may be said to comprise two separate devices. One device reads and then interprets instructions, and the other device carries out the instructions and manipulates the data. Thus we have both *instruction time* and *execution time.*

To conclude this discussion, we will look at the two methods adopted by computers to represent characters, using binary coding. These are:

● the pure binary approach
● the binary coded decimal approach.

The majority of computers are able to adopt working methods for both of these.

Pure binary

Each number is represented by a specific group, i.e. the number as a complete whole. So we might have:

1980 is 11110111100

and 1989 is 11111000101.

Binary coded decimal

In this approach, each character is converted into six bit, so that

1989 is	00 0001	00 1001	00 1000	00 1001
	[= 1]	[= 9]	[= 8]	[= 9]

Compare this date with the way it is expressed in pure binary above, where we have 11 bits constituting the year. In binary coded decimal we have a total of 24 bits. The computer can also work at a higher speed in pure binary.

We also adopt what is known as a *parity bit.* This makes the total amount of 1 bits an odd number. In other words, there is always an extra bit which can indicate a fault in the computer created during data movement or storage. So a character incorporating an even number of 1 bits has a parity bit of 1, thus providing, for example,

parity bit	character
1	10 1011

whereas 0 would be the parity bit in the case of an odd number of 1 bits:

parity bit	character
0	10 1001

If a character which has an even number of bits is read it is incomplete. This parity checking is undertaken as an automatic procedure whenever the transfer of data is carried out.

Review of the information processing methods

Broadly, from what we have said already, we have three categories of methods for the processing of information:

● manual
● mechanised
● computer.

To provide an overall review of these categories we shall examine their implications for a firm which holds a range of products in its warehouse and which has a factory supplying the warehouse in accordance with a pre-determined schedule.

Manual system

Various documents bear orders received from customers. The details of these are checked and transcribed on to a special form to assist processing. Here, the task is to ensure accuracy and completeness – addresses and particulars being compared, using, perhaps, trade directories or telephone directories – and the use of the firm's catalogue is probably a key activity here.

The standard order form is transferred to the warehouse so that the products may be extracted from stock and can be prepared for delivery. Now the task is to identify the products, obtain the right quantity, pack them and despatch to the proper address.

The order form is transferred to the finance department in order that an invoice may be provided. Sale particulars are recorded in the customer accounts as necessary. The task involves reference to files, arithmetic calculations, and also the updating of relevant records.

The goods, plus invoice are despatched.

A statement of account is sent on a monthly basis to the customers and payment is received. Again, the task involves file reference, calculating and updating.

The manual system is:

* relatively slow in operation
* error-prone (thereby requiring strict monitoring)
* restricted in load capability but flexible and easily altered in procedure.

Control is undertaken using the data which is recorded during the processing. For instance, information relating to cash flow would be obtained from the ledgers, and marketing/sales analysis would be aided by information from invoices.

Mechanised system

This category includes all devices which assist calculation, the preparation of standard forms and file reference. So it means calculators, accounting machines, ledger card systems, VRCs, and so on.

Customer names and addresses, and product price and details could be stored on magnetic tape and used in conjunction with an electronic typewriter. On the other hand, a word-processor (WP) could be used.

The accounts department may very well adopt the same approach for invoicing procedures to print customer details (using an accounting machine, perhaps). Calculations would be undertaken by the accounting machine. Note that invoice details would be transferred manually to ledgers, perhaps with the use of a 3-in-1 device.

A mechanised system is:

* relatively fast (compared with the manual version)
* less error-prone
* able to bear greater loads, provided that there are enough of the devices to cope with a higher input of data at times, and also provided that spare capacity is available
* flexible.

Control is undertaken on a similar basis as for manual systems, and the provision of mechanical devices does not contribute greatly to this area.

Computerised systems

Staff input coded data (in various ways, as we shall see in later chapters) and the computer provides an on-screen display of particulars for checking.

The computer itself completes preparation of the customer invoice, enters transaction data of the sale on the customer account, and updates the control file.

Information concerning the order is transmitted by computer to the warehouse, in detail.

Statements are prepared on a regular basis by the computer.

The computer system is:

* very rapid in operation
* an incorporation of the various procedures, and, thus, not very flexible (i.e. to modify the procedures there must be program modification and so on)
* expensive, requiring cost-effectiveness analysis prior to initial installation.

Control information is obtained from files maintained by the computer, and, as processing continues, so actual sales performance, customer payments, credit levels and so on are updated. The computer may be programmed to advise management when certain levels (e.g. credit) are reached so that action may be taken.

Note that various devices not directly connected to the computer system (i.e. *off-line*) are used to assist in the initial data preparation. The punched card system, discussed earlier, is one example, but there are many others. This leads us on to our next section.

Processing modes

A processing mode is the manner in which a computer system copes with data for processing (for transformation into information). We have a number of different modes, usually expressed as:

- batch processing
- on-line processing
- real-time processing
- interactive processing.

Batch processing mode

In fact, this particular approach is not at all confined to use by computer systems but is commonly encountered in all kinds of commercial applications. It is certainly generally adopted by organisations using computers to process their information requirements.

This approach means that the data to be input is gathered together into a group or *batch* and then processed as a group at one time. So there could be a collection of related documents of some kind which have been gathered over, say, a period of a week or a month. These are then input. The classic example of this idea is the payroll procedure, in which the timecards for a week's attendance are processed as one batch to produce payslips.

Each batch has its own *batch control slip* which contains:

- the number of the batch
- any relevant code for identification purposes
- the *control totals* (i.e. the number of records in that batch, the total value of the transactions in the batch, *hash totals* – which are simple totals of invoice numbers, dates and so on for the computer to utilise as a check for accuracy)
- authorisation (date of preparation, name of person who prepared the batch and keyed in the data).

The batch control data is input with the data on the source documents and it will be used continually by the system to ensure that only the correct data is processed.

Let us take a simple batch example. Suppose LSS plc uses a computer-based sales ledger:

- all sales invoices are prepared manually and a copy is retained; all invoices are collected at the end of the working shift with a batch control slip attached, with the batch number (the next unused one in the batch control book), the total number of invoices, and the total value of all the invoices in this batch; the control details are entered into the control book
- the batch is transferred to the computer department; the control clerk records receipt
- details (invoice and control data) are input to the computer (perhaps via punched cards, perhaps keyed on to magnetic tape then verified)
- the computer checks (edits) the data and lists all the invoices accepted as valid, producing a document count and total value, also listing any invoices it rejects as incorrect
- totals on the slip are reconciled with the computer's list by the control clerk
- the computer sorts the data into customer account number sequence, and then updates the ledgers
- the computer produces a printout of the total invoices dealt with, and the control clerk reconciles this with the batch totals, then transferring all the documents output by the computer to the sales department, where totals are checked by the sales clerk once again.

There are *advantages* to batch processing:

- very rapid processing is not required because this mode usually deals with periodic processing (e.g. as we said, payroll)
- the approach is relatively easy to construct
- the computer is able to cope with one task at a time.

Disadvantages are:

- delay arises between transaction origination and information output
- management information is not up-to-the-minute or current.

On-line processing mode

The major aspect of this mode is that the data is input to the computer directly from the point of data origin. The usual input device here is a terminal linked with the computer (on-line) and because of distance between them this is described as a *remote terminal*.

The data is usually collected together on some kind of *backing storage* (e.g. magnetic tape or disk) until input for actual processing. It is common, therefore, for the remote terminal itself to have such storage facilities so that input to the computer can be in bulk at a given time. Note that this involves *batching*.

Another form of on-line processing relates to the approach known as *demand processing* for file interrogation (i.e. direct access to information held on computer file), and the updating of files using batch processing at *off-peak*, more convenient periods. The UK clearing banks adopt such a mode, the system permitting all enquiries to be made from files, and overnight transaction processing (batch).

The terminal is also used to initiate the undertaking of complex calculations by the computer, and also for receiving a response when the processing has been completed.

Real-time processing mode

This mode can be explained as one in which the data is input and processed, and output (results) is transmitted so rapidly that the environment or situation originating the data is able to be influenced. This is by no means unusual in human experience! If a human being stumbles the situation is perceived by the brain and a reflex action arises to prevent falling. That is a *real-time* mode! It is sometimes called *on-line real-time* (OLRT).

It follows that a real-time mode must also be on-line. The *response-time* is the period elapsing between the final digit of input and the first digit of output (response). So, in plain language, it is the time taken for the computer to react and carry out an instruction from a terminal.

This is obviously the direct opposite of batch mode, since in real-time mode each transaction is processed at once, upon input, and so all the batch stages (inputting, validating, updating and outputting) are applied to that transaction.

These systems are common, and some examples of them are:
- nuclear power-generating control
- retail stores, for stock control (e.g. John Lewis, Argos)
- air-traffic control systems at airports
- missile control
- bank cash-dispensers
- British Airways Booking System (BABS).

Characteristics of the real-time mode are that:
- there is rarely a source document since transactions arise and are dealt with at once
- output is transmitted to where it is required
- remote terminals are needed at the point of origin
- information is stored on-line and so files may be updated at any time as well as interrogated
- processing is immediate, upon receipt of the data.

Advantages gained from this mode are:
- instantaneous processing yields a better service for customers and can contribute to improved cashflow
- information is simply obtained by interrogating the linked files
- up-to-date information for management exists which can provide early warnings of problems and in many cases provide more efficient stock-holding levels (i.e. extra stocks are sometimes held in case there are delays in the stock-level reporting system, but the real-time approach eliminates this measure).

Disadvantages are:
- costs of developing and installing the system are high (e.g. storage facilities of the required type are essential in large amounts)

- there is a need to provide extra processors (and duplication of files) to avoid breakdown difficulties
- failure (of hardware, i.e. devices or software, i.e. programs) within the system can cause severe problems.

Interactive processing mode

This allows a question and answer routine to be developed, and thus there is a *dialogue* between terminal and computer. A hotel receptionist, for instance, may use a terminal to find out if accommodation is available at another hotel in the chain.

Selecting the information processing mode

Various considerations must be taken into account when the decision to adopt a specific mode is to be made. These are:
- the overall cost (hardware, software, locations, staffing) has to be looked at in the form of a cost-benefit analysis (CBA) approach, bearing in mind the benefits conferred by the mode in question
- the availability of funds for acquisition (whether direct purchase, leasing or renting)
- response times required by the users, and the level of accuracy sought in the responses
- the storage media necessary (we discuss backing storage in its various forms in Chapter 3)
- how often information changes arise, i.e. the need for regular and frequent updating
- current facilities for data collection, and future needs for these (e.g. data preparation staff, machines, communication methods, etc.)
- processing security (confidentiality and accuracy).

If the response times required are rapid, then obviously the need would appear to be for the real-time mode. On the other hand, existing computer equipment may be unable to cope with that. So can the organisation afford the financial investment to achieve this? Would it be worth the investment in terms of cost-benefit analysis?

In our next chapter we look at the computer itself, in greater detail.

Summary

In this chapter we have discussed:
- the stages in the information processing cycle, common to all information systems:
    origination
    preparation
    input
    processing
    output
    using storage and control
- information processing methods:
    handwritten (manual)
    accounting machines
    VRCs
    punched card system (URS)
    computer systems
- the operation of the computer and the binary approach, with the binary digits being translated through on/off switches
- the general aspects of the three broad categories of methods:
    manual
    mechanised
    computerised

• the processing modes:
  batch
  on-line
  real-time
  interactive.

Self-test Questions

Answer these questions, then check back to assess your answers.

1 List and describe the stages in the information processing cycle.
2 Explain the activities, in outline, necessary to produce punched card input for a computerised system. What does the collator undertake?
3 How is the base two system utilised to represent characters input by human beings? How does pure binary differ from binary coded decimal?
4 What would you expect to discover in a 'mechanised system', and what advantages may be derived from this system?
5 Discuss the major characteristics of two categories of processing modes.
6 Describe the operation of a batch processing mode.
7 List the advantages and disadvantages of real-time processing.
8 What matters have to be considered when deciding what processing mode to adopt?
9 Explain the following terms.
  a) VRC   b) byte   c) character   d) bit   e) URS
10 Give examples of these.
  a) the parity bit   b) real-time systems   c) interactive mode   d) n bits $= 2^n$ symbols

CHAPTER 3
Computer hardware 1

Introduction

We have reached the point where we must now look more closely at the computer and its components. We have already given a simple definition of the term *computer* as:

> *any device which is able to accept data on an automatic basis, apply a series or sequence of processes to this data, and provide the results of this.*

Just like any other information processing system, the computer's operations can be simply looked upon like this.

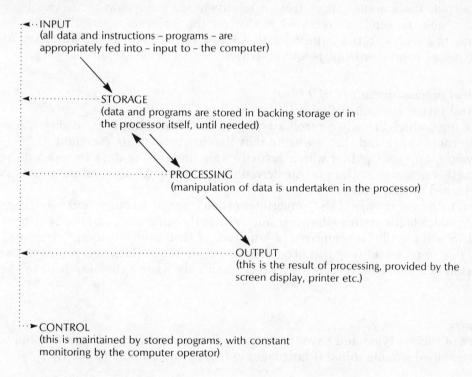

INPUT
(all data and instructions – programs – are appropriately fed into – input to – the computer)

STORAGE
(data and programs are stored in backing storage or in the processor itself, until needed)

PROCESSING
(manipulation of data is undertaken in the processor)

OUTPUT
(this is the result of processing, provided by the screen display, printer etc.)

CONTROL
(this is maintained by stored programs, with constant monitoring by the computer operator)

The computer configuration

The configuration is the name given to the collection of physical (hardware) devices which constitute the computer system, basically of five categories. These are:
- the central processing unit (CPU) which incorporates the control unit, the main storage or immediate access storage (IAS), and the arithmetic logic unit (ALU)
- the control console
- the input unit
- the output unit
- backing storage.

In diagrammatic form we have this.

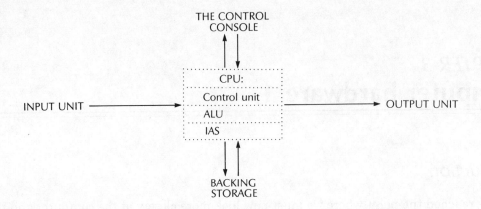

Now we will consider the five elements of the configuration in more detail.

The control console

This acts as the interface between the computer operator and the computer. Not used to input or receive output, the console ranges from a relatively simple typewriter device by which the operator is able to send instructions modifying the program controlling the computer's operations, to a sophisticated terminal with a visual display screen and an automatic logging device to record computer timings and activities.

The central processing unit (CPU)

The central processing unit includes:
- *control unit,* which literally controls all components of the computer, reading the program in the internal storage and then ensuring that the instructions are executed
- *arithmetic logic unit* (ALU) which actually does process the data in terms of logical and arithmetic calculations. Data is transferred from internal storage and the processing results are returned to that storage
- *immediate access storage* (IAS), sometimes called internal memory, and wrongly called 'core storage' which holds or stores the program(s) currently being used, and the data for processing. This IAS will usually be comprised of hundreds of thousands of storage elements, each one being able to represent 0 or 1 in accordance with its state. Data and programs can thus be processed and executed respectively when – and only when – they are held in the internal storage.

Input units

These are of various types and have the major task of accepting the data input and converting this to machine-readable (binary) language, to make it acceptable to the CPU.

Output units

Of various types, including printers, these have the task of converting what the CPU has produced through its processing into the format required by the users.

Backing storage

This has the task of holding files in the form which is appropriate to the computer processing activities. Sometimes referred to as *auxiliary storage, external storage* or *secondary storage,* it provides support to the IAS which cannot ever be large enough to hold everything needed for a given computer application or *job.* This storage, as we shall see later, is in the form of magnetic tapes or disks.

Note that, strictly speaking, we have been looking at the configuration in broad terms, as components which constitute the computer system. However, devices (in our diagram these would be input and output units and backing storage) other than the CPU itself are called *peripherals*.

The computer activities

In order to gather all the points we have studied concerning the computer together, here is a brief survey of how the computer carries out its processing function, from start to finish.

1 The program(s) and all data are converted into machine-comprehensible language and recorded on an appropriate medium for input.

2 The encoded data (monitored by the control unit) is transferred to the IAS (either via some input device or from backing storage) to be retained until needed for processing.

3 The initial program instruction is taken from the IAS by the control unit, and the appropriate units are directed to carry out necessary activities. Required data is taken from storage (*store addresses*) and placed in a given location or *accumulator* in the ALU.

4 Any required manipulation or calculation is carried out and afterwards the processed results are transferred to an *intermediate storage area* in the IAS (i.e. a *working store address*) reserved for data during processing stage.

5 The control unit, as required, supervises a given output unit (e.g. printer) to convert processing results into human-readable format.

6 Program instructions are individually carried out from first to last in strict sequence as directed.

Types of computer and their uses

It is very important to be aware of the different types of computer used today. We begin this section by examining the main categories of computers and then go on to look at the kinds of devices which are commonly encountered today in business.

Digital and analog

Digital

The digital computers handle data which is held as a number of *discrete* or distinctly separate items. They carry out all activities in a sequence of stages (instructions) to undertake mathematical calculations on the discrete items.

The digital clock shows the time by displaying the hour and the minutes, e.g. 12.39. The pocket or desk calculator is also digital.

In this study we are concerned with digital devices since they are the ones used in commercial organisations.

Analog (or analogue)

These computers accept an item of data as a quantity which varies over time, i.e. not as a group of discrete items. This means that they are able to measure continuous developments such as voltages, acceleration, deceleration and speed of a vehicle (a speedometer in a car is an analog device) and temperature.

In these computers, input numbers are represented by varying a physical quantity, e.g. the number 9 may be represented by varying the voltage by, for example, producing a voltage nine times stronger than the voltage representing 1.

We also encounter the *hybrid* computer which combines both digital and analog approaches, so that this machine can accept a varying input and convert it for digital processing.

Computer sizes

The distinction between the various sizes of computer is not as straightforward as it may appear. The actual physical dimensions are less important than the general performance and storage capacity of the individual machines. There are also extremely rapid developments in computerisation generally and the tendency is for computer size to reduce and performance capability to rise.

The actual rate of operation of the typical current (*fourth generation*) computer for normal processing is measured in terms of *picoseconds*.

$$1 \text{ picosecond} = \frac{1}{1\,000\,000\,000\,000} \text{ seconds}$$

The latest, very powerful processors have their performance measured in *millions of instructions per second* (MIPS), and usually expressed as tens of *nanoseconds* (one billion or 10^9 nanoseconds constitute one second). The large mainframe computer with one processor (CPU) is usually rated at anything from 10 to 20 MIPS. As we shall see later, some mainframe computers have more than one CPU. Thus computers are able to undertake millions of instructions in one second, which accounts for their incredible ability to provide answers to queries very quickly.

Memory is another factor. Size of main (IAS) storage is measured in *addressable locations*, 1024 of these being represented by a *kilobyte* (K). The small home computer sold in the high street will have anything from 4K to 64K memory size. On the other hand, the large computer system is likely to have storage of one million K. Most of the small office microcomputers today have storage capacity of at least 256K.

A further distinction is made concerning storage. Current computers have a memory divided into *random access memory* (RAM) and *read only memory* (ROM). The former is the working area, whereas the latter contains certain permanently stored instructions which are not able to be erased or amended (often referred to as *firmware*). Some computers have areas in their memory which may be programmed, i.e. instructions which are routine and permanent may be stored in that part of the memory but cannot then be erased. These are *programmable read only memory* (PROM).

The advances made in computer and information technology generally have made it hard to categorise computers conveniently. Before we look at the three basic categories, however, we have to look at just such a major development – *parallelism*.

The parallel system

The traditional kind of computer has what is called a *Von Neuman architecture,* named after the Hungarian-born US mathematician. This signifies a *single processor* (CPU) which performs all its operations in sequence (*sequentially*). The program concerned and the data to be processed are both held in the same store, and so each individual operation requires several accessing activities. Thus, in order to improve the single processor's performance generally, we have to make an improvement in the processing capacity and the speed (in MIPS) of that single CPU.

This has given rise to the *supercomputer.* Fundamentally, the supercomputer is simply a machine at the top of the range which carries out the functions of the digital computer using very sophisticated hardware. As well as providing enormous computational power they also offer very large memory systems for data storage. The typical version of the supercomputer is the ETA-10 which consists of up to eight processors all linked to a very big shared memory. The supercomputer performance is not measured by the rate at which the computer is able to deal with instructions (MIPS) but by the rate at which it is able to carry out useful work. This is normally expressed as the *number of floating point operations completed per second*, divided by 1 000 000 to put these figures on a manageable level. The abbreviation for this measure is MFLOPS. If we take the total power of all the processors of the ETA-10, we have a figure of 4600 to 9200 MFLOPS, depending upon the version of the architecture.

The idea of the supercomputer, then, is to boost computer power. The *hypercube*, however, aims to achieve the capability of the expensive supercomputer (which, for a restricted range of jobs would cost up to $1 million) for the cost of a minicomputer of normal dimensions. The hypercube developed from the idea of *parallel computing*. The idea of parallel computing (or *parallel processing*) is to use a combination of the power of a number of separate processors.

The hypercube (or *binary n-cube*) is a special design for a network of processors which are in some way interconnected. To distinguish this technologically from parallel computing it is generally termed *concurrent*. Each microprocessor is linked to its nearest neighbours. A typical example is the Arrow Computer Systems' NCube/10 which provides the power of a major super-computer at the price of a top-of-the-range minicomputer and is able to operate within the usual office environment.

Micro, mini and mainframe computers

The usual way of classifying commercial computers is by using the terms *microcomputer* (PC), *minicomputer* and *mainframe computer*.

Microcomputers

This commonly-encountered range of computers was made possible by the big advances in technology and miniaturisation of electronic circuitry which arose in the late 1970s. They range from the cheap domestic computer used in households (often for games such as *Space Invaders!*) to advanced and sophisticated office computers which are certainly familiar to all accountants.

The smaller minicomputers and the larger microcomputers are not easy to separate in classification. The major characteristics are:
- they are usually of desktop dimensions
- the prices are relatively low
- additional (peripheral) units may be attached
- input is usually by keyboard, output is on-screen usually supported by printout if required.

We are, of course, referring here to business computers. These are able to supply up to ten megabytes of storage and communicate with others. Microcomputers are also able to act as terminals and be linked up with minicomputers or large mainframe systems. The microcomputer which is independent (*standalone*) and not connected to others is still able to accept application packages (ready-written programs) so that it can undertake word-processing, procedures for accounting and so on.

Apart from the large microcomputer, there is also the *transportable* which can be carried to the boot of a car and transported to another location without difficulty.

A further type is the *truly portable*. The machine not only can be carried about (in a case) but can be operated by batteries. The truly portable (or *laptop*) machine is usually more expensive than desktop versions (e.g. the Toshiba T311 costs about £4000, whereas desktop personal computers of equivalent capability can cost around £2000 or less). However, for the much smaller laptops with small memory (e.g. 64K) and relatively limited capability – the whole unit being the size of a notebook – the price may be around £800.

The small portables are used by sales representatives, for instance, and others working away from their offices. Provision of an *acoustic coupler* allows the portable to transfer information (via an ordinary telephone line) to the headquarters computer, a useful concept for sales representatives who have to communicate customer orders rapidly.

Minicomputers

These are similar to mainframe computers, having the same basic structure. Thus the distinction between them is somewhat vague, but the effective volume of the mini's output is only a small part of that of the mainframe. The minicomputer is compact and can be installed in an environment which is not as protected as that of the mainframe. No air-conditioning is needed, for example, except in the case of the largest minis.

The cost of the minicomputer is, of course, lower than that of the mainframe. They can also accommodate a large number of users and one model, the Vax, is able to support 256 terminals linked to its network. However, the minicomputer is mid-range, competing to a large extent with smaller mainframes and larger microcomputers. Some experts have suggested that the mini will disappear as a category in a few years. It is also very likely that a new type of minicomputer – a supercomputer which is already being termed the *supermini* – will be popular, using the technique of running several processors together.

A further challenge to the minicomputer stems from the *workstation* (see below).

Mainframes

Mainframes consist of various devices which, acting in concert, constitute the major structure of a large data processing unit. It is usual to discover products of different suppliers making up the mainframe. They must, of course, be able to work together (*compatible*). In the late 1980s it became usual to find that a mainframe incorporated several processors, or CPUs. Mainframes are frequently found at the heart of a large network of microcomputers, which can total hundreds of machines.

Workstations

We must now look at the concept of the *workstation* because they became very important during the 1980s. The term is often used very loosely to mean any kind of sophisticated computer terminal or microcomputer situated on the desk of an organisational executive.

However, devices are also marketed which are workstations, as distinct from microcomputers. The main distinction between them lies in the fact that workstations provide access to remote computing power and microcomputers provide it from within themselves. The workstation must thus be capable in the area of data communications, but should also possess a limited capacity for calculation.

A typical facility offered by the workstation is that of the personal executive diary. Another is the ability to connect with remote private or public computers, the latter being provided as a public service to offer such information as train times, the weather and so on (*viewdata*), using the ordinary telephone network.

Workstations may also provide *computer conferencing* facilities, in which a manager using the device is able to communicate questions and receive answers from other workstations.

A typical workstation is ICL's OPD, which is a powerful but cheap microcomputer (created by Sinclair Research), using a set of powerful business applications software (created by Psion), with extensive telephonic capabilities (devised by British Telecom) and produced as an entity by ICL.

Input to the computer system

You already know that the computer will only accept data in machine-comprehensible format, so that if the original or *source* document is not acceptable, then it must be transcribed. This means that data collection and input can be a problematic and expensive activity.

The term *data collection* can be taken to mean the process of gathering the data. Here we use the term *data capture* to signify the obtaining of the data at its source in machine-readable form. Data collection and preparation involves:

- originating the data on some clerically-prepared document (unless direct input methods are adopted, e.g. the computer receives the data directly via the keyboard – terminal – input)
- transmitting the data, transferring the data from the section or unit originating it, to the computer installation. This may mean conveying the documents physically on a trolley, or electronic transmission of data
- preparing the data, prior to actual input to the CPU, by converting it to machine-readable language; this is undertaken by the input unit itself, or as a separate activity, as in card-punching
- inputting the data, the input device reading it and then placing it in internal storage.

Methods of data input may be categorised as:
- *off-line data input,* using punched cards, paper tape, magnetic tape or disk, 'by-product' techniques
- *on-line data input,* using keyboard, point of sale (PoS) cash registers
- *special approaches,* using bar coding, plastic cards, kimball tags, optical mark reading (OMR), optical character recognition (OCR), magnetic ink character recognition (MICR), voice input.

Off-line data input

Punched card input

In Chapter 2 we looked at the punched-card system, and this is exactly the same in terms of input methods. The punched cards are stacked into a special tray-like container (the *hopper*) and fed into the card-reader one at a time. This method has advantages:
- the equipment is basically simple and relatively cheap
- the cards can be handled – prepared, sorted and so on – off-line
- the card data may be read by human beings because the contents can be printed on each one
- the system is flexible.

On the other hand:
- the cards take up a good deal of storage space in offices
- the input speed is relatively slow (1000 to 2000 cards per minute)
- card-punching and verifying is very time-consuming
- the cards are fixed in length and so some columns will be unused
- equipment used is noisy.

To produce really efficient input, the operators must be highly trained, the source documents themselves must be efficiently designed, and the machines used must be in themselves very efficient and well-maintained.

This approach is still adopted in many computer systems, largely because it was originally adopted for accounting systems and the equipment was already present when the system was installed.

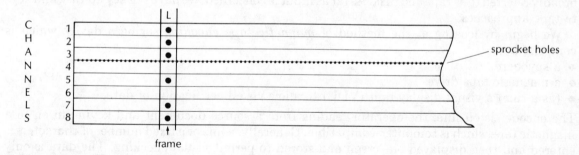

Paper tape input

Paper tape is found in reels up to 300 metres in length and is an alternative to the punched card. Each character is formed by punching holes in a row across the width (about 2.5 cm). Each hole position lies in a track along the length of the tape, and the rows are called *frames.* Each frame will have five, six, seven or eight holes depending upon the method adopted. A special code is used for computer input. Below is a diagrammatic view of punched tape.

The diagram is intended to show the principle of hole-punching. The channel numbered 8 is the *parity* channel, and a system of even-parity checking is present here. This means that (as in the case of the parity-bits we looked at earlier) when the code consists of an even number of holes, a blank is left in channel 8. When the code is made up of an odd number of holes, an extra hole is punched there.

Like cards, paper tape has to be punched using a special device, and also verified prior to input. Verification occurs when source data is retyped on a tape verifier which makes a comparison with data on the original tape. The verifier also produces a new tape, normally of a different colour to identify it. If there is a discrepancy, the device locks and the operator has to make an alteration to correct the error.

Data transfer rates for tape are usually somewhere between 1000 and 2000 characters per second.

Paper tape is used for special purposes, such as the point of sale unit, or PoS, which is a cash till recording transactions as a by-product on paper tape for later reading by the computer. In many cases, although paper tape is used initially, the data may be converted into a more rapidly-handled medium, such as magnetic tape for computer input. This idea also applies to punched cards.

A comparison of paper tape and punched cards shows us the following:
cards
- may have human-readable information printed on them
- can be pre-punched with information
- are more durable than tape (although the latter is now made stronger by plasticisation)
- may be resorted prior to input
- can be individually corrected without disturbing other data;

paper tape
- systems are cheaper
- can contain variable length records (whereas cards have fixed record length because of their format)
- takes up less storage space
- allows a parity track to improve accuracy
- prevents the data from becoming out of sequence
- does not suffer from possible loss or misplacement of a single set of data (cards can be lost!).

Magnetic tape or disk (disc)
We shall be examining the nature of magnetic media when we take a look at backing storage. However, for the time being, we need to know that there are various kinds of magnetic media, broadly referred to as tape and disk. As far as input is concerned, we have the key-to-disk and key-to-tape approaches.

We begin by looking at the method of *magnetic tape encoding,* using a device which is comprised of:
- a keyboard
- a magnetic tape drive
- (as a rule) a visual display unit (VDU) to allow visual verification of data.

The encoder is off-line, the operator reading from a source document and keying in on to a magnetic tape which is computer-compatible. Generally, a line or a fixed number of characters is entered and then displayed on-screen and stored to permit visual checking. The data is only entered on to the tape itself when a special key is depressed to signify that the operator is satisfied with the accuracy.

Magnetic tape encoding is adopted where large volumes of data have to be collected in batch processing (see Chapter 2). The tape approach is more efficient than cards or paper tape. The advantages are:
- the relatively low cost of magnetic tape
- speed of input to the computer
- high storage capacity
- easy verification
- the format is not of fixed length (as in cards) but is variable.

The *key-to-disk* approach is characterised by the existence of:
- workstations (keyboards and VDUs)
- a small processor (computer)
- disk storage

- supervisor's console (in large systems)
- magnetic tape units.

For large systems, the supervisor's terminal will be used to schedule the data to be transcribed, controlling both the input and loading into files. The small processor uses a small collection of programs to undertake validity checks on the data input to the disks, and to control the encoding. The actual procedure is as follows.

1 An operator at one of the workstations (or keystations) identifies the number of the batch and the number of the station; data is keyed in, validated by the processor, and, as accepted, is written on to the disk.

2 For very important data, a second operator will verify the data's accuracy.

3 Completed batches of data are now grouped in order to create the total transaction file, and this file (i.e. the collected data to be processed by the computer) is written from (transferred from) the original working disks to either another disk or magnetic tape (for input to the main computer).

The input speed of the disk method can be higher than 300 000 characters per second (cps). This system is costly to obtain and to maintain, and, of course, if the small computer/processor *goes down* (fails) then the entire system is immobilised. However, there is a greater productivity rate from this approach and the system is highly flexible. There is also minimisation of operator error.

Diagrammatically, the system may be expressed as below.

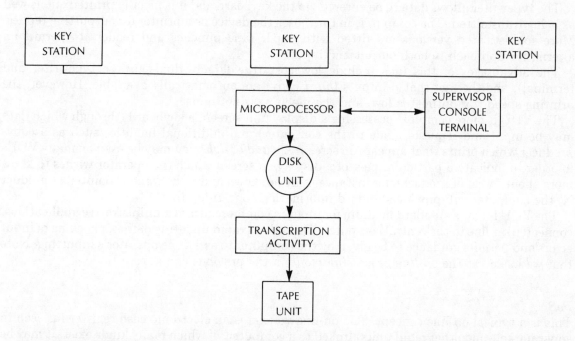

There are smaller systems, of course, which consist of individual keystations, not interlinked at all, each one using *floppy disks*. As we shall later see, these are small magnetic disks.

By-product techniques

Data to be input is prepared as a result or by-product of some other operation. A key-punch, or some form of encoder, is linked to, for example, a cash register (we referred to the PoS system when we looked at paper tape), accounting machines, invoicing machines and receipting machines. Input is prepared at the same time by the device. The data created is then input as a separate operation.

The clear advantage is that this approach eliminates any extra keying in.

On-line input

In this area we have two basic concepts – the use of the keyboard and the PoS unit. Note that the keyboard (*terminal*) is used in various ways, including off-line approaches; these are either special terminals, or dual-purpose which can be used off- or on-line. In the same way, the PoS method can be on-line or can create by-product data off-line. Here, we are only concerned with the on-line approach.

Keyboard

We have already noted the use of keyboards. Strictly speaking, a *terminal* is at least able to be linked to a computer, whether it can adopt an off-line mode or not. Basically, terminals are used for three purposes:
- on-line input of data
- giving instructions and controlling the computer
- reception of output.

Terminals may be *remote* (situated a distance away from the computer, perhaps hundreds or thousands of miles away) in which case *transmission links* (e.g. satellite, or telephone lines) are essential.

There are two types of terminal: the *teletype* (or teletypewriter) which may, in smaller offices, be an electronic typewriter which can be used as a terminal, perhaps able to be linked to a micro-computer, and the *visual display unit* (VDU).

The typewriter allows data to be entered via the keyboard and it is usually printed out as well as being transmitted. The computer, in turn, uses the device as a printer for outputting replies. More sophisticated versions are fitted with paper tape punches and readers to permit an alternative approach to both output and input.

The advantages of this idea include low cost (the largely dual-purpose typewriter and terminal), and the fact that printouts (*hard copy*) are automatically available. However, the printing speed (for output) is low, and the machine is not quiet.

The VDU is more complex, possessing a display unit screen, a keyboard (through which data may be input and requests made to the computer) and additional facilities such as a copy-producer which prints what appears on screen. A *wand* or *light pen* may be used on many VDUs in order to indicate a particular part of a display on screen which the operator wishes to know more about. A list of products, for instance, may be shown and if the wand is pointed at product X, the computer will provide standard information concerning that.

The VDU is now a standard medium for input in commercial and administrative applications, connected on-line to the central computer. This allows rapid updating of files, checking of input errors and permits guidance to be given by the computer to assist the operator's inputting. Note that we looked at the *on-line processing mode* in the previous chapter.

PoS

This is a typical on-line concept. The on-line version is an electronic cash register (as seen in supermarkets and other retail units) linked to a computer, of which many kinds exist. It may be fitted with a wand or lightpen to read optical bar coding (see the next section), or a device to read magnetic strip coding on cards. It may be linked to a minicomputer which receives direct, on-line input and updates stocklists immediately.

The disadvantage here lies in the relatively high cost, both of the system devices themselves and of transmission to the central computer. The latter point leads to the establishment of the off-line PoS approch.

Special approaches

These approaches, again, are very different from each other and our list simply includes the major ones.

Bar coding

This may be optical (consisting of black and white vertical strips) or magnetic (magnetic strip on a card).

In the bar code on the left, white represents 0 and black represents 1. Usually it is printed as part of the packaging, for example on the back page of a book cover.

9 780859 501712

In the magnetic version, the magnetic strip is encoded with binary patterns relating to size, price, origin.

Plastic cards and badges

The *badge* is a document which is pre-punched and usually (for durability) made of plastic. It provides fundamental information for identification. A remote *badge reader,* usually an on-line computer device, identifies the holder of the badge. This is clearly useful for security purposes.

Associated directly with another badge, or card, the system may be used to record particulars of a job undertaken in a factory. The holder inserts the badge or card into the reader which transmits the time of commencement and termination of the task. Inserting the badge or card will also allow access to the keyboard attached to the reader so that further particulars may be input to the computer.

Kimball tags

These are small tickets attached in a retail store to the price labels of items for sale. The tag has a section with perforations in it and, when the product is sold, this part is detached and then read by a device which converts the punched data to magnetic tape, paper tape or punched cards.

Optical mark recognition

Optical mark recognition (or reading) is based upon the assignment of values to marks placed upon a specially designed document. So we might have the choice of the number 5, indicated thus:

| 1 | 2 | 3 | 4 | 5̸ | 6 | 7 | 8 | 9 | 0 |

This approach is seen on meter-reading sheets for water, gas or electricity consumption. However, special forms are necessary, and mistakes can be easily made, and much space is required on the form, since each possible character needs a separate location.

A number of professional bodies and educational establishments adopt this method to evaluate multiple choice examination answers. The point about OMR is that the computer itself can produce the output in the form of a document, and this can then be marked to transform it into machine-readable input. The marking may be undertaken in ink or by pencil or typewriter.

Optical character recognition (OCR)

OCR is somewhat less popular today because of the relatively high cost of the equipment and the broad impracticality of the system for general usage. It is, however, well-established in certain areas.

Two major OCR *fonts* or typefaces exist for this method: OCR-A, which is American, and OCR-B, which is European. Some OCR readers will actually read ordinary typed letters and digits and printing in books. A device exists which combines OCR and voice output, for example to assist blind persons by reading to them. Hand-printing is also acceptable to some systems, but this has to be undertaken very carefully and is somewhat restricted in range.

OCR documents, like OMR, are able to be *turnaround documents* in that they can be printed by an appropriately equipped computer as output and then, after additions have been made manually, returned for reading (i.e. as input). The *optical readers:*
- are able to read documents, including cards and continuous stationery, of differing thickness and dimensions
- can display characters which are not recognised, for correction
- may include a sorting facility so that the documents can be directed to several stackers (or pockets, for grouping them together under special headings)
- are able to operate at a speed of 100 to 400 characters per second (cps), or, for document readers, at 1000 documents per minute
- can usually output on-line to a mainframe computer, or otherwise to tape or disk in off-line mode.

High volumes of text and graphics input are dealt with by a device known as an *intelligent character recognition reader* (ICR) which can read literally thousands of typestyles from A4 sheets. An example of this is the Kurzweil K5000 document scanning system, costing around £12 000, designed to assist the printing and publishing industry, but used for any type of high volume task. The advantages of this method are that:
- the system is a natural one, especially to the person on the staff who is not technically-oriented, and so the documents may be easily understood
- data is captured at source (no intermediate stage requiring keying in of data)
- printing by hand is acceptable, given that care is taken to conform to standard.

Disadvantages are:
- the high cost of OCR equipment
- the need to redraw the document used when the items listed on it are subject to change
- printing by hand is restricted to less than the complete alphabet.

Magnetic ink character recognition (MICR)
In MICR the human-recognisable characters are printed in special, magnetisable ink which permits a reader to recognise them. Examples of one form are given below.

$$0 \quad 1 \quad 4 \quad 9$$

The most frequent usage is by UK banking institutions. A line of MICR print is seen at the lower edge of cheques and this gives the serial number of the cheque, the bank and branch, the number of the account and, when the cheque goes through the system, there is the manual addition (using a device called the *inscriber*) of the sum stated on the cheque. The other items are all pre-printed.

The *magnetic ink readers* (or *document processors,* or *magnetic character sorter-readers*) recognise the imprinted characters and transfer the result to storage, or transfer data directly on-line.

Documents may be *stacked* or *pocketed* (grouped) by sorting, so that in the case of the banking application, cheques may be thus processed according to the account number. The sophisticated reader can, in addition, accumulate and print totals and also check the documents to make sure they incorporate a specific number and are stacked in sequence.

A speed of up to 2400 documents per minute can be attained, and this explains the adoption of the system for clearing bank operations.

Voice input

The idea of *voice* or human speech input is now coming into use. The development of sophisticated workstations linked to each other and to central computers tends to demand more and more ways of linking people with computers.

The major problem of voice input is *speech recognition.* Some systems are *speaker dependent* (they can recognise only one speaker's message); others are *speaker independent* (recognising the words of a user who has not previously been involved in the system). However, these usually have only a small vocabulary of a dozen or so words.

Advantages gained from the adoption of speech recognition systems include the fact that accuracy of input is achieved at a higher level than is the case for keyed-in data. The reason is that when the user is carrying out a basic task he or she is not interrupted by the need to key in data. Instead the user's voice indicates the data to be input. 'Eyes and hands busy' is the way we now describe such an activity, the speech being the input method.

An example of this idea is seen in parts inspection and quality control. Traditionally, the inspector concerned would be obliged to interrupt the activity by reporting defects on a form, or using a keyboard. Using voice input, however, part numbers and defects may be recorded without pausing in the inspection activity. At present the office environment has a very limited range of voice technology. Despite this, market opportunities worth billions of dollars have been forecast in the area of speech technology for the early 1990s.

Summary

In this chapter we have discussed:
- the simple division of computer operations into:
    - input
    - storage
    - processing
    - output
    - control (a constant process)
- the basic configuration of the computer:
    - the CPU
    - the control console
    - the input unit
    - the output unit
    - backing storage
- types of computer and their usage:
    - digital and analog
    - the parallel approaches
    - microcomputers
    - minicomputers
    - mainframes
- the idea of workstations
- input methods:
    - data collection and data capture
    - off-line input (punched cards, paper tape, magnetic tape and disk, and by-product techniques)
    - on-line input (keyboard, PoS)
    - special approaches (bar coding, plastic cards, badges, kimball tags, OMR, OCR, MICR, voice).

Self-test Questions

Answer these questions, then check back to assess your answers.

1 What is the computer configuration comprised of?
2 Explain the following terms.
    a) CPU   b) IAS   c) ALU   d) peripherals   e) computer
3 List the basic computer activities undertaken in processing.
4 How can we distinguish between various sizes of computer?
5 What is parallelism?
6 Explain the nature and functions of the workstation.
7 What are data capture and data collection?
8 List the methods of data input, categorising them as off-line, on-line, special approaches.
9 Distinguish between OMR and OCR.
10 How does MICR work?

CHAPTER 4
Computer hardware 2

Introduction

In this chapter we continue looking at computer hardware by examining output methods. There are basically four categories of these:

- visual display (transient messages) on VDU
- computer output in microform (COM)
- printing
- voice, or audio response.

After we have discussed these methods, we shall consider what aspects have to be taken into account when a choice is made from both input and output alternatives.

Output

We have already said that we are able to categorise output methods by placing them in groups according to their specific methodology. But we can also categorise overall by listing them under the headings of *human comprehensible,* and *machine comprehensible.*

As far as human comprehensibility is concerned, the methods listed in the introduction belong to this category (although note that in COM a reader is necessary for humans to read the results). On the other hand, in the machine comprehensible category we include magnetic media (tape, disk), optical media (optical or laser disk), punched card and paper tape.

From this it is clear that the output's purpose is to provide *processed data* (i.e. information) either for immediate use or for storage. Machine comprehensible methods, therefore, tend to relate to the latter purpose.

Visual (transient) display

The message received by the visual display unit (VDU) is *transient* or temporary. We discussed terminals previously and saw that they usually also have printout facilities as well. The size of the screen will restrict the use of displays. Normal VDU capacity is 20 rows per frame or *page*, at a maximum of 80 characters a line. The advantage of this form of output lies in the fact that a dialogue can be conducted and rapid responses obtained from the computer. VDUs are not actually used as commonly as one may think. The reason for this is there is a difficulty in training non-specialist staff in their effective use.

There is also the problem of fatigue which can be caused by prolonged use of the VDU. Some organisations have agreed with trade unions to restrict the viewing period for an individual at any one time. Two features of the VDU are *paging* and *scrolling.* The former means that the screen is used to display a complete page at a time, rather like turning over the pages of a file or book. The latter refers to the ability to move the display upwards or downwards, a line at a time, similar to the movement of film and television titles on screen.

The VDU has a specific *repertoire* of displayable characters. Usually it consists of the American Standard Code for Information Interchange (ASCII), applied to 64 characters and symbols.

In addition to characters, graphic displays may be provided; both can be presented in combinations of the three primary colours (thus offering seven in all), also incorporating differing levels of brightness.

COM

COM is computer output in microform (i.e. in the form of microfilm or microfiche). It refers to direct recording of output from the computer in microform. The microfiche is a sheet of film 15 cm × 10 cm (6″ × 4″), capable of holding several hundred pages (A4). It is the degree of reduction which governs the number of pages able to be held, and it is possible to store 3000 pages (A4) on a microfiche (an *ultrafiche*) given that the reduction ratio is high.

The microfilm is a roll of film (16 mm or 35 mm) and each one is capable of storing 2000–5000 frames or pages. The microfilm is less compact than the microfiche, and it is usually easier to use the latter, especially if and when a page has to be modified. In the case of microfilm, it is likely that the complete roll would have to be replaced; you will recall that the same problem applies also to punched cards and rolls of paper tape.

The *reader* or viewer magnifies the film or fiche to a size which permits the information to be read. Some readers are capable of accepting differing kinds of microform (including short film lengths known as *strips*), and also of making copies.

A good example of the use of COM is seen in a building society which has four million depositors and 330 branches. It films over 480 000 documents per month and produces 30 000 microfiches. The COM installation processes information from two different mainframes (a Burroughs and an ICL) which have different fiche formats. Data to be processed is held on magnetic tape, and a minicomputer controls the processing.

Information held through COM operation is obtained from storage by *computer assisted retrieval* (CAR), as an alternative to manual viewing. The advantages of COM are:
- the actual medium is less costly per page than paper is, and dissemination of information (where postal services are used) is cheaper than using the paper medium
- storage space is saved (the exact saving being dependent upon the ratio of reduction)
- microfiche and microfilm are durable (more so than paper)
- a COM recorder is more rapid in operation than the average printer (operating at about 1000 pages per minute if it is 'top of the range').

The disadvantages are:
- unless CAR is adopted, each location where users wish to read microfiche or microfilm must be equipped with a reader
- updating can present a problem if required on a frequent basis
- microform reading can (as in the case of VDUs) cause the user to suffer from fatigue.

Printing

The categories of printers originally consisted of two basic types of devices (daisywheels and matrix printers), but, over the years, new technology has been developed and this has been augmented by new business requirements for higher printing quality.

Today we can adopt three broad categories, for the sake of simplicity:
- character
- line
- page.

Each one of these, in turn, has individual kinds of printer. The diagram expresses this in simple form. First of all, let us get some definitions clear. You will notice that the terms *impact* and *non-impact* are used here.

Impact printers use mechanical pressure to transfer a character through an inked ribbon. In other words we have the principle adopted in typewriting.

Non-impact printers do not use this approach. Instead, they produce the output by various means including the use of special, sensitive paper which changes colour when voltage is applied to the writing component. These printers are quieter.

Character printers

These are also called *serial printers,* and they print a single character (letter, figure, symbol) at a time. The most commonly-encountered version is the electronic typewriter.

The *non-impact* devices under this heading consist of solid ink, ink-jet, bubble and electro-thermal printers.

Solid ink printers This idea was developed in the late 1980s and uses a solid ink pellet which is provided in a small cartridge. The ink is heated until it becomes liquid and is then ejected from the print-head. Upon striking the paper it penetrates and solidifies quickly. This printer can operate at a speed of 480 characters per second (cps) but, if used at half that speed the *resolution* (or clarity) of the printing is of higher quality. The price is around £2200.

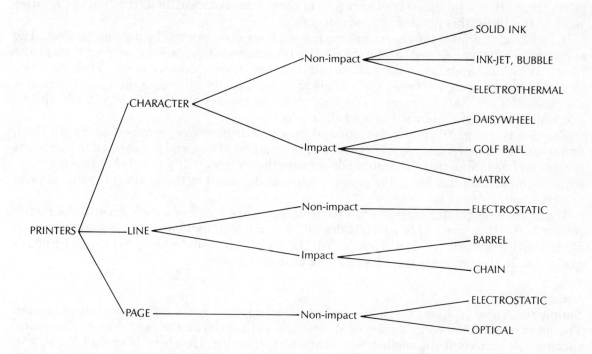

Ink-jet, bubble printers Usual ink-jet printers eject special ink from a thin nozzle, controlled by an electric, variable field. The jet of ink is thus *painted* on to the paper (which does not have to be of special type) in the same way as if someone were to use a spray (aerosol) can.

The latest version is the *bubble jet printer* (produced by Canon, and referred to as the BJ-130). This device ejects ink using thermally-generated bubbles. It is capable of printing over a wide area and has two speed modes: 220 cps, and 110 cps (for high-quality print). Each ink cartridge used (40 cc) has sufficient ink for 1 000 000 characters of high-quality mode. The price is about £800. Other ink-jet printers include Hewlett-Packards *Thinkjet,* the Xerox 4020 colour-printer, and the Diconix (Kodak) Model 150 which is half the size of a telephone directory, battery-powered and very versatile.

Electrothermal Here we have an array of elements, some of which are heated electrically to cause a chemical modification in the paper in the shape of dots. This creates the impression of a given character. Special paper has to be used, and the printer cannot produce more than one copy at the same time (a typewriter, for instance, can do this, using carbon copying).

Impact printers under this category of character devices are daisywheel, golf ball and matrix.

Daisy wheel Sometimes known as *petal printers* because of the shape of the print wheel (a central circular hub surrounded by stalks or petals like the daisy flower), these are very common and possibly account for up to 50 per cent of the market for printers, although rapid changes occurred in the late 1980s. The dominant producer of daisywheels (also popular for electronic typewriters) is Brother.

The principle involved in this printer is for each of the print hammers to carry a specific character outline. The hammers are arranged around the perimeter of a rotating print wheel. When the appropriate hammer is in position, it strikes through the ink-ribbon on to the paper. Speed is around 30 cps.

There is also a need for high-quality print which *impacts* indelibly on to paper. This applies particularly to such organisations as banks, insurance companies and legal partnerships, who need printers which make such a definite mark that the imprint cannot be erased from the paper.

Golf ball The ball is of plastic or metal and has on its surface the embossed character outlines. The ball rotates and changes its angle so that the appropriate character presses against the ribbon.

Matrix These are *dot matrix* printers, sometimes known as *wire matrix*. Early in their development, these printers produced relatively poor quality print, not ideal for letters, but in the latter years of the 1980s, this problem was overcome.

In this kind of printer the characters are formed from dots, printed by a group of wires. The appropriate wires are selected to form the required character outline and they impact through the ribbon on to the paper. Most dot matrix printers have a *letter quality mode*. The characters formed by the group of wires are clearly made up of dots, so, the more dots there are, the clearer the characters are. Early printers of this type produced characters with the dots clearly visible, and which were slightly blurred around their edges.

The speed of the matrix printer is around 100 to 480 for *draft mode* (i.e. lower quality printing), and around 40 to 100 for *letter quality mode* (higher quality). The speed is measured in characters per second (cps). Note that the draft mode is faster than letter quality simply because the latter requires the actual print-head (the group of wires in this case) to travel along the line of print several times.

The price of the printer ranges from £200 to £2000. An example of a sophisticated dot matrix printer is the Honeywell 4/66, which is described as a *multifunction colour matrix printer*. It offers a choice of *character attributes*, such as the use of italics, underlining to provide emphasis and so on. It also produces graphics (e.g. pie charts) in colour.

Line

Simply put, these printers print a line (not a character) at a time in a very short space of time. The speed of operation varies a great deal according to the need for the printer to create vertical spacing and horizontal spacing between characters. However, the speed is around 150 to 3000 lines per minute.

This kind of printer tends to be standard equipment for minicomputers and mainframes, but may, of course, be supplemented by other types as well.

The *non-impact* category consists of electrostatic devices.

Electrostatic This needs special paper and an array of wires which produce an electrostatic charge on the paper. This causes carbon particles to collect on the charged points where a chemical solution is then applied. This gives the shape of the characters.

This approach is used for *graph plotters* but not normally for printing needs in offices.

The *impact* versions are barrel and chain printers.

Barrel Alternatively called *drum*, this printer is comprised of a cylinder which rotates very rapidly and has the characters embossed upon its surface. Each individual print position has the complete set of characters embossed. There may, for example, be a total of 160 print positions horizontally, i.e. the *line of print* consists of 160 places either for characters or spaces. If there is a total of 64 characters in the set, then the device would have to have a total of 10 240 (i.e. 64 × 160) embossed characters on its drum.

The barrel printer often produces slight irregularity in the straight shape of the line and slight blurring of the printed characters. This is because the hammers have to strike the carbon ribbon very rapidly to produce the characters upon the paper, but the rings or bands of characters are moving all the time. This method is called *fly printing.*

Chain The printer operates by using a horizontal, rotating chain upon which characters are set. Each print position (as in the barrel printer) has a hammer which impacts through the ribbon to coincide with the arrival of the appropriate character.

As in the case of the barrel printer, effective timing is vital. However, the line produced is always regular because the chain works from a constant lateral position.

The chain can be changed to provide an alternative type of print character if the user so wishes.

This category of printers is sometimes referred to as if it included some character printers. In fact this tends to be the case, where the character printers are capable of operating speeds equal to the *lower end* of the line printer market. But the real *line printer* incorporates a separate mechanism for each individual print position along the width of the sheet of paper.

Page

Page printers are, by their very nature, non-impact. There are electrostatic and optical (laser) printers.

Electrostatic We have already seen how this device operates. As a page printer, it creates dots (80 per centimetre or 200 per inch) of a sufficient density to produce high quality characters, in accordance with the programmed codings. Business letterheadings, and *logos* can be created in this way.

Optical The optical (or laser) printer operates by creating the image of a page of print on the surface of a special drum, using a laser beam of low power. A *toner* (special ink) is then attracted to the drum areas exposed to the laser beam and this is transferred as a permanent entity on to the paper. When this is done, the drum is cleared of that image, ready for the next page, and so on.

The laser printer arrived on the market in the mid-1980s, and fairly rapidly became accepted as a fast and sophisticated letter quality printer. This *high resolution printing,* plus the ability to print graphics, means that the printer can be used to produce reports, charts and complex documents (e.g. newsletters).

Most laser printers are founded upon the principles of photocopying. Even though they are rapid in operation, they are, in comparison with other methods, at a disadvantage in that they take around one minute to formulate a page in memory prior to printing it. After this the laser printer prints at the rate of about eight to ten copies of that same page per minute. Note that the traditional line printers we were looking at print at the rate of around 20 pages per minute at least.

There are various models of laser printers available, ranging from the Siemens 2300 (price about £200 000) with a declared output of 200 pages per minute to various small versions such as the Sony OA-P5108 at around £2500, for use with Sony word-processors, at eight A4 pages per minute. However, most laser printers cannot handle anything other than A4 paper size.

The printer of the future is likely to be able to cope with a number of completely different applications, producing magnified or reduced images as required. Note that there are rival technologies being researched, operating quite differently (e.g. magnetography, ion deposition, etc.).

Voice output

The idea of speech output is actually simpler than voice input, simply because machine recognition and comprehension of speech requires a complex technology. Outputting speech messages by computers is likely to require a vast amount of storing by the computer; for technical reasons, ten minutes of computer speech would require nearly 38.5 million bits of storage! There are ways of reducing this level, though.

In given circumstances speech (voice or audio) output provides an advantage, although it is not considered as an alternative to the other methods. This is especially the case where the user is disabled, blind (devices are able now to read – *scan* – text and convert this to speech, although the voice sounds mechanical and unemotional) or where the user is working under conditions requiring intensive use or hands and eyes.

Selecting input and output methods media

We have reached the point in our study where we need to take stock of the aspects which have to be considered when a selection from the complexity of input and output methods has to be made. For example, input methods constitute a vital and large expense within the computer system. On the other hand, output devices are also vital keypoints to the system, especially the printers which are workhorses of the computer, always being used.

Input and output media

Of course we can adopt different methods for both input and output but we also have to look at different kinds of hardware devices. So, we should examine the methods first, and then find the best devices to undertake the method chosen.

In the case of both input and output we should bear in mind the following areas:
- finance, the availability of funds and the need to minimise cost
- information needs of management and staff
- data volumes and frequencies of input/output
- the level of complexity of the data
- skills possessed by user staff
- the situation with regard to human resources available.

Input

Specifically, we need to discover:
- *costs* data collection and capture do constitute a major cost area and so we should look at the cost of media, operator(s), and space taken by the device(s)
- *data* the quantity of the data for input (magnetic media are able to cope with large input volumes efficiently), once preparation has been undertaken
- the timing involved (how long data collection takes, recalling that data conversion is time-consuming)
- flexibility needs (what changes in data may occur in future?)
- accuracy requirements – data must be prepared *and* input correctly (OCR is a help here because it reduces the possibility of human error)
- *reliability* the risk that the data collection system will break down has to be minimised as far as possible
- *applicability* the method and the medium must be directly appropriate to the work to be done (e.g. the concept of bar coding is applied to a specific task).

Output

It will be useful here if we regard *printers* as a special case for consideration, largely because in general all computers have some kind of printout device, irrespective of the presence of other forms of output. So, to select printers we should need to know:
- *requirements* a daisywheel, for example, is not suited to graphics, but is excellent for letters
- *speed* as a rule, the faster the machine the more expensive it is

- *noise levels* non-impact printers are quieter than impact printers, although some printers have a 'quiet mode' which can be adopted when needed
- *printout materials* impact printers are usually flexible, but some non-impact ones can only print on special paper
- *quality* how much printing is required to be of letter quality (usually, a dot matrix is suited to draft mode, a daisywheel to letter quality)
- *colour* some printers provide this as an optional extra
- *interface* what devices the printer will need to link up with (network), and how compatible they are
- *maintenance and support* the assistance available from the suppliers in the case of problems, and the extent of maintenance required by the printer (how often, how costly?)
- *size* is only desktop space available, or is the printer a separate unit on the floor?

The selection of visual display units (VDUs) may be regarded in the same way, with special considerations such as:

- *message size* the number of characters per line, and lines per page (displayable at the same time)
- *screen* the colour combinations available (e.g. yellow on a green background), and the level of brightness (is it adjustable?)
- *display acceptability* if viewed for long periods of time, how acceptable this is
- *ergonomic considerations* since ergonomics (the study of human beings in relation to their psychological and physiological environment) is important, how suitable for the users is the design and positioning of the keyboard (adjustable?).

We have looked at enough computer system hardware to make us realise that there is a great array of high technology devices available to assist organisations in the provision of information. What we will look at now is the idea of information technology (IT).

Information technology

Information technology (IT) has an official UK definition which originates from the Department of Trade and Industry. It is:

> *the use of computers, microelectronics and telecommunications to help us produce, store, obtain and send information in the form of pictures, words or numbers, more reliably, quickly and economically.*

The term *office automation* (OA) is also commonly used and, strictly speaking, this suggests that there is some form of automatic, logical sequence of activities adopted from source to final completion, this being held to incorporate the discovery and correction of any errors. In fact, this is not (yet!) possible for the entire office. However, there are certainly in existence forms of OA in the office for given activities; word-processing (WP) is a good example in which there is control by the processor of the format, correction of any errors in spelling and so forth.

In this section we look at the significance and components of the typical IT or OA approach in the office.

IT devices

Before we go on to look at the major devices used in IT, it has to be said that, according to a survey conducted by the National Computing Centre (NCC) in 1985, about four out of every ten micro-computers stand idle within twelve months of being purchased. This does indicate that wrong decisions are taken concerning selection of equipment (you will recall that we stressed the considerations involved in selection of input/output methods and media).

There is a widespread idea that, for example, the microcomputer is the best possible answer for all OA needs. However, statistics derived from *The PC market in the UK* (Wharton Information Services, end 1980s edition) show that three out of ten micros used by professional businesses are used in the main for word and text processing. Certainly, though, for accounting and other calculation-based activity, the micro does constitute a great step forward. We shall now look at these devices:

- wordprocessors (WPs)
- desktop publishing (DTP)
- electronic mail (Email)
- facsimile (fax)
- videotex.

Word-processors (WP) and desktop publishers (DTP)

Before we go on, we have to consider the point that word-processing is different from desktop publishing. The latter is the logical successor to the former and is a more sophisticated development allowing text and graphics to be produced. First of all, however, we shall deal with word-processors.

Consider the fact that every human being is actually a processor of words, a WP! Humans are less efficient at this when they are not assisted by the WP device, simply because with the device one is able to deal with all the documents to be produced in transient form – on screen – and then instruct the machine to print a page only when everything is in acceptable form (and correctly spelt!).

There are dedicated WPs available (i.e. devices which undertake WP activities and nothing else), but the tendency in the late 1980s was to make use of a *software package* (a readymade and supplied program) to allow the microcomputer to undertake word-processing.

Where the idea of WP is part of the general computer system within the organisation, then there is access to central files, and access also to particular printers available (for, say, letter quality production). The WP also usually has its own dictionary so that it can automatically compare the words input with the words listed. Standard sentences and paragraphs are also stored in the WP, so that the user can merely instruct it to print one – or a combination of – these for inclusion in the text. Dictionaries in WPs range from 20 000 to 100 000 words, and some permit additions of special terms by users.

A further facility in WPs is *mail-merging,* which prints out standard letters incorporated with files of names and addresses.

Desktop publishing (DTP) is the natural development from what is known as *wysiwyg* (what you see is what you get). Certainly this concept applies also to WPs, but in the case of DTP, the use of what is called a *machine-independent page description language* (pdl) allows the idea to apply to page printers linked to the DTP device, and thus to produce high-quality printing of the formalised pages. It conveys requirements to the print-control unit.

DTP is able to mix both text and graphics on screen and on the printed page and is thus aimed at creating more effective communication. An example of DTP is seen in the Macintosh PageMaker desktop publishing system which allows the user to design and lay out a publication on the microcomputer's screen, amend the text, add graphics and mix typestyles and typefaces without difficulty. Standard items of text can, if required, be inserted on each individual page, or on selected pages.

Electronic mail (Email)

We have here a slightly confusing issue, because, to many people, the concept of Email signifies *telex* and/or *facsimile* (fax). We shall be treating fax separately in this study, but we will deal with telex now, to avoid difficulties.

Telex is a universal service with a large number of worldwide subscribers (about one million). It is an advanced form of text service which uses relatively slow and basic equipment. Subscribers are each assigned a unique telex number and can seek information from directories and from operators. However, there is also *teletex* (don't confuse this with *teletext,* which is quite different and dealt with below). This is sometimes referred to as *supertelex,* and this is probably the device of the future in terms of Email. Transmission using this device is undertaken at about ten seconds a page (or 3500 words per minute), some 30 times faster than basic telex.

The complete set of transmissible characters has 300 members, including capital letters, accents and non-English characters (although they must be based on the Latin format, so Russian and Greek transmissions in those languages are not yet possible).

It is also suggested that a *gateway* (i.e. a link between two dissimilar systems) could now be established between teletex and fax.

The approach to Email is sometimes called *mailboxing,* i.e. at some point or other in the system, the subscriber has a *mailbox* to which all other subscribers are able to despatch mail (letters, notes, etc.) which is only accessible to the individual supervising that mailbox. The large mailbox systems in the UK include British Telecom Gold. This is an electronic mail system linking telex with a text editor, a noticeboard (drawing attention to important issues) and a device to check spelling. There is also Istel's Comet which is a privately-operated bureau service.

Note that in the case of both these services, Gold and Comet, there is no need for a special terminal to be used. Given a connecting device (this is a *modem* which we shall be looking at when we discuss networks), WPs and microcomputers can be used for Email purposes.

We have been looking here at Email for external (national and international) communication, but it is also commonly used for large organisations internally. A number of computer suppliers offer this facility with their OA systems.

Facsimile (fax)

This approach has been called *photocopying down the telephone.* The typical late 1980s version (no bigger than the office typewriter) is able to transmit any page of text to any remote location which has a telephone linkage and a compatible machine. This includes diagrams, signatures, rough sketches, handwritten messages and so on. The more advanced versions link the fax to computers and to electronic document storage.

It is also possible to transmit hard copy images (including graphics) of text from a fax device to a microcomputer. The latter stores the text received and it can thus be displayed on-screen, merged with WP documents, amended and edited, and then returned to the fax unit for distribution. The material can also be stored on the micro's disk memory, sent to other computers and/or printed out (using any kind of printer).

Various versions of fax exist; one example is the ITT 3536 (at a price of around £4000), which has a memory facility. Data from the scanned documents may be stored in memory for extraction and transmission at some later time. For security purposes, the receiving fax allows the document to be stored at once and extracted only when the authorised recipient – using a special four-digit code – wishes. It is also capable of adopting *encryption units* which scramble or mix up the text before transmission, and then unscramble it when it is to be read.

There is also a portable fax version (Xerox 7010, price just over £2000) which plugs into any British Telecom square-type telephone socket and uses power from the nearest socket plug providing electricity. This can transmit two pages of graphics and text in less than 60 seconds.

Videotex

The name *videotex* is given in general to teletext and viewdata. The former is a one-way transmission, broadcast in the UK as Ceefax and Oracle. This offers *switch-on* access by the user to business data such as foreign exchange rates and other data such as weather forecasts. It may be received via a television set, or as part of a range of facilities provided by a terminal.

The central core of a viewdata system is a central computer storing information and with appropriate software to handle and edit pages. Viewdata terminals exist to communicate (two-way) with the computer, using standard telephone links. These *dedicated* terminals have simpler technology than computer terminals do. Alternatively, microcomputers or workstations can be used. Travel agents, in particular, use the viewdata approach, and this is a private system.

A system (Vistec XSELL) has been developed which aims at assisting sales management activities. It links the headquarters computer with remote terminals to provide a multi-way communication network. Senior managers are thus able to obtain immediate feedback reports for analysis to allow them to modify, as need be, marketing plans. It also eliminates some paperwork for sales staff in the field and any changes may be communicated at once from head office.

The advantage gained by use of the viewdata (as opposed to the computer system) concept lies in the fact that viewdata requires much less training. Also, viewdata may be accessed anywhere where there is a telephone (no need for special cables) and the dedicated viewdata terminals cost around one third of the price of a computer terminal, and less than a microcomputer.

Comment

It has been said that if UK banks did not use computers, then they would have to employ 50 per cent of the country's adult population to write up the books for today's current accounts! This does indicate that IT, or OA, is virtually indispensable to firms in this and other countries. Statistics indicate that the world has in operation some 10 000 000 computer systems, and in the UK alone some 5 000 000 workers use computers.

A classic example of the use of a computer system is seen in British Airways, which is able to make passenger reservations (26 classes of fare) one year in advance on over 750 flights per day. However, we have to realise that although computers and the other electronic devices we have been looking at in this chapter are helpful and of great importance, they are not to be taken as substitutes for human control. They are intended to assist humans but not in such a way that humans are subordinate to the devices.

We still have to carry out a great deal of work on systems, software, and the ergonomic implications (remember that ergonomics is the study of the relationship between humans and their psychological and physiological environment) of computers. Only by accomplishing this shall we be able to ensure that IT machinery will provide more assistance and less stress.

Summary

In this chapter we have discussed:
- methods and media for computer output, broadly expressed as human-comprehensible and machine-comprehensible, but in detail listed as:
     visual display on VDU
     COM (computer output in microform)
     printing
     voice response
- the categorisation of COM into fiche and film, and of printers into impact and non-impact, and as:
     character
     line
     page
- the selection of input and output methods and media, bearing in mind:
     finance
     information needs
     data volume and frequencies
     data complexity
     staff skills
     availability of staff
- specific considerations when considering individual media:
     IT and OA
     WPs, DTP devices
     Email
     fax
     videotex (teletext and viewdata)
- the significance of IT, OA for human beings.

Self-test Questions

Now tackle these questions, checking back afterwards.

1 Explain the terms human comprehensible and machine comprehensible.
2 List advantages and disadvantages in adopting COM.
3 Distinguish fully between impact printers and non-impact printers, giving examples of each kind.
4 Produce a diagram illustrating the various kinds of printers available for use with computer systems.
5 How does a matrix printer differ in operation from an ink-jet printer?
6 When considering the selection of input/output methods and media, what must be borne in mind?
7 What special aspects have to be considered in choosing a VDU?
8 Define IT.
9 What is DTP and how does it function?
10 How does teletex differ from teletext?
11 What do the following abbreviations stand for?
    a) VDU   b) OA   c) COM   d) wysiwyg   e) DTP   f) cps   g) fax

CHAPTER 5
Files and their storage

Introduction

Having looked at a good deal of the hardware involved in computer and IT systems generally, we must now consider the very important question of files (their content, their structure, their organisation) and also methods of storing data. When we have looked at this area, then we can go on and look at *networking* and other practical aspects. But, what *is* a file?

A *file* is a collection of data items which have been organised into records so that individual data items or records may be retrieved as required for processing. Or, expressed more succinctly, the file is a collection of related records.

A *record* is a group of facts which relate to a given thing or aspect. The group of facts is regarded as a complete unit.

The activity of *filing* means arranging, storing, indexing these records with the aim of making them easily accessible. This means that:
- records must be preserved intact
- the grouping of the records must be convenient for access
- access should be able to be immediately undertaken
- the files are updated on a regular basis.

We are talking here of *all* files, not only computerised versions.

The filing system

Irrespective of the kind of system the office has, for the sake of efficiency it must be:
- simple (to operate and understand)
- secure (e.g. using fireproof cabinets)
- operated with a system of classification which is appropriate
- up to date
- expandable
- integrated (using some form of cross-referencing)
- cost-effective.

To this end, the concept of *central filing* is often adopted, with all documents which relate to the same topic-area held in common files, located in a central filing unit. Sometimes there is a compromise, and departments and sections hold their own current files, with the *historic* or outdated information located centrally.

Central filing

Advantages of this approach are that:
- there is uniformity in filing methods
- filing activity is more closely monitored
- improved management control of the records is obtained
- the files are clearly organisational, and not the property of parts of the firm

- all documents/records relating to a given area may be filed collectively
- specialist staff and equipment may be maintained effectively.

Disadvantages are:
- information may be less rapidly accessible, certainly in the case of manual (non-computerised) files
- staff engaged in central filing lack specialised (departmental) knowledge of files
- the possibility of loss of records is increased for large systems.

Categories of file

We have to identify the various file categories.

Master files

These incorporate vital system data which is permanently held with the given system and processed as required. Master files relate to important subjects such as customers, personnel, products, etc.

They include names, addresses, reference numbers and so on in the case of customer and personnel master files, and usually items such as product names, prices, descriptions in the case of the product files. There are two sub-categories of master files:
- *reference files* containing static records, which are not very likely to alter very much, e.g. addresses, account numbers, product codes
- *dynamic files* here the information needs frequent updating, as in the case of a bank's current accounts held by customers.

These two kinds of file may be held separately or joined to form a kind of hybrid version.

Input and output files

These files convey data *to* the system and information which has been processed *from* the system, respectively. In the case of a computer system, an input file could include *hours worked* for input to the wages system. An output file could contain the processed results to be printed.

Transfer files

These are files used by the computer system in processing activity. They carry (transfer) data between systems as necessary, or from one file to another file, or from one computer activity to another. It may be that data has been extracted from a master file, prior to printing, for instance.

Transaction files

These carry data which is, by its nature, transient, and which relates to individual happenings in a given period of time. The contents of the transaction file are, after a specified period, used to update a master file, for instance. An example of this is a transaction file of stock movements used at the end of a day to update stock level records.

Work files

These are, again, transient files and they contain data obtained from other files which must be treated in some way before the contents are useful. For example, data could be obtained by the computer and held on a work file. There could then be a *sort* process which takes that data and puts it into a given (e.g. alphabetic) sequence. Thus, data from the work file would then be transferred (in accordance with the need for sequence) on to a sorted file. Work files, then, are intermediate.

Dump files

These files are used to maintain a copy of the results obtained by a system up to a given point. The file holds the processing outcome as a security measure. The results would not be lost if the computer for any reason became out of action.

Library files

In computer terminology these files hold the programs which are needed for a given application or job by the computer.

The structure of computer files

Although what we have said when talking generally may be applied to all sorts of files – manual or computerised – we now concentrate upon the files which are incorporated within the computer system, and then we go on to look at the various categories of computer storage media.

The computer file is simply, like any other file, a collection of related records, held in some form of sequence related to the *key field* (i.e. a specific aspect of the record used to identify it). In the case of, for instance, a file of customer records', the account number is likely to be the chosen key field, so that the records are in account number order, or sequence.

Consider the diagram below.

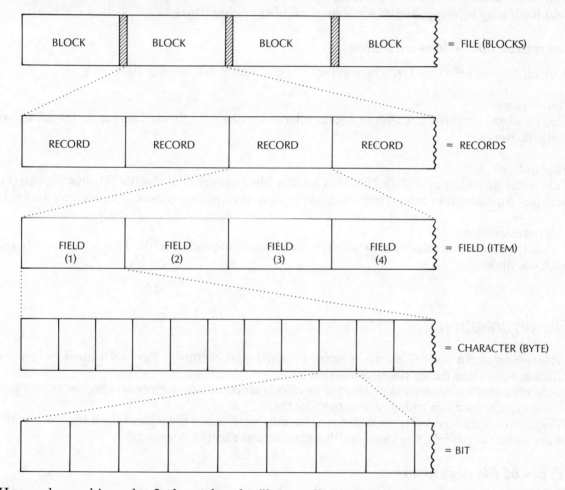

Here we have a hierarchy. It shows that the *file* is a collection of records, a *record* is a collection of fields (one common to all being the key field for identification purposes), a *field* consists of a number of characters (bytes or words), and a *character* is constituted by a number of binary digits (*bits*).

Suppose we take a typical record, with, say, six fields.

PRODUCT

		Number of characters
NAME:	Workdesk	8
MATERIAL:	Steel	5
CODE NUMBER:	WS234A	6
PRICE:	£65	3
MODEL:	3-drawer	8
COLOUR:	Black	5

In this example, for this particular item in the file, we have a total of 35 characters (plus spaces between) to account for. Perhaps the description could be written more efficiently to reduce the total, but without causing confusion?

This brings us to the fact that records may be of *fixed or variable length.*

In *fixed length* records, there is the same number of characters, neither more nor less. But, to take our example, suppose the material were *plastic,* instead of *steel*? The data field would have to be wide enough to take two additional letters (characters). This applies to every field, of course. The fixed length record has a given space assigned to it, and so if smaller numbers of characters are used in some cases, then space is wasted.

In *variable length records,* each record is able to accept a varying number of fields and each field itself may be comprised of a different number of characters.

Computer operations and files

Basically, there are three types of computer operations which involve files.

File enquiry

This consists of scrutinising files to obtain information held by them. There is no modification of file contents.

File update

This is the amendment of data held in a master file, in order that the file reflects the current position. An example of this is the posting of the sum received in payment of a customer account.

File maintenance

This is the continuing activity of deleting or adding standing data in a file. This is often combined with file update.

File organisation

We are now about to look at the manner in which the computer file is designed to operate efficiently. We can define file organisation as
   the relationship between the values of key fields on consecutive records, and the location on
   the storage medium which is occupied by these.
What has to be understood is the direct relationship between the file organisation and the method of accessing its records, i.e. between file organisation and the access mode.

Types of file organisation

There are five types of file organisation:
- serial
- sequential
- indexed-sequential

- random
- chained.

Serial organisation

There is no logical sequence whatever – the data is inserted as and when it arises. Neither is there an index for reference. For instance, orders arriving during the day may well be punched onto paper tape (unsorted) and then copied to a magnetic medium. The only order or sequence in this case is chronological.

Sequential organisation

The records are held in the key field sequence. Master files are organised in this way, as a rule. There is no index, but the principle involved in seeking items from this file is based upon logic. If the sequence is alphabetical, then the name SMITH would be found before SOUTH but after SAVIDGE.

Indexed-sequential organisation

Here we have an index system founded upon a particular key. This index is consulted to allow location. There are usually unfilled locations to cater for additional records.

Random organisation

This concept establishes a relationship between the key field of the record and its address (location). A straightforward instance (but not very common!) is where record number 1177 is actually found in location number 1177. Usually, the key of the record is used to calculate the address. No index is required.

Chained organisation

In this type, a given record has a linkage (is *chained*) with another one and this, in turn, leads to a further record. The program pursues the trail, one record leading to another.

File processing

We have said already that file organisation is the manner in which the computer file is arranged (and, sometimes, indexed).

File processing is the way in which the computer program retrieves records from a file, transfers these to memory (for the purpose of updating, perhaps, or transacting in some way), and transfers these back (if necessary) to the file.

Note that the file can only be organised in one way, but it may well be possible to process the records in several different ways.

File processing methods differ according to whether all records are read into (taken into) the memory of the computer, and are read in the actual sequence in which they are stored. Main types of file processing are:

- serial
- sequential
- selective-sequential
- random.

Serial processing

Each record has to be read, until the last record is dealt with. So any file *organised* according to the serial concept must be read serially, i.e. processed in that way.

Sequential processing

In the same way, data which is *organised* sequentially can only be processed in that way. As in serial processing, each record is read one after the other; although, of course, the records are in sequence of some kind.

Selective-sequential processing

Once again, the file can only be processed sequentially, one record after another, but here only the records which are required are taken into memory. Records not sought are ignored.

Random processing

This approach allows records to be selected at random. It is used where on-line systems process transactions as they arise and thus do not have the chance to sort or sequence them prior to filing. For a randomly-organised file, this is generally the only logical approach.

Before we consider the factors involved in selecting a file organisation approach, we must examine a couple of different kinds of storage media. Whilst we shall be looking at the types of organisation in detail, it is necessary for us to appreciate the way in which *serial access devices* and *direct access devices* operate.

Serial and direct access

These two categories are very important. The difference is simple to understand once we realise that direct access is the way we look up the meaning of a word in a dictionary, for example. We do not, if we want to have the word *whittle* explained, begin at word one, page 1 and then go through every single line until we reach the Ws! The same applies to any manual set of files. Human beings always adopt direct access. If they want to select a given track on a record to play it, they look at the index and then move the needle to the point which they estimate is appropriate. They may have to adjust the position for accuracy, but at least they do not begin at track one and play them all.

Only computerisation introduces serial access in reality.

Serial access

This arises where we have a single strip used for storage, such as we find in the case of magnetic tape, punched cards or paper tape used as storage media.

Using magnetic tape as our example, the structure is as follows.

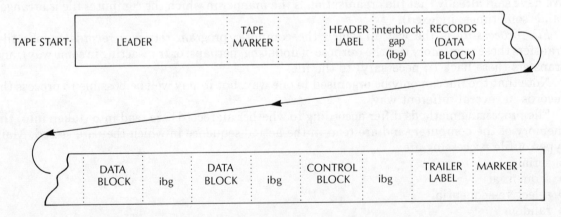

What we see above is the manner in which a file is stored on magnetic tape. Note that:
- the *leader* is comprised of the first length of tape – usually two or three feet – provided to allow the operator to handle it. It does not contain data
- the *tape marker* is a physical sign impressed on the tape to show the beginning of the area used for recording data
- the *header label* is the first block (group) of data, and it is read by the computer to allow it to identify the file
- the *records* or *data blocks* constitute the majority of tape space. The blocks are simply a number of records

- the *inter block gaps (ibg)* separate the blocks and exist to permit the computer to pause as necessary between blocks
- the *control block* incorporates 'control totals' (the total sum of the transactions, say, stored in the file) to act as a check
- at the end of the tape there is the *trailer label* (indicating that the stored data terminates there) and the *marker* (indicating the actual termination of the tape itself).

So, in order to process the file, all of it must pass the *reading-heads*. The unwanted records cannot be skipped or omitted. Records have to be processed in the manner in which they are stored. The same principles apply to both paper tape and punched cards.

Because of these points, the disadvantages in adopting serial access are that:

- time is consumed in passing through unwanted records
- rapid reference to records is not possible (remember we are using the term 'rapid' relatively here)
- the input has to be sorted to match the file order.

Direct access

Magnetic disks allow direct access, which means that records unwanted for reference may be ignored, and records can be processed in any sequence at all. Let us look at the layout structure of data on disk. In the diagram below, note that there are (conventionally) eight blocks. There are also concentric circles which are tracks, numbering from 1 to 200. Eight blocks constitute a complete track.

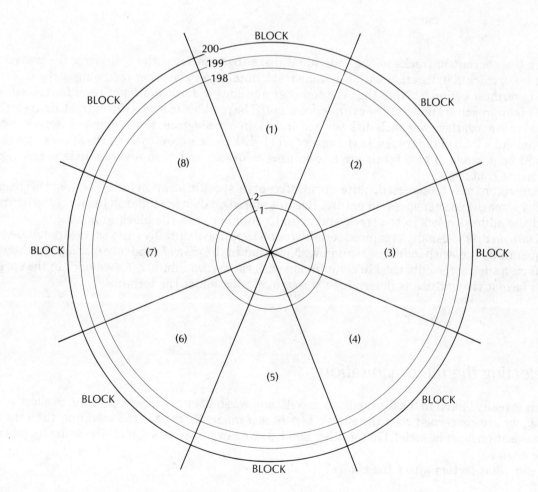

Note that some suppliers divide the disk into eight blocks (sometimes referred to as *buckets*), while others manufacture disks to allow the user to decide upon the number of blocks and the block size. The first type uses the *fixed length block* approach, whereas the alternative uses the *variable length block* version.

There are also *disk packs,* incorporating six or eleven disks mounted on a spindle and the drive mechanism. An idea of how these operate in terms of file access is given below.

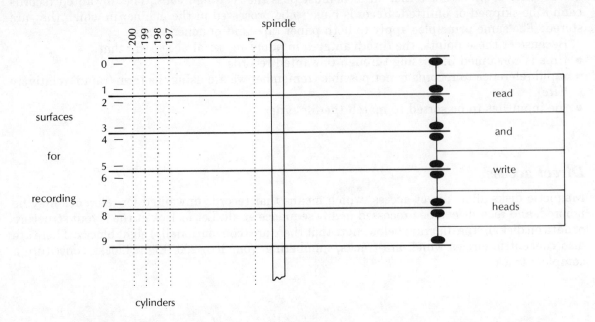

Here the concentric tracks of the individual disks together form the *cylinders.* So, recording surface 0, track 200, together with the same track number for the other recording surfaces, form the outermost cylinder. Note that the topmost and lowest surface are not used for recording.

This approach is known as the *cylinder concept.* The read/write heads (for extracting/inserting data) move together over each disk surface and so, in our diagram, it is possible to access in one movement a total of ten tracks. In the case of an 11-disk pack, access to 20 tracks at the same time would be possible. These totals are known as *seek areas,* and form a very efficient and rapid means of contact.

Any record may be accessed, quite irrespective of its specific location (*address*). For this reason this approach is direct access in nature. Records stored on disk are indexed (again, to save time) and the address refers to the track and cylinder number, and the block number.

Data on disk is usually organised serially (as on tape), sequentially (also as on tape), indexed-sequentially (i.e. with index) or randomly. Note that in the case of random organisation there is, in fact, a special formula used in conjunction with the record number. As we said, in the case of this format the address is determined through application of the formula.

Selecting the file organisation

This is really linked to the file medium as well, and we shall be dealing with this area shortly. For now, we are concerned with the simple fact that if magnetic tape is the medium, then the file organisation must be serial. On the other hand, as we saw just now, a direct-access device extends the choice.

But what factors affect the choice?

Factors affecting choice

The list of factors includes:
- file activity
- file volatility
- file size, and subsequent rate of growth
- format of data to be held
- blocks
- file density
- file maintenance.

File activity

By *file activity* we mean the number of records accessed on a run, divided by the total number of records in the file. This is the *hit rate*. Thus, if the total number of records on the file is 50 000 and the records accessed on average per run amount to some 1000, then the activity rate expressed as a percentage is only 2 per cent.

For a low rate of activity, the file ought to be organised so that an extensive search is not necessary. To avoid making the computer examine every record to find the right one, we would adopt a direct access method.

The records which are most often processed should logically be the ones which can be located most quickly.

For high activity files, processing of the indexed-sequential kind is a sound idea, or some form of serial processing.

The *active file* is used very often and so careful organisation is able to save a good deal of time. On the other hand, an *inactive file* is referenced much less often, so time is not a major consideration.

File volatility

This relates to the extent to which records are deleted from, or added to, the file. The *volatile file* has a high percentage of additions or deletions, whereas at the other end of the range is the *static file*.

Some types of file organisation present problems in this area. With direct-addressing there is no difficulty, except for the fact that there may have to be an *overflow* (i.e. a special provision for storing extra items which do not fit into their related block of records). So an addition may need to be put into the overflow location and this will have to be examined with the other records related to it. This takes up useful time and thus extends the access time.

File size and subsequent growth

It is possible for a file to be so small in volume that the kind of organisation adopted is unimportant. This is obviously due to the fact that the time taken to process it is relatively brief in any event. However, it is also possible for a file to be so large (in some computing systems, at any rate) that it cannot all be on-line simultaneously and so it cannot be processed randomly. In these circumstances a file could *only* be processed serially; it would need to be a sequential file processed sequentially.

The bigger the file the more important is its organisation. But at what rate will existing files grow? If a file will grow steadily, then the organisation of the data must be able to cope with this, and accommodate additions. In the case of serial organisation the size of the file does not really matter. In the case of other categories of organisation, however, allowances for growth – or *expansion space* – must be made available within the total area taken up by the records.

As a general rule, we would plan files on the calculated estimate of their future rate of growth.

File format

Really, this is the format of the data within the file. Here, we refer to the block size and also the packing density.

As far as *block size* is concerned, where magnetic tape is the medium the block can be as long as necessary. In the case of a disk, block size must relate to the extent of space wasted (bearing in mind also that a block must not be divided between two tracks – this would offset the cylinder concept).

Packing density is the measure of the extent of space remaining for inserting records without causing overflow (which would have to be located elsewhere in the file). So, there has to be a compromise between density so low that file space is unused, and density so high that expansion and insertion is not a simple matter without overflow.

For a serial or sequential type of organisation, a high level of packing density (virtually 100 per cent) is permissible, especially if the file is a temporary one. For the indexed-sequential kind, overflow arises again. If such a file has a *low volatility* then it can have a high packing density, but where there is the likelihood of a good deal of amendment to the file, then overflow will cause processing time to be increased.

Blocks

You will remember that choice is usually available to the user of fixed or variable-length blocks. A block consists of a number of records (including the possibility of its being a single record). On magnetic tape, the block can be as long as necessary. As far as disk is concerned, however, the size of the block has to be considered in line with the amount of space wasted where a multiple of the block size does not fit neatly into the limited length of the track. On the disk, blocks are of a fixed size; so, if we want, for convenience, nine blocks per track, it may simply be that a track will have space unused. In fact, *blocking* (i.e. determining the size and number of blocks) may easily offset the advantages gained in randomly organising a file. Since direct-addressing can be used anyway, the actual physical location of the required record can easily be determined without further organisation.

File density

File density may be defined as the proportion of space on the storage medium allocated to a file which is used by the records on file. So we have:

$$\% \text{ density} = \frac{\text{number of data characters}}{\text{number of positions for characters}} \times 100$$

Broadly speaking, the lower the density of a file, the higher the costs of storage.

File maintenance (frequency)

This is defined as the number of updates required by a given file within a particular time period. Files may be maintained on this basis in one of two ways:
- on a real-time basis (as and when the transactions arise)
- transactions are held until an appreciable number have accumulated and they are then undertaken in a batch.

Generally speaking, the first decision to be made will relate to the choice of processing (*access mode*). This will usually be determined by the application (*task to be done*). Following this the storage mode and the storage medium can be looked at.

File size and file access time

We have referred to the size of the file, but we must now list the influences which affect that size. These are:
- the size of the records
- the total number of records
- any additional space needed for direct-addressing pointers
- extra space needed for any index
- packing densities, expansion allowance
- purging activity frequency, i.e. how often the file is examined to delete items no longer relevant.

Access time (time taken to access data in the file) will always relate to:
- record size
- number of records contained in the file
- the file organisation itself
- the hit rate
- and for serial/sequential files, the location of the records.

Database

We cannot leave the topic of computer files without referring to the database concept, and so we now look at this briefly. It is dealt with more fully in *Analysis and Design of Information Systems.*

The nature of a database

We have to make a clear distinction between a database and a databank. A databank may be regarded as a library, and the idea of what we discussed as *videotex* is also a databank approach. The user receives what there is to receive in the form in which it is despatched or created originally. If the user wants the facts to be presented in graphic form, then he or she must carry out this operation himself or herself, unless the original presentation of the facts and figures was in that format already.

A database is different in that it provides a structure, framework or base of data for the computer to work on and present in the format sought. Thus, the effective and efficient database is a collection of data which satisfies all the needs of all the applications which may access the database. The true database system (DBS) is a unit which holds (files) data for the whole organisation and is a storage and retrieval system.

Where there is no database within an organisation, individual sections and functions supply their own informational requirements. This approach is inflexible, slow to respond to queries, and causes the duplication of data, which in turn gives rise to the need for duplication in updating the files.

The Data Base Management System (DBMS) is the software which supports the database and translates the files into meaningful information for the user. There are three database structures. These are:
- relational
- hierarchical
- network.

The relational database
In this approach, the database system presents its data in the form of tables (called *relations*) and the data is then manipulated in accordance with needs of the user.

The hierarchical database
Data is arranged in hierarchies or *trees* with *branches*. If, via the terminal, we insert a query concerning, say, Product X, then the system will list any characteristics associated with it, such as basic materials, and these will lead to further characteristics such as countries of origin for the materials and so on.

The network database
This developed from the hierarchical database and is complex. It relates items through linkages. Product X, for example, may be made of steel but this database can point out all other products manufactured from steel, together with other aspects sought.

Summary

In this chapter we have discussed:
- the concept of the file and filing
- the filing system's checklist for efficiency. It must be:
    simple
    secure
    appropriate
    up to date
    expandable
    integrated
    cost-effective
- the idea of central filing
- file categories:
    master (consisting of reference and dynamic)
    input and output
    transfer
    transaction
    work
    dump
    library
- computer file structure:
    bit – character – fields – records – file
- computer file operations:
    file enquiry
    file update and maintenance
- file organisation categories:
    serial (no logical sequence)
    sequential (logical sequence)
    indexed-sequential (index according to a specific key)
    random (relationship between key field and address)
    chained (linked with other records)
- major types of file-processing (access mode):
    serial
    sequential and selective-sequential
    random
- serial access
    (e.g. as required by magnetic tape)
- direct access
    (required as a rule for rapid access on disk)
- selection of the file organisation, considering:
    file activity (hit rate)
    file volatility (rate of record deletion/addition)
    file size and growth (related to packing density)
    data format (also related to packing density)
    blocks, file density (space assessment)
    file maintenance
- factors affecting file size and access time
- database.

Self-test Questions

Answer these questions and then check your answers from the chapter.

1 To be efficient, what characteristics must a filing system possess?
2 List the various categories of files and explain them.
3 What basic components constitute a computer file?
4 What are the three kinds of computer activities involving files?
5 How does serial file organisation differ from random file organisation?
6 Explain the meaning of file processing and describe sequential processing.
7 Draw a diagram illustrating the way data is structured on magnetic tape.
8 What is the cylinder concept and why is it important?
9 What factors affect file organisation?
10 Explain the term *database*.

CHAPTER 6
The storage media

Introduction

The storage of information has always been a major problem for computer systems. In the late 1980s the user had an extremely wide selection of media available because of the great advances in technology.

Programs are becoming very much more complex and systems now require larger and larger memory capacity. There is also the need for data security, especially where there is a *multi-user system* which would cause problems for a large number of individual users if there should be a breakdown (i.e., if the system *goes down*). All this adds up to a great demand for high quality and high capacity storage of data. There is also an increasing demand for systems able to store and display more information *at the desktop,* at lower cost.

When referring to the capability of the media we use measurements such as 2 Mb (i.e. two million or *mega*bytes), and 80 kcps (80 000 characters per second), and we shall be adopting these in this text.

The microcomputer (PC) and memory

In order to explain the various important aspects of computer memory, we are going to use the personal computer (PC), which was introduced in the late 1970s, as our theme in this section.

The term *computer memory* really signifies two types: permanent and temporary.

ROM and RAM

The permanent memory is the read-only memory (ROM) which cannot be changed in any way. If the ROM is not programmed well, then the computer will work relatively slowly.

The temporary memory is the random access memory (RAM). As a key on the keyboard is pressed, the character is placed in a specific area – a compartment, as we might call it in popular speech. So, if we type a total of 1024 keystrokes, then we use 1 kilobyte of memory. The term *kilo* in *this* context does not strictly mean 1000 because the computer adopts binary mathematics, and 2^{10} is, as we said, 1024. It is commonly abbreviated as K, not k.

Note that the RAM contents can be altered, or erased. In fact, if the power is switched off, the RAM is completely blanked out, unless, of course, the contents are previously held on some form of backing storage.

The typical PC has 1 Mb of memory, but only some 640K of RAM is able to be used of this total. The rest is held for ROM. Since its onset, the PC has become progressively more powerful, with great increases in the available addressable (RAM) memory, and a greater need for large capacity backing storage.

Early PCs used additional units giving up to 100 Kb, whereas today, in the case of the *supermicros* like the IBM PC AT, that figure is 1200 Kb.

Storage media

We are going to look here at the full range of storage media which is available for the computer market generally. We shall describe and discuss two basic categories – magnetic and optical – and then a third category of *special* media versions.

Magnetic media

In this category we have:
- magnetic tape
- magnetic disk
- drum
- bubble.

In magnetic media, the data is recorded in magnetic patterns on a surface which can be magnetised. The magnetised surface is moved past a *head* which is able to *write* data onto this surface, or, alternatively, *read* data from it (hence the name *read/write head*). Note that writing means transferring from internal memory to the medium, and that reading is the reverse of this. If the head writes, then it automatically overwrites (and erases) existing data in that location. This means that magnetic media may be used over and over again (as, indeed, we can re-use audio or video tapes again and again).

Basically, the recording is accomplished by making magnetic marks horizontally along the line of recording track. The bits, or magnetic particles, are therefore placed longitudinally. The latest technology is now offering greater capacity (density) by storing vertically. This *vertical recording* concept is to be available in the early 1990s.

Magnetic tape

We looked at magnetic tape in Chapter 5, together with magnetic disk. Tapes are of varying lengths, conventionally up to 1097 metres (about 3600 feet), and 1 cm (0.5 inches) wide. During reading, the tape is transferred from one reel to the other, just as for an ordinary tape recorder.

Tape is still a major method of providing back-up for data but over the years its technology has not advanced very far. There are three basic tape sub-system categories available:
- reel-to-reel tapes
- cartridge and cassette tapes
- video data cassette tapes, or cartridges.

An example of the video version is Gigastore, launched in the UK in 1987. This is a low-cost tape storage device with a capacity of 2.5 gigabytes (i.e. 2500 Mb). This medium is regarded as being best suited to *archive* storage (i.e. storing historic data as permanent records), and it can provide rapid back-up of disk data without difficulty – or operator supervision.

A *magnetic tape drive* (unit, deck, transport) is comprised of the drive mechanism, which winds the tape from the reel upon which it is stored, the *exchangeable reel* to the *take-up reel*, and the read/write heads transferring data to and from the tape.

For a reel of tape, the exchangeable reel is loaded on to the deck, so the end of the tape can be threaded to the take-up reel by the computer operator. At the end of the data-read, the tape is rewound onto its original reel and the operator removes it. Tape on this kind of reel is usually referred to as *streamer tape,* as opposed to cassette or cartridge tape.

Standard video cassette records (VCRs) are often used to provide back-up. The advantages of using magnetic tape are that:
- input speeds are about as high as for disk input, reaching around 320 000 bytes per second
- it provides storage for large quantities of data at relatively low cost
- the updating of the tape offers a useful approach for security (this is the *grandfather, father, son* technique discussed below).

Disadvantages are that:

- file updating takes a good deal of time because data has to be sorted to correspond with data order on the reference file (due to serial organisation and access)
- for low activity (hit rate) files, the efficiency of the tape system is reduced since all records have to be read
- tapes cannot be used for real-time, on-line enquiry systems.

We referred above to the *grandfather, father, son* updating technique. Tape records are often in the form of a master file which will need to be updated using transaction records held on another tape, in the identical sequence. The process of updating will therefore mean that brought-forward records are read from one tape so that they are updated and then written on to the carried-forward tape. This means that there are three tapes in use at the same time.

- The *grandfather tape* is maintained for security and is the brought-forward tape of the previous run.
- The *father tape* is the brought-forward tape of *this* run and so is the carried-forward tape of the previous run.
- The *son tape* is the present, carried-forward tape of this current run.

Capacities of frequently-encountered tapes are around 60 Mb, 80 Mb and 100 Mb. A typical 60 Mb unit for a typical PC would cost around £900.

Magnetic disk

This is currently the most common kind of storage used, and we have a choice of a number of categories, floppy (flexible) disks and hard disks.

Floppy disks (floppies) These are sometimes called flexible disks, or diskettes, and are orientated to the PC user. They have existed from the early 1970s. They are made of thin, tough plastic and are contained in square envelopes. The floppy disk rotates inside its envelope and the read/write head moves over a slot in the envelope cover.

These disks began with an 8-inch diameter, but there are now versions which are 5.25 inches and 3.5 inches respectively. The smallest one has a capacity of 1.4 Mbytes (twice that of the 8-inch version).

The introduction of new generation *super* PCs (e.g. the IBM AT) demands special floppy disks with higher data storage density capacities. The early PCs used a floppy disk drive with a capacity of under 100 Kbytes, whereas the later versions provided 1200 Kbytes. Today we have a capacity of one megabyte and more. It is useful to know that one megabyte is roughly the equivalent of 30 pages of a newspaper the size of *The Sunday Times,* but printed with no space and no paragraphs! Statistics show that a total of some 240 million floppy disks are sold annually in Europe alone, a small percentage of these being the new high density versions.

Hard disks These disks (basically referred to as Winchesters – the location of the IBM laboratory where they were developed in the late 1960s) are sold as self-contained, *clean* units which must not be interfered with once they leave the factory. Their capacities have increased over the past five years, culminating in a capacity of 100 megabytes at the end of the 1980s. Micro-Winchesters are 3.5 inches in diameter, with a 10 megabyte capacity. For systems which have a single user, normal capacity is 5, 10 or 20 megabytes, larger capacities being needed for use in a network where access is sought for a number of different users.

Hard disks are externally or internally fitted. The former are placed separately from the computer, with their own power cables and plug. Prices range from about £500 for a standard 5.25 inch drive to around £35 000 for a mainframe device with 400 megabytes of storage.

There are some 200 different types of hard disk available in the UK and thus the decision to use a hard disk at all, and especially what *kind* of hard disk, is one requiring careful consideration. Usually the large capacity of hard disks is the major reason for use and expansion of data must be allowed for.

There are also removable *disk cartridges.* The disk drive is permanent, but the cartridges themselves are exchangeable, and this idea clearly offers a virtually infinite total capacity. The typical cartridge capacity is 10 megabytes.

An additional point to bear in mind is what is known as *time before failure,* i.e. how long the disk operates before it has to be replaced. An acceptable average is around 25 000 hours.

Magnetic drum

This device still exists but the capacity is relatively limited when compared to that of the disk. The drum is divided into tracks along its length, usually with one read/write head to each track.

Bubble memory

This is a non-moving magnetic unit of storage which uses microscopic areas on a very small surface which are magnetised and demagnetised to provide binary coding (the *on* and *off* concept). A single 10 mm chip will hold one megabyte.

At the end of the 1980s, Hitachi introduced improvements which have increased demand for this medium. The earlier versions had relatively slow access times. It is in cartridge form, is robust and requires no maintenance.

Optical (laser) storage

Here, we are concerned with what is referred to as *laser* technology (laser means *light amplification by stimulated emission of radiation*).

The basic idea is that a high-intensive laser beam literally burns holes into the pre-established tracks of sensitive metallic layers lying between two glass disks. The presence or absence of a hole is thus translated into the binary coding format. This approach is the digital optical recording (DOR) concept.

We have two products available: *Compact Disk – Read Only Memory* (CD-ROM) and the *Write Once, Read Many* (WORM), but a third version has emerged in prototype form which is erasable and thus allows data on disk to be amended and updated or completely erased.

CD-ROM This type of disk is a standard 4.75 inch version developed from the audio compact disk player. Digital information can be read by computer, instead of being converted to an audio signal. This is a highly cost-effective method of distributing, for example, copies of large amounts of information for access on a PC microcomputer.

Typically, it is used for the dissemination of reports, price list information, catalogues of parts, maps and so on where the information is likely to be of a static nature.

The 4.75 inch disk mentioned earlier holds 552 megabytes of data (broadly equal to 1500 floppy disk storage, or 270 000 pages of text). The Post Office was one of the first organisations to adopt this system. They have stored 23 500 000 names and addresses on a single CD-ROM. Access time is rapid – any address can be found (from only partial information) in two seconds.

The *player* or *driver* required to utilise these disks will differ in price according to the computer concerned. For a PC the cost would be about £1500. Main suppliers are Sony, Hitachi and Phillips who, in association with Control Data, form LMS.

CD-ROM may be used as a mass storage device, but can also combine, on one disk, software for all types of computers and specific software for specific computers. Again, a mass storage of data may be linked to databases through this system.

A further example of the use of CD-ROM is to store maps of all oceans and seas in the world on ten CD-ROM disks. These would be part of an integrated and automated *on-board* system for navigation, linked to satellite, sonar and radar transmissions and to engine-room control.

CD-ROM technology is fully compatible with large and small computers.

WORM This concept is designed for the DP area, especially in relation to back-up and archiving (long-term storing) of information.

The important point to make here is that users are able to write to disk, whereas in the case of CD-ROM, information has first to be recorded on magnetic media and is then *mastered* by an organisation offering the service of recording the data using the laser. The CD-ROM mastering activity costs about £4000 to the client, but copies may be made cheaply.

The WORM disk is basically of plastic, coated with a thin metal layer. It usually has two sides, whereas the CD-ROM disk has one for usage. Storage capacity for the 5.25 inch disk is a total of 400 megabytes for the two sides together.

Note that the name *WORM* is likely to be interpreted as *write once, read mostly* as the erasable disks become less expensive and more marketable.

The erasable version uses magnetic-optical recording in that when the write laser strikes the surface it alters the magnetic polarity of the surface. The erasable disks (manufactured by 3M) use the same format as 5.25 inch WORM disks with a total storage capacity of 400 to 600 megabytes for two sides.

A system called Laser Optic 1000 Filing System now in use allows some 4000 A4 pages to be stored on one disk 5.25 inches in diameter. This is WORM technology which links a PC with the optical disk. This system allows input from and output to a number of users, i.e. it can adopt input and retrieval workstations which are forming a network. This is, in fact, an *optical disk filing system* which is simple to operate.

The system incorporates a workstation with a 5.25 inch optical disk drive, a monitor, a laser printer, a document scanner, and an IBM PC/AT (or compatible version) with a 70 megabyte hard disk. The scanner digitises diagrams, photographs, graphs, signatures, text, handwritten notes, pre-printed forms. It uses a feeder tray capable of containing 30 pages for continuous scanning. When scanned, the image is displayed on the monitor and checked for clarity and format. All documents may be stored on the hard disk and then indexed and saved by putting them on the 200 megabyte optical disk. Even inexperienced users are able to load the optical disk with documents to provide a rapid-access filing system.

It is also worth noting that Olivetti announced their fully integrated and automatic system for storage, retrieval and handling of documents using optical disk in 1985. This is known as the Filenet Document Image Processor. It is capable of holding in its memory about 20 000 000 A4 pages (in computer language this is 128 gigabytes). It has a document entry station (where all types of documents can be entered on to optical disk cartridges and software), the workstation (which permits information to be stored, accessed and manipulated, e.g. documents can be compared), and also a document printing station using a laser printer (outputting at 12 pages per minute). The cost of this system, aimed at large organisations dealing with large volumes of paperwork requiring distribution, is about £250 000.

Special storage categories

We use the title *special* for this category overall simply because the devices involved use different technologies peculiar to themselves. Here, we shall look at:
- COM
- solid state storage
- card storage.

COM

In Chapter 4 we looked at the idea of Computer Output in Microform (COM). Then we were considering it as an output form, but we now concentrate on the storage aspects.

COM systems found a higher level of acceptability with users at the end of the 1980s than at any other time. This is due to the fact that there have been considerable developments in optical disk storage. The awareness on the part of users, promoted by optical storage technology, has given rise to a higher interest in the application of automated systems to organisational filing and storage, with special reference to computer-aided retrieval (CAR).

A typical CAR system is the Agfa version, using 16 mm microfilm. It comprises a DEC minicomputer, a hardcopy printer, lockable film storage cabinet and a microfilm reader/printer. The system permits a number of users to interrogate simultaneously and is compatible with most user networks. Data is input via a keyboard and the material can be indexed in differing ways to suit user demands (e.g. by customer number or name). The software is used to identify the microfilm reference. The system is linked to computer databases and accurate, rapid retrieval is achieved with the ability to provide A4 copies at the printout speed of 12 per minute.

Solid state storage

A problem relating to direct access mass storage is that *bigger is slower*. Thus, the greater the volume of data on a disk spindle, the longer is the average disk access time. If we take mangetic storage, disk capacity has increased some 50 times over the past 15 years, yet magnetic disk access time is not much more rapid than it was in the early 1970s.

One answer to this difficulty has been the arrival of *semi-conductor* mass storage devices which have no moving parts. At the top of the range, storage capacity reaches 1.5 gigabytes, but cost is a major factor at present.

Card storage

This device is similar in both shape and size to a credit card, and it contains integrated circuits so that it may be used as a solid stage memory device. One version is called the Astron IC card and it has a 38-pin connector at one side of it.

There is a ROM and a RAM version. In the former, the information stored cannot then be altered. The RAM card allows changes to be made. It is possible to store programs and data on this small card.

The Astron card is durable and is not affected by magnetic/static forces, extreme heat or cold, scratching or humidity.

A kit for the IBM PC may be obtained from Card Devices Ltd. It includes a PC adaptor card and four 16K Astron RAM cards, called EEPROM cards. The cost of this in 1990 was under £100, plus the price of the adaptor card (£50).

Storage media characteristics

Studying the characteristics of the various categories of storage media is clearly important in deciding which to adopt for an organisation. We said earlier that this selection is necessarily connected to the total budget available for the acquisition and the processing modes to be utilised. These, in turn, relate to the quantity and the frequency of the data inputs and the need for speed.

As far as storage is concerned, the characteristics sought have to be the result of a compromise. The major characteristics relate to these following aspects.

Capacity

There has to be sufficient storage to cope with the application being dealt with by the system, enough, that is, to deal with all concurrent data.

Access time

The mean time needed to obtain access to the stored records must relate satisfactorily to the processing time. A rapid and efficient processing system must not be unduly delayed by media possessing relatively sluggish access times.

Security

There must be security of data retention – no loss, damage or other corruption should arise.

Interchangeability

The storage device considered must be interchangeable for data required for a given output, or specific application. This is known as *reloadability*.

Cost of storage

Here we mean the cost per stored unit of data. This must be acceptably low so that it does not render the storage medium cost-ineffective. This cost is expressed as so many cents per bit, e.g. for optical disk this is around 0.000 001.

Rate of transfer

Data has to be transferred between the storage unit and the central processor (either way) at an acceptable speed so that undue sluggishness is not experienced. The rate is measured, as a general rule, in terms of thousands of characters per second (i.e. kch/s).

Summary

In this chapter we have discussed:
- the concept of the computer memory, using the PC as our theme, noting the importance of ROM and RAM
- the storage media available:
    magnetic media, tape and disk, drum, bubble
    optical (laser) storage, CD-ROM, WORM (noting the examples of optical filing systems)
    special storage, including COM, solid-state, cards
- the media characteristics of capacity, access-time, security, interchangeability, storage cost, rate of transfer.

Self-test Questions

Answer these questions, then check your answers in this chapter.

1 Distinguish between ROM and RAM.
2 Explain the way in which magnetic tape operates to store data. What is the magnetic tape drive?
3 List advantages and disadvantages in the use of magnetic tape.
4 What is the grandfather, father, son technique?
5 What is meant by these terms?
   a) hard disk   b) bubble memory   c) a megabyte
6 Explain, with special reference to WORM, what optical storage is.
7 What is CD-ROM technology?
8 How may COM be used in an organisation?
9 What is card storage?
10 List storage media characteristics.

CHAPTER 7

Communications and networks

Introduction

In this chapter we shall be looking at the idea of computer communications and networking. The term *communication* is a massive subject in itself, embracing data transmission and also sound and video transmission using telephone lines, satellite linkages and radio. Here we use the term *data communications* to mean the control and transmission of organisational data as it is transferred from one point to another.

The components involved in computer communication

We begin by looking at the various ways of transmitting data (i.e. the methods by which the data is to be communicated), and the devices which have to be used to accomplish this. We then look at the considerations which have to be examined before selecting the method.

Decisions taken by organisations concerning their communications and information systems are certainly among the most critical they ever have to take. Speeding up installations of equipment to assist in this, and adopting a given technology rapidly, may well solve some local problems, but can prove costly eventually. Most organisations use separate, dedicated communications linkages to deal with telephone, data and telex *traffic*. Quite often, because different functional managers have different responsibilities (and budgets!) there may also be quite different, and usually overlapping, approaches, or else there will be pointless duplication.

As far as computers are concerned, where there is a great distance between the computer and the terminals, electronic data transmission must be adopted. For a restricted geographical area, a local area network (LAN) is adopted, and for wider areas we have the wide (or wider) area network (WAN). We shall be looking at these later.

In the UK there are two types of transmission lines: *private lines* and *public lines*. The former use the telephone network with a special line being provided in addition to the ordinary telephone (annual payment of a fixed charge being required). The public lines relate to the ordinary telephone network, charges being made for the kind of service used and the length of the call.

Now the use of the private automatic branch exchanges (PABX), which has been developed to use all-digital (instead of analogue) technology, enables an office to link up not only telephones but microcomputers, word-processors, teletex, Email or fax.

Data transmission devices

The *transmission modes* available are:
- simplex, which allows transmission one-way only
- half-duplex, for two-way transmission (not simultaneously, but one after the other)
- full-duplex, allowing two-way transmission at the same time (an ordinary telephone conversation is of this kind since it allows interruption of someone's speech by the person at the other end of the line).

Devices required include the modem and the multiplexor.

The modem

The term *modem* means *modulator/demodulator*. Computers, as we have already seen, represent data by using electrical pulses. However, operating in this digital mode and using the digital, binary code can cause problems. Remember that the mode translates numbers and letters into various combinations of eight bits (0 and 1). This group of bits is a byte. The speed at which the signals (bits) travel along the transmission line is a *baud*, i.e. the number of bits per second. A baud is therefore one bit per second, so that a 2000 baud line transmits at the rate of 2000 bits per second.

The receiver has to begin accepting the transmission at the correct moment, i.e. at the first data bit of the first byte. If the receiving device does not do this, then it will be out of step and will completely misread every byte which follows. Two ways of making sure that the bytes at the receiving terminal correlate to the bytes actually transmitted are:

- *asynchronous transmission* – adding an extra bit to the beginning and the end of each byte (forming an *envelope,* that is, ten bits) to act as signals, so each character has
  1 start bit + 7 data bits + 1 parity bit + 1 stop bit
- *synchronous transmission* – instead of inserting extra bits, the stream of bytes is preceded by two or more *sync bytes,* which have an agreed pattern to be recognised.

In practice, the asynchronous method is adopted for shorter transmissions of data, whereas the other kind is used for long transmissions of data.

The most common medium for transmission is the telephone system, either through private circuits leased from British Telecom or other *international carriers,* e.g. Mercury, or through dialling on the PSTN (Public Switched Telephone Network). Any telephone network is designed for voice transmission (thereby operating in analogue format) using constantly varying electrical currents to interpret speech tones. Data transmission is in digital format, not yet universally acceptable to the telephone networks. The task of the modem is thus to translate, in electronic terms, the data presented digitally to analogue format, therefore allowing the line to cope with this.

The telephone circuit to which the modem is linked may well be worldwide, or perhaps just a few kilometres long. For this reason, modems must be able to use techniques which enable them to communicate with each other, and so modems must be made to comply with standards issued by the International Telegraph and Telephone Consultative Committee (known as the CCITT).

The original data modems of the 1960s were both expensive and bulky, providing transmission speeds of some 300 to 1200 bauds. Today, speeds of some 9600 bauds (or bsp) are available (e.g. the V.32 modem). Full-duplex circuits adopt two wires (one for each direction) and the late 1980s version of Datacomms V.33 modem could provide speeds of up to 14 400 bauds.

However, other transmission technologies are emerging (e.g. voice-data, allowing simultaneous despatch of analogue and digital messages) which may, in time, alter the market for modems. In addition to the basic function of transmitting data, there are now modems which are *intelligent,* allowing automatic dialling by the modem, automatic answering and other features. The basic cost of a simple modem in 1990 was around £80; the price of the more sophisticated versions may be over £3000.

Note that there is also the *acoustic coupler,* for use with the portable microcomputer (see Chapter 3, p. 29). This costs around £100, and may be used to effect the transmission of data from an ordinary telephone in a hotel room – or anywhere else. The telephone handset is clamped on to the coupler which is the modem. The use of the acoustic coupler does, however, produce a transmission of lower quality than that of the fixed modem, because of the physical connection to the telephone handset.

Costs of modems tend to decrease, whilst their capabilities increase over the years. In selecting which modem to adopt, the user must first decide what device he wants to communicate with (e.g. electronic mail, database) and then list modems which suit these needs. The baud rates will be a consideration, together with the data volumes and frequencies, and the distances involved. Small business users may not consider the extra cost of a sophisticated version of the modem worthwhile.

Multiplexor or mux

This device is used when and where it is necessary to send data from several different sources along the same transmission line. It is able to code the data in a particular way so that it can be unravelled at the destination for which it is intended.

This is vital where there is only a single transmission line but there are several terminals linked to the control computer. They range from very basic devices which are not really more than modems with two *ports* or entry/exit points, to major systems which run on minicomputers.

The mux permits data from more than one source to be sent along a single channel and it consists of a multiplexing device (to mix signals) and a demultiplexing device (to sort them out, or unmix them).

We may take firm ABC plc as an example of the use of the mux. Let us say that this firm has a minicomputer and remote terminals. The warehouse has five terminals but only a single communication line to the minicomputer at HQ. If the firm did not use the mux, then only one terminal could be linked to the minicomputer at any one time. This would mean that the users had severely limited access to the HQ computer (the *host computer* as it would be termed), or the firm would have to invest a line for each terminal – five lines. In the latter case this would not be cost-effective because a single terminal would not use its dedicated line to full capacity. A mux would allow all five terminals to connect at the same time with the communications linkage. In our example, there would be a demultiplexing at the host end to unmix the signals and allocate the messages.

The mux is therefore a device which saves expense. The diagram below gives you an idea of the outline of a data transmission system, using modems and muxes.

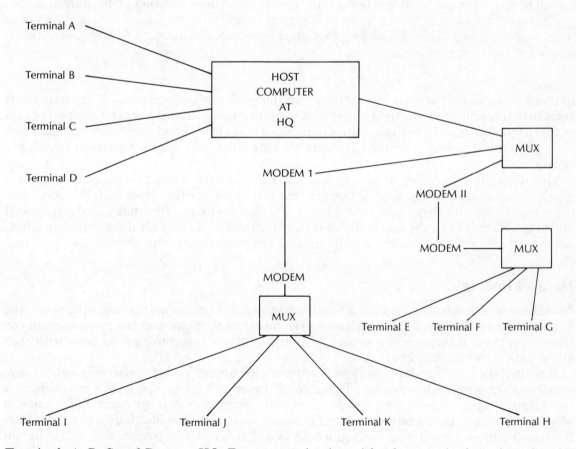

Terminals A, B, C and D are at HQ. For communication with other terminals modems I and II are used because of their remoteness. Note that the muxes lie between the source of the message and the modems. Modems I and II are at HQ.

Front-end processor

This device is normally either a micro or a minicomputer placed between the host computer and the multiplexor. Its task is to take from the host computer the work involved in undertaking error procedures, the labelling (serial numbering) of messages and so on. The greater the frequency and volume of the transmitted data, the more important is this role.

The concentrator or dataplexor

A transmission line is likely to be under-used for at least part of the time, largely because of the speed at which the human terminal operator can input data and the speed at which the line can transmit. A 300 baud line has something like seven times the capacity of the operator. The concentrator *concentrates* or gathers the bits from each terminal and holds them in its *buffer store* (memory) until there is enough of a collection to warrant transmission. This means that it accepts bits at a low rate and then transmits them at high speed.

Protocol and polling

These are two terms you should know about.

Protocol

Communications protocol is the method adopted to detect and correct errors, and some form or other of this is devised for transmission over long distances. The reason for its importance lies in the fact that both public and private telephone lines can produce some form of distortion or loss of message. Everyone has experienced noises, for instance, when using the telephone which occasionally obliterated what was being said. This can and does happen to data transmissions.

The method used has to identify the existence of errors in the transmission (e.g. data not in sequence, or missing data) and adopt a procedure to recover the lost data (e.g. request retransmission of the corrupted areas).

Polling

In many cases, where there are several terminals linked to the host computer, if any terminal is allowed to transmit whenever data is prepared for transmission, then the central computer could be taken by surprise and lose some or all of that data. On the other hand, some terminals may well share common devices on a common line, but they are not able to use the devices at exactly the same time.

This difficulty may be coped with by *polling*. The computer will access each terminal on a regular, routine basis to find out whether the terminal needs to have access to it. If it does, then the computer accepts all (or some) of the input. This is done extremely rapidly, and no terminal operator feels that he or she is actually sharing the attention of the central computer! In effect, the central computer determines which terminal can have access, and when.

Data switching

As we have seen in this chapter, data is very often transmitted from one location to the next using a permanent transmission link, e.g. as between an office terminal and the central computer. Obviously, this is a very sound approach when the locations communicate regularly with each other, with no other occasional users.

It is often the case that data has to be communicated unpredictably to users. Telephone conversations are switched by circuitry. The circuit between point A and point B is established for the duration of the conversation only. As far as data communications are concerned, a superior way of providing links of a temporary kind is *packet switching*. The idea here is that a message is divided into *packets* of data of fixed length (e.g. 128 bytes) and transmitted in this format together with the control data (i.e. largely the sender's identity and the address of the recipient).

The packet switching system (PSS), or packet switching exchange (PSE) accepts messages, reads the *address header* and sends them to their destination. The PSS is a computer network, each computer directing the packets received to the computer which is next in line along the route to the message's ultimate point of destination. Despite the breaking up of the original message into the packets, the PSS delivers the message in its complete and original form to the ultimate recipient. The PSS can duplicate packets for transmission to a number of destinations.

Computers used within the PSS are referred to as *store-and-forward* computers. This is due to the fact that they possess storage units (buffers) to contain packets waiting for onward transmission.

Centralised, decentralised and distributed systems

We are now looking at the old, original kind of computer system and contrasting it with the much later and present trend. As a general rule, we can say that development in computer systems commenced with the centralised version (a single, large computer receiving input from units within the organisation which was physically transported to the central installation for processing). Then followed the development of remote terminals and, ultimately, the distributed system, a series of interconnected, linked locations with computing capabilities, sometimes working quite independently of each other as the occasion demanded.

The centralised system

Generally, the mainframe computer is situated at the headquarters of the organisation. All activities undertaken by the computer were originally in batch processing mode (see Chapter 2, p. 20). Input was sent to the installation where data was processed and returned to the user when completed.

An important issue here is that the EDP management was, as a rule, responsible to the Director of Finance. This was simply because the computer was originally installed in order to undertake processing of financial data (mainly preparation of wages).

Eventually, remote terminals were developed and the centralised system received most of its input keyed-in, thus eliminating the necessity of physical transportation of input data. This also meant that the central computer now tended to be accessed for information as and when this was required. The usage of interactive terminals became known as *teleprocessing*.

The decentralised system

This system is comprised of totally independent (unconnected), or *stand alone* computers which undertake their operations completely separately. The contemporary decentralisation system is likely to consist of a number of microcomputers, although most organisations tend to link these together – or, at least, some of them.

The distributed system

This may be thought of as a decentralised system which, if required, allows an individual unit to be linked with other units and/or with a central mainframe or minicomputer. Thus, each individual department/section in the organisation has its own computing facility but still has access to the central computer if necessary. The term *departmental computing* has arisen, signifying that there is an emphasis in the system on the specialist and functionally-orientated computer activities. Usually these are micro-mainframe linkages. The falling costs (and increased power) of smaller computers have allowed organisations to obtain a number of microcomputers or minicomputers to undertake processing activities which had hitherto been carried out by the central mainframe.

Distributed computing implies that the department using its own computer facilities must assume responsibility for the accuracy and completeness of the source data and the resultant output.

Distributed computer systems may be either *lateral* (or horizontal) or *hierarchical* in format.

Lateral
This consists of a number of minicomputers, or microcomputers, which are autonomous but can intercommunicate in order to provide back-up services for each other or obtain a more powerful processing system, or perhaps only to exchange messages.

Hierarchical
Here, we have several computing levels. The heart of the system is the mainframe (not necessarily only one of these) able to cater for the requirements of the lower levels of the hierarchy, e.g. remote job entry.

Next is the level comprised of a minicomputer (or several of these) able to control the network and pass messages from and to the other levels and also to cope with interactive terminals and batch processing on a local basis.

The third, and lowest, level in the hierarchy is a number of microcomputers, intelligent terminals and other devices which are to perform special tasks (i.e. they are *dedicated*), such as PoS (point of sale) terminals in supermarkets.

The distributed system is commonly encountered today and offers a number of advantages and disadvantages which we must examine.

The advantages are:
- the general processing speed within the organisation as a whole, and in units within it, is higher than for centralised systems
- individual computer failure can be compensated for by the other units – the system does not rely upon one device completely
- each unit within the organisation has its own store of information, and can access this without delay
- the distributed system has a twin orientation – to the total organisation *and* to individual departmental needs.

The disadvantages are:
- the cost of storage is high because each individual department has its own information store, so that duplication exists
- management and maintenance costs are higher than for a centralised system, because of the system's complexity.

Networking

The concept of communication between computers which are geographically dispersed was, until comparatively recently, a difficult one to approach. But the falling cost of computer hardware invites the idea of computers sharing resources and computing power generally.

The computer communication network incorporates the host computer, communication interface devices (e.g. modems, muxes) and the communication processor (the special-purpose computer which copes with protocol conversion, error handling and so on, referred to earlier as the *front-end processor*). There is, however, a certain amount of confusion concerning the terms *network* and *multi-user system*. In fact, the latter is actually a basic computer serving several users. This system operates so rapidly that each individual user considers that the computer is dedicated to that specific task. In the case of a network, each computer is able to send to or receive from the other devices.

A network *or* a multi-user system could be adopted to solve the same problem in many cases. For example, PCs could be installed in every section of the organisation, linked to a network and be thus able to share information and produce reports founded upon facts retrieved from all or some of the devices linked. On the other hand, adoption of a multi-user approach would mean that a computer is installed in the organisation and terminals are located in each section and linked to that computer.

Obviously, a multi-user system must use some form of network. A typical example is the Rank Xerox Virtual Micro. Microcomputers are installed in a central location and the users each have a basic terminal (screen, keyboard). This provides the illusion of working with one's own individual PC. Files are accessed from centralised disks, peripherals (e.g. fax, printers) which are also shared. Fifteen PCs are deemed sufficient to cope with one hundred users.

LANs and WANs

In the case of a collection of computers located at a single site, e.g. a headquarters office or a hospital, where these are linked together then we have a local area network (LAN). The LAN is also able to link up with other LANs.

A much wider, national – or global – network is a wide area network (WAN). This may involve satellite transmission between continents.

Network architecture

This may be defined as the layout (*topology*) and the function of the components of the network. The layout relates to the way in which the components (*hardware devices*) are interlinked, and the function relates to the role.

A network is either *broadcast* or *point-to-point* in form.

Broadcast
Here, the computer sends out a message along the network, and this may be received by any or all of the components. But this gives rise to the problem of *contention,* i.e. data can collide if the computers in the network broadcast at the same time!

Point-to-point
This entails sending the message to a specific destination within the network, and it can only be received by that unit. The most widely used method of communicating in this form is what we looked at earlier in this chapter – packet switching.

There are three major examples of network architecture.

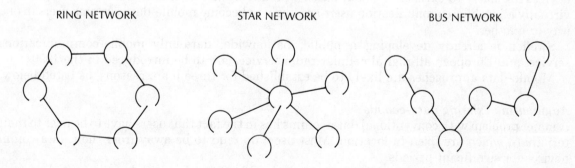

RING NETWORK   STAR NETWORK   BUS NETWORK

Ring
Each unit or *node* can communicate directly with two others. Where one node is *down* (fails) then the ring has to be disconnected until repairs are undertaken.

Star
The failure of the central unit would cause a breakdown of the whole network, but this is an efficient way of direct communication using the central controller. It does utilise more cable than either the ring or the bus.

Bus

This type uses less cable than the other two and can be added to easily.

There is also the more complex and expensive version known as the *fully connected network* in which the nodes are so arranged that any transmitted message never has to pass through more than one component to reach its intended destination.

Primarily, what we have been talking about in this section refers to LANs. A number of firms now offer LANs as a product able to link up a wide variety of computer makes and types. In addition, of course, computer suppliers themselves offer their own particular and individual versions.

Management of networks

As networks develop in an organisation so that they spread throughout the various departments and sections, then there is an even greater need for control within the configuration and the monitoring of the distribution of the shared resources throughout the networks. The original concepts of PC networks only related to up to 20 microcomputers, being departmental in nature. At the present time, however, the organisation-wide networks are aimed at connecting hundreds – and perhaps, soon, thousands – of PCs.

Where the network is purely departmental, then management monitoring is restricted. Most of the users are undertaking similar work and they will need access to a number of network users and the shared network resources. But, where this network incorporates many departments, supporting a very broad range of users and differing applications, then, of course, management facilities have to be more comprehensive.

Mobile data communications

Up to this point we have discussed networks in terms of cabling and wiring, although we did refer also to WANs utilising satellite communications. But radio links are now a real alternative for data networking applications, especially in relation to mobile terminals and users. In fact, developments in mobile radio technology generally are providing important new systems opportunities because they release data communications (or *data-comms*) from the limitations of fixed-location wiring and cabling.

By the mid-1990s it is believed that some ten million mobile-communications users (i.e. those using radio-telephones in cars and so on) will exist in the UK. Some 250 million users of these devices are likely to exist on a global basis. The importance of this is that it is thought that virtually all mobile-communication users are likely to become mobile-data systems users in one way or another.

Sweden is already developing a public, nationwide, data-only mobile-communications service, and European all-digital cellular-radio services are to be introduced in the 1990s.

Mobile-data approaches are likely to be established for three main reasons, as listed below.

Augmenting existing data-comms

A major problem with conventional data-comms lies in the fact that users have to be near to their terminals, which are fixed in location. Most users do tend to be away from their data-comm devices for significant periods.

When mobile-comm linkages are established, this difficulty will be eliminated and so efficiency and effectiveness will improve.

Augmenting existing mobile-comms

Here it is suggested that conventional speech transmission can be supplemented by transmission of print-out text and/or displays on VDU.

Extending IT facilities

Small receivers provide radio-teletext services, and there are pocket telex devices available.

Modems would still be necessary, and there has been considerable development in this area. Radio links are much more difficult to use as transmission devices than cable links are. In particular, the error correction is more complex.

Value added and data network services (VANs)

Our heading is the correct and current name; nevertheless the abbreviation is *VANs*, simply because *VADNs* is not easily pronounced! This is a term which you will often meet in the future and it signifies a range of services, organised and offered by individual bodies for access by subscribers of different kinds. The services include such diverse aspects as viewdata (see Chapter 4) and voice services (for which the user dials a telephone number to receive information, e.g. Citycall, offering one of eight specialist news bulletins read out to the user).

The oldest and best-known VAN is probably *Prestel,* and one of the most recently-introduced is British Telecom's *Telecom Gold.* Other VANs are:

- ICL's Late Availability Service providing holiday tour operators with a database of air flights available so that agents may book right up to the last moment
- IBM's Unidex which links brokers directly with computers of the insurance companies with which they intend to have dealings, with special reference to pensions and life assurance
- ICL's Drugwatch, offered to pharmaceutical firms engaged in drug clinical trials.

The Department of Trade and Industry (DTI) in the UK has issued licences for the operation of over 600 VANs to a total of 140 firms.

Summary

In this chapter we have discussed:
- the components involved in computer communication:
    transmission modes being:
    - simplex – one-way only
    - half-duplex – two-way, but not at the same time
    - full duplex – two-way, simultaneously
    devices:
    - modem – translating data from digital to analogue format (bearing in mind asynchronous and synchronous transmission
    - multiplexor (mux) – allowing simultaneous transmission of signals (e.g. terminals are able thus to connect with the communication linkage at the same time
    - front-end processor (micro- or minicomputer) to take the burden of following procedures (e.g. labelling)
    - concentrator, to gather bits from communicating terminals for later (more economical) transmission
- protocol for detection/correction of errors
- polling (routine checking, in sequence, or devices to determine their need to communicate)
- packet switching (a data switching approach, using packets of data for transmission through store-and-forward computers)
- centralised processing, decentralised processing, and distributed processing
- networking – multi-users and networks, network architecture: ring, star, bus, 'fully-connected'
- network management
- mobile data-communications
- VANs.

Self-test Questions

Answer these questions, then check your answers in this chapter.

1 What are the transmission modes?
2 Distinguish between synchronous and asynchronous transmission. Why are they important?
3 What is the role of the modulator/demodulator?
4 Draw a diagram showing the relationship between terminals, host computer, modem and mux.
5 Explain the function of a data concentrator.
6 What is the meaning of protocol and of polling?
7 How does packet switching work? Why?
8 Contrast a decentralised system with a distributed system.
9 How does a networked system differ from a multi-user system?
10 Use diagrams to explain ring, star, bus.

CHAPTER 8
Software

Introduction

Hardware means, as we know, all the physical devices used for data purposes. Software has various definitions, but the one in common use is taken to be all the programs used in the computer system, irrespective of their origin (i.e. whether they are provided by suppliers or written in-house, within the organisation whose computer is to use the program(s)).

In our text we shall use it to mean *all* programs.

Software has to be used to operate and control the system hardware. In fact, there is no other machine which has to rely upon human instructions quite so much before it can function at all! On the other hand, it would be very hard to name another device which could be regarded as more sophisticated than the computer!

We can categorise software into a series of basic groupings:
- operating systems
- utility
- sub-routines
- aids to programming
- application packages and programs
- Data Base Management System (DBMS)

We shall be looking at each one of these in turn.

Software categories

The categories are arbitrary divisions purely for your convenience in studying. There is no generally accepted way of dividing the software into groups!

Operating systems (OS)

An operating system is a *suite* or collection of programs aimed at undertaking activities which would otherwise have to be carried out by the human operator (thus wasting computer time because of the low speed of human working!). The whole point of the OS is to monitor the operations of all the hardware (and of other programs, incidentally) to speed up – and make more efficient – the tasks involved in DP. This objective has been made more and more significant due to the faster operation of computers and their developing sophistication.

The main tasks of the OS are:
- communication (operator and computer)
- monitoring and controlling peripherals
- software monitoring and multiprogramming.

A part of the OS called the *executive* is held permanently in the IAS part of the CPU, in main storage and is called *core resident*. Portions of the OS required for access less often are contained in some form of external backing store (usually disk pack) and are called in to the main storage when needed. We refer to the external storage of programs as *virtual storage,* and the executive program is often called the *control* or *supervisor* program.

In fact, consideration of the overall effectiveness of the OS must be made when a computer is being selected for an organisation. Suppliers rarely standardise their OS with other suppliers, and these programs are provided initially as part of the CPU.

Looking at the main OS tasks, we see them as vital activities.

Communication

This is undertaken through the use of the console terminal, but is maintained at the minimum level. Typical communication aspects include:
- indication that an activity has been completed by the computer
- request by the computer for more stationery
- indication of error in data input
- instruction from the operator to start and stop.

Note that the dialogue between the operator and the computer is permanently recorded to act as a *log* of the work undertaken. Records are established by the machine of the timing and the programs utilised. This is often used to apportion the cost of using the system to the various user-departments.

Peripheral control

The OS monitors and controls all peripheral devices, including microcomputers on the network to make sure that all of them are carrying out their operations correctly. This incorporates:
- checking header labels on magnetic tapes
- monitoring the size of the blocks which are output to tape
- assigning storage space to data, program instructions and so on
- dealing with *interrupts,* which are temporary halts caused by program or machine problems
- error checking.

Software monitoring, multiprogramming

As far as software is concerned, this concerns the monitoring of the programs of various types in order to ensure that the instructions are present when required.

One important aspect to be looked at here is the fact that the CPU will have to wait – be *idle* – whilst a peripheral carries out its own task, at its own speed. This means that the CPU is constrained or *bound* by the device. *Multiprogramming* is one answer to this waste of time, i.e. storing more than one program at one time. The OS monitors the application (job) program. The OS is provided with the timings needed for the task on hand, and the control may thus be passed from one program, which is perhaps temporarily halted, to another program.

Once a given program is completed, then the OS will *call in* another program, selecting the one which is the most appropriate.

Note that the hardware and the application programs can only function in the way they were intended if the OS is itself efficient and effective.

We may also note at this stage that the great speed of the CPU can also be freed from hindrance by two further approaches:
- *simultaneity,* the use of more than one peripheral device, on a simultaneous basis
- *buffering,* where input is stored in part of the main storage called a buffer, on a temporary basis, and where output is held also until the output device is prepared to accept it.

This means that the CPU can continue its high speed activity, and, simultaneously, input devices are inputting new data and output data is being dealt with by the output units.

We also have *spooling.* This stands for *simultaneous peripheral operations on line* and it relates to two activities:
- the process of transferring data from a slow input medium to a faster one (e.g. from punched cards to magnetic tape) before inputting to the computer

- programs need a much higher proportion of time for printout than for inputting or processing, and so output is stored on tape or disk ready to be printed out some other time (perhaps as a background task for programmed activities not needing the printer).

Utility software

Sometimes referred to as *service programs,* utilities undertake tasks which are necessary to each and every computer system. Again, these are provided for users by the supplier of the computer. The major kinds of utility software are:
- file conversion
- dumping (file and memory)
- file maintenance
- file reorganisation
- sorting/merging
- housekeeping routines
- debugging
- edit.

File conversion
This is actually file copying, or media conversion. It is the transfer of the contents of a given file from that medium to another kind. So, data may be read from magnetic tape to disk, for some special reason. Usually, this activity will incorporate validity checks. The transfer may be of all the data in exactly the same format, or with some editing and change.

Dumping
File dumping is simply the transfer of the contents of one file to another file of exactly the same medium and type, e.g. disk to disk. This is usually a security precaution so that data is not lost.

Memory dumping is copying the main storage contents on to a device used for output (e.g. magnetic tape, or printer of some kind). The point is that a program being undertaken on computer may not be completed for some reason. If some failure or fault arises, then it would be wasteful to have to start all over again.

For memory dumping, *stop and start* routines have evolved. Dump points are established at predetermined intervals during the run (the program's operation). When one is arrived at, the *state* of the memory (main storage) is dumped or copied on to, say, magnetic tape. When a failure of some kind arises, the operator recommences the operation at the point at which the last dump was carried out, so the whole application does not have to begin all over again. The dump is read from the tape back into storage as it was originally.

File maintenance
This permits updating by addition or deletion of file records.

File reorganisation
This occurs when a file has grown too large for its present format. Up to a point, *overflow* can be used, i.e. the particular records may additionally be sited in another part of the file. However, there are limits to this and when these are reached, the whole file must be reconstituted in orderly fashion.

Sorting/merging
This permits records to be put into required key-field sequence. This program, then, rearranges records into a sequence which matches master file data. This *sort routine* will also be able to merge several files into one, as needed.

Housekeeping routines

These are basic activities such as writing disk file labels, or clearing main storage by removing unwanted data and so on.

Debugging

This refers to aids to tracing the operation of a program so that a program error can be tracked down. It also assists during the development of a program and contributes to the correction of errors in programs.

Edit

The routines undertake tidying-up tasks by preparing data for output. Inserting decimal points and various signs such as £ or $ or % is carried out.

Sub-routines

A sub-routine is a group of instructions which exist for the purpose of undertaking very specific logical or arithmetical operations, or repetitive operations (e.g. PAYE tax calculations for wages applications).

Sub-routines may be written independently of the organisation's programmers – provided usually by the computer manufacturer – or they could be incorporated by the programmer within his or her own written, coded instructions.

The sub-routines, when used for repetitive operations, are stated once and then referred to as and when necessary. This facility saves storage space because each routine is written and stored once only and then used as needed.

Programming aids

This is a group of routines which are intended to help programming activity. There are three major types:
- assemblers, compilers
- generators
- simulators.

However, we will look more closely at this type of aid at the end of this current chapter when we deal with *programming languages*. For now we can explain that:
- *Assembler programs* assist in translating terms in the program such as ADD or MULT (multiply) into precise instructions to be comprehended by the computer. They are for *low-level language* programs, written in symbolic form, and the assembler program makes the programmer's task easier because he or she is now able to use a range of easily understood instructions.
- *Compiler programs* also have a translation function, expressing a *high level language* program in machine code so that the program is now machine understandable (comprehensible). In other words, the programmer writes in a language he or she has learnt and the compiler program permits the machine to understand the instructions.
- *Generators* are special programs which are used to generate (i.e. write) other programs from a given outline.
- *Simulators* are programs which are used to allow a particular program written for a specific computer to be used on another model.

Note that there is a hardware device, the *emulator,* which is attached to the new and different computer and which allows it to use programs written for another one. Do not confuse this with the simulator which is a program, not a device.

Application packages and programs

The idea of application software is simply that a complete system is provided for a specific application, or job to be done. The system is a set of programs (or, more rarely, a single program).

These programs can be written within the organisation wishing to use it (*in-house*) or by an external (*ex-house*) body such as manufacturers, software houses (specialising in this activity), trade associations, research bodies and so forth.

Such packages available for commercial usage include:

- payroll
- warehousing control
- production control
- accounting (financial, sales, purchase, auditing, network analysis (PERT))
- word-processing.

Specific application packages have also been produced for use by specialist bodies such as building societies, stockbrokers and local authorities.

Packages purchased by organisations will usually require some kind of modification prior to use, but it must be said that there are direct gains to be derived from buying-in such programs. These are:

- there is a reduction in the cost and effort expended on programming itself
- the package will already be tested and should therefore contain no errors
- the package provides expertise not usually available to the smaller user.

Obviously, the application package purchased must be carefully selected, and so we have to be aware of the considerations to be borne in mind when making this choice.

- Does this package actually carry out the specific job in question, completely and fully?
- Does the package include unnecessary activities (i.e. not actually required by the organisation)?
- What modificiations are needed before the package can be used?
- Can it be used without difficulties?
- What are the running times? maximum times? mean times?
- To what extent has the package been used by other installations?
- Is any special hardware needed?
- What are the terms of the contract (price, supplier assistance available, the documentation accompanying the package)?
- Could the package cope with expected future requirements?

DBMS

In Chapter 5, p. 61, we took a brief look at the idea of the database. We saw that the DBMS is the *database management system*. During the past few years databases have become extremely popular, and they use DBMS software which is able to construct the records of the organisation and maintain them in the widebased file known as database. The programs used are very complex.

Models, graphics and spreadsheets

In this section we deal with special kinds of application software which have become very commonly used in all areas of the private and the public sectors. Here we are going to examine three of the major categories of software which offer assistance to management in the area of use of information.

The term *decision support system* (DSS) has emerged to refer to computer systems which are designed to produce information in such a way that they can be used to assist management to make better decisions. This term can be used to mean a wide range of approaches from the spreadsheet to highly sophisticated *artificial intelligence* (AI) techniques used to evaluate the pros and cons of situations which have to be decided about.

A very popular approach is the *Executive Support System* (ESS) which serves top executives. This is basically a workstation which is programmed to provide management information with a miniumum of fuss.

We shall be dealing with three very important application software developments and their capabilities, within the concept of the DSS.

Models

We must be careful to give a meaningful definition of *model*. We mean by this term a representation in mathematical terms of the relationship existing between the significant variables in a specific situation to which the model relates.

Examples of some of the models available through IT technology are:
- technical design models, such as the computer-aided design (CAD) approaches
- marketing models, used to forecast sales results and market developments and incorporating results of market research, the consumer expenditure statistics available, and so on
- corporate planning models, analysing particular long-term courses of action in terms of the effects they have on specific areas in the firm, e.g. corporate liquidity, cash flow
- econometric models, mathematical expressions of the economic situation (used by the UK Treasury).

A particular version of modelling is the *simulation model*. This tries to predict behaviour by imitating or *simulating* the major aspects and characteristics of the entity being modelled. This approach is used in order to discover what changes in inputs have what results in outputs. Simulation techniques are adopted for all kinds of organisational purposes including the flow of traffic and the appraisal of capital investment.

Graphics

We use the term *business graphics* to signify using computers to translate numeric data into graphs, pie charts, histograms and any other representation of this type. A special form of this is *computer-aided design* (CAD), which is extensively used by technical specialists in the motor vehicle and other industries.

The whole point of graphics is to produce an understanding of complex data as far as the user is concerned. The idea is that the graphics are actually accessible *on site,* where they are required. Graphics assist the user because:
- differences and comparisons are generally drawn to the attention of the user
- the image presented may be directly linked to the area being studied (e.g. *comparative sizes* may be demonstrated by blocks)
- there is a wide range of graphics available.

However, there are some drawbacks, in that techniques for computer graphics are very complex, and greater storage capacity is required than for numerical data (around a hundred times more!).

The most popular form of package connected with this area is the microcomputer graphics package. The typical microcomputer configuration used in relation to graphics would be:
- the microcomputer itself
- a printer for text-based output, in addition to the screen
- a plotter which would cooperate with the printer to produce the graphics on the text (paper)
- some type of input device.

Some microcomputers possess separate storage for graphics in addition to the main storage, because of the popularity of this type of use. One micro (Research Machines *Nimbus*) has one Mbyte of main storage (RAM) plus 64K of dedicated memory for graphics. Many Japanese machines also have the same facility.

Colour displays are also very common today and this facility adds to the value of the presentation of data in graphic format.

The essence of graphics is to define unambiguously, hold in storage, manipulate, interrogate and output *images* or *pictures*. Because these are much easier to comprehend than numbers, graphics offer considerable assistance to information communication.

As far as mainframes are concerned, there are also *visual early warning systems,* these being *graphic decision support systems.* This idea assists management to receive information in graphic format, but without the need to construct charts and graphs themselves. In this approach graphic information is presented on-screen by depressing a terminal key.

This approach incorporates collections of reference tables and charts which are updated as an automatic procedure when the data alters. Any one of these may be accessed at any time. In addition to display on VDU, printout copies, overhead projector transparancies (OHP) and 35 mm film can be produced as needed.

At the present time, the mainframe is able to provide the services offered in this DSS version, and it is often used to form part of a network to link management workstations.

Frequently there are *micro-mainframe linkages* which permit a microcomputer to be used as a terminal for accessing and communicating graphics information formats.

Spreadsheets

A *spreadsheet* may be regarded as the computer version of a sheet of financial analysis paper. The user is provided with a *worksheet* which has columns and rows in this manner.

```
        a    b    c    d    e    f    g    h    i    j . . .
   1
   2
   3
   4
   :
   :
```

The precise number of these depends upon the *package* we are dealing with.

The intersection of a column and a row is a *cell,* and each cell has an identification (number/letter, e.g. b3). Each cell may carry words or numerical values (or even formulae). Thus, a cell could contain *February* if, for example, this was the beginning of a cost report on a monthly basis.

Whenever the contents of the spreadsheet are modified in any way, then the other values related to it are automatically amended too. This allows *what if?* analysis (or *sensitivity analysis*) to be a major use of the spreadsheet. Given that we have all the cells containing relevant figures, we can ask what if . . . b2 were £1200 and not the present figure? All the other cells which would be affected by this change would immediately indicate their new, related, values.

The spreadsheet is a DSS tool. Strangely the concept has little, if anything, to do with computers!

The main attributes of the spreadsheet are speed and flexibility. The first spreadsheet package was known as Visicalc, now no longer available. Current packages include Lotus 1-2-3, Microsoft Excel, and Multi Plan. Spreadsheets may also be linked to other applications, especially graphics packages.

The spreadsheet made a major impact upon the accounting profession in the 1980s, and its success is linked with the success of the microcomputer. Today we have *integrated packages* which are available to permit data and files to be transferred from spreadsheets to word-processing, communication and database programs – and in the other direction. This means that data from a database application is usable within the spreadsheet package. In the same way, part of a spreadsheet may be included in a report which is being compiled using a word-processing package and then transmitted to another workstation or site by the use of a communications package.

Some of the uses of the spreadsheet are:
- cashflow forecasting
- budgeting
- management accounts (variances, cumulations)
- standard calculations (e.g. leasing, NPV)
- estimating
- auditing.

Spreadsheeting has also cut down the time taken by accountants in professional offices to prepare and amend cashflow and profit forecasting for their clients. Larger firms in industry are now incorporating microcomputers and spreadsheets into their MIS. Smaller firms have discovered that the spreadsheet may be utilised as an automated cash book, for costing activity and even wages calculations.

Note that what we call *dedicated financial modelling software packages* can today offer an alternative to spreadsheeting. The idea of financial modelling is to provide managers with projections of future business activity which have a high order of probability, in order to assist in decision-making of an informed kind.

The model applies a range of calculations intended to forecast the outcome of present and current business activities and demonstrate the effect provided by the adoption of new ones which are being considered. In fact, the software we are discussing now incorporates complex, sophisticated modelling, and mathematical routines. By comparison, spreadsheets are less helpful in that the user is obliged to create his or her own models by the process of defining the macro-instructions and the necessary functions needed to result in the required calculations.

In the use of the spreadsheet, the user must site each and every calculation in a given *cell,* thus rendering it less easy to track down the model's logic. In the case of the model, however, the user is able to evolve the model needed with no reference at all to the cell locations. In fact, for the most part, simple statements are used to develop the model stage by stage.

In the spreadsheet, the outcome of complex calculations will usually be based upon earlier ones, and these earlier ones, in turn, will relate to previous versions, and so forth. The degree of probability of error in spreadsheeting can be high.

Some financial modelling programs allow English-like statements to be used. Some also provide the facility of print/display of logic hierarchies, to reduce error and to allow the user to return to the model at a later date and still understand what was done to arrive at a given conclusion, without difficulty. This specific clarity, which not only allows new users to comprehend the origin of the figures, but provides clarity of the business activities themselves, is a major gain over the spreadsheet approach.

The outcome of all this appears to be that spreadsheets are sound devices for gathering, presenting and reporting data and also for more basic models and calculations. On the other hand, the financial modelling approach is best suited to more complex approaches.

Programming languages

It is important to remember that the computer cannot accept, hold on to and manipulate data *unless* that data is in binary format.

In the same way, the program held in storage has to be in binary code. That binary code is *machine code,* of course. The original computer programs had to be actually written in that code, and it was a long, tedious and error-prone activity. Today, easy-to-write programming languages are used because we now have translating programs to undertake the conversion of those instructions into machine-comprehensible coding.

Today, there are four categories of programming language in use:

- machine languages
- low-level languages
- high-level languages
- fourth generation languages (4GLs).

One way of expressing the relationship of these gradings is by bearing in mind the *software hierarchy,* which is shown in the triangle which follows.

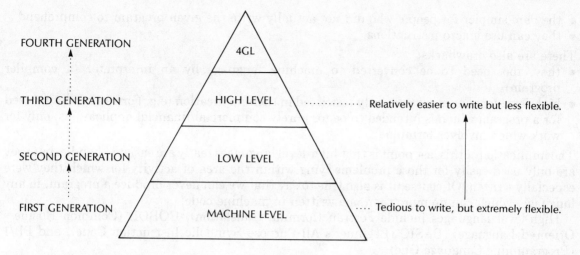

FOURTH GENERATION   4GL

THIRD GENERATION   HIGH LEVEL   Relatively easier to write but less flexible.

SECOND GENERATION   LOW LEVEL

FIRST GENERATION   MACHINE LEVEL   Tedious to write, but extremely flexible.

Machine languages

Using machine code – the computer's own language – programming can accomplish anything of which the computer is capable. This language permits instructions to go into absolute detail for every location within the machine. It also allows the computer to work at its fastest possible speed of operation, simply because the instructions do not have to be interpreted by another program before the computer is able to comprehend them.

Problems arising with this language approach are:

- difficulty in programming
- slow progress and tedium in writing programs
- likelihood of error
- difficulty in changing programs at a later date.

Machine languages are *machine dependent,* that is, each make of computer has its own individual version. Very little of this type of programming is done today – except for very technical and special applications.

Low-level languages

Historically, low-level languages developed simply because of the failings of machine languages as far as programming is concerned. The kind of programming adopted here is referred to as *assembler level programming* and it introduces mnemonic coding for the appropriate machine coding instructions.

As we saw earlier in this chapter, *assembler programs* have to be used in order to translate the mnemonic coding into precise machine-understandable instructions. An example of mnemonic coding is MULT meaning multiply, or SUB meaning subtract. Low-level languages used today include Honeywell's Easycoder, and ICL's System 4 Usercode.

There are special instructions called *macros,* which are stored on tape or disk to cope with, for example, file access. These macros are standard terms which convey a number of specific machine language instructions.

To write a program in a low-level language gives the advantage of being able to use the machine efficiently, but it does require a very thorough knowledge of the computer's workings.

High-level languages

In developing high-level languages, computer scientists were seeking languages which were less time-consuming to learn and simpler to use generally. Today their use is very widespread and they have significant advantages:

- they can often be used on more than one make of computer (or, at any rate, they need little modification)

- they are simpler for people who did not actually write the given program to comprehend
- they can use macro instructions.

There are also drawbacks:

- they, too, need to be converted to machine language by an interpreter (a compiler program)
- high-level languages are relatively restricted in their application (e.g. Fortran cannot be used for a program which is intended to be for purely commercial/financial applications, only for work which involves formulae).

The implication of this last point is that high-level languages really are easier to handle, but they are only used easily for those problems lying within the area of activity for which they were especially written. Of course, it is also true to say that we can never produce a program, in any language, which can do more than one written in machine code!

High-level languages include Fortran (formula translation), COBOL (Common Business Oriented Language), BASIC (Beginner's All-Purpose Symbolic Instruction Code), and PL/1 (Programming Language One).

Fourth generation languages

These are commonly referred to as *4GLs*. The term has unfortunately become a generic one covering a wide range of concepts and methodologies, and software products. Today there are around 150 different products under this heading. Students will see a number of articles in the press asking what a real 4GL actually is!

The best approach to understanding this area is once again to examine the three categories of machine, low and high-level languages. We find that each one is concerned with telling the computer *how* to cope with a particular problem. In other words they deal with the computer strategy to be adopted. 4GLs, however, are concerned with telling the computer *what* the problem is.

3GLs (you will realise that here we mean high-level languages!) are obliged to use a compiler to convert an abbreviated kind of *statement of how* to tackle an activity into a larger, machine-understandable and detailed statement.

4GLs use a generator to transform a *statement about what is needed* into a machine language *statement of how* to tackle this. It does this simply by referring to a *library* or collection of *templates* which already have the strategies written on them. A *template* is the name we give to a list of commands which refer to a given job. We describe 4GLs as *non-procedural languages*. This means that they are not concerned with procedures – these have already been listed and prepared on the various templates. The logical weakness here is that users of 4GLs are limited to the problems dealt with by the templates. However, there are also *hybrid 4GLs* which now combine compiling and generating, but they have to be used by professionals.

The 4GLs simplify the development process a great deal and they also allow the end-users to become more involved in their computer system, thus offering a higher degree of motivation.

Some of the 4GLs (alternatively referred to as *program generators* and *application generators*) have evolved from programming languages such as Cobol (e.g. the 4GL called Micro Focus Source-writer) and some form database languages (e.g. Cullinet's ADS).

Fifth generation languages are now beginning to evolve, and conventional programming languages are being developed further and linked up with, for example, *object-oriented development*. This means that the analyst identifies the objects with a system, their properties and the things they must do, instead of simply looking at functions. Examples of new languages connected with this are Ada, Object-Pascal and Smalltalk. The Ministry of Defence, and its US counterpart, both use ADA for real-time applications.

Incidentally, it is interesting to note that the fifth generation languages differ greatly from earlier generations. They specify the processing required in mathematical equations. The gain from this is that a small amount of text permits programming of complex systems.

Summary

In this chapter we have discussed:

- the important categories of software: operating systems (OS) for communicating, monitoring/controlling peripherals, and monitoring software and multiprogramming; and the terms multiprogramming, simultaneity, buffering, spooling
- utility software: the tasks of file conversion, dumping, file maintenance, file reorganisation, sorting/merging, housekeeping routines, debugging, editing
- sub-routines
- programming aids: assemblers, compilers, generators, simulators, emulators
- application packages/programs and models, graphics, spreadsheets
- programming languages: machine, low, high, 4GLs and beyond.

Self-test Questions

Answer these questions, then check your answers in this chapter.

1 List the categories of software.
2 Explain *virtual storage* and *OS*.
3 What is the purpose of buffering?
4 What is *dumping*?
5 What is the difference between assemblers and emulators?
6 What advantages are derived from the purchase of application packages?
7 What does a DDS do? How?
8 Explain the accountant's use of a spreadsheet.
9 What does the software hierarchy set out to explain?
10 What do 4GLs do?

CHAPTER 9
Flowcharting, decision tables and programming

Introduction

This chapter contains our study of two separate and yet associated areas: flowcharting and decision tables, and then programming. In the former we look carefully at two very important devices for the analysis and demonstration of procedures and flows of work in various categories, and in the latter section we look at the broad principles of the writing of the computer's sets of instructions.

Flowcharting

What is a flowchart? It is a diagram which uses easily recognisable symbols to denote various activities and which are linked by *flowlines*. They show the purpose and the direction of the general movement, or *flow* of whatever is being described.

These diagrams are extremely useful and there are many different kinds in existence. They are intended to assist the user's comprehension by presenting the facts in a clear manner, thus eliminating the use of a lengthy narrative to describe the sequence of events, activities or operations.

A major difficulty is that, although attempts have been made to standardise the categories and the symbols adopted in flowcharting, not much success has been achieved in this quarter and, in fact, it is fairly easy for someone to identify a flowchart drawn by a colleague because of the individuality of its design!

Flowchart categories

We can place flowcharts into several alternative categories, but the simplest and most convenient are probably:
- *the system flowchart,* concerned with the main inputs, outputs, files and their linking up in a particular system, and this includes the clerical procedure flowcharts (which are intended to indicate procedures within a given clerical system)
- *the program flowchart,* indicating the logical sequence of decision and activity in a given program.

Note that the symbols used in these two main categories are to a *limited* extent standardised, as we shall see. A necessary device for flowcharting is the *template,* which is a plastic sheet with symbols cut out so that it can be used to draw those symbols as required. As a rule, it has the significance of the symbols printed on it.

In addition, there is a *block diagram* which, in order to avoid pointless semantic argument, is accepted as a flowchart. This is intended to indicate the major processes to be carried out (usually in respect of a computer program), but it does not necessarily *flow.*

Typical flowchart users

It is useful to note that flowcharts are very frequently used by various groups of people within an organisation. Here are some of these users.

Managers

They use flowcharts to:
- assist in training of staff
- apply effective control and coordination of effort
- comply with organisational and/or statutory needs (e.g. relevant accounts, reports and so on)
- assess the appropriateness/relevance of management information and its timing.

Auditors

They use flowcharts to:
- carry out a check of procedures and the overall system
- assess the degree of internal system control
- develop the audit program itself.

Systems analysts

They use flowcharts to:
- determine *actual* activities and their actual purpose
- analyse any bottleneck situations, any superfluous activities
    (e.g. causing duplication of effort)
- any ineffectual controls and/or problems existing.

Programmers

They use flowcharts to:
- plan the sequence of decision/action in a given program
- demonstrate the activities within the program to other individuals concerned with it
- place on record the way in which the program actually functions.

Rules for flowcharting

These rules attempt to produce an acceptably useful flowchart if they *are obeyed.*

1 Indicate the *subject* of the flowchart, the *date* of its creation and the *name* of the person creating it, as well as the *meaning of symbols* used (i.e. insert a key) and use only one symbol per activity (i.e. be consistent).

2 State clearly the *work-units* (departments, sections, etc.) involved in the system, the *procedures* (which unit and which person carries out a given activity upon receipt of information) and the *documents* (invoices, reports, and so on) and where they originate.

3 Establish a very clear *definition of any controls.*

4 Determine in the flowchart the *logical sequence* of each and every activity and the flows involved, making a distinction between information obtained from a document and the document itself.

5 *Neatness and clarity* of the flowchart is essential.

6 The flowchart must *flow* either vertically (top of the page to the bottom) or laterally (left to right).

7 *Incorporate special detail* (required, say, by a given part of the chart) in a separate flowchart, indicating its existence on the main flowchart by cross-referencing.

8 The flowchart must be *free of error, logical,* and *include everything* relevant.

Standard symbols

As we saw earlier, there are a few generally accepted standard symbols like these.

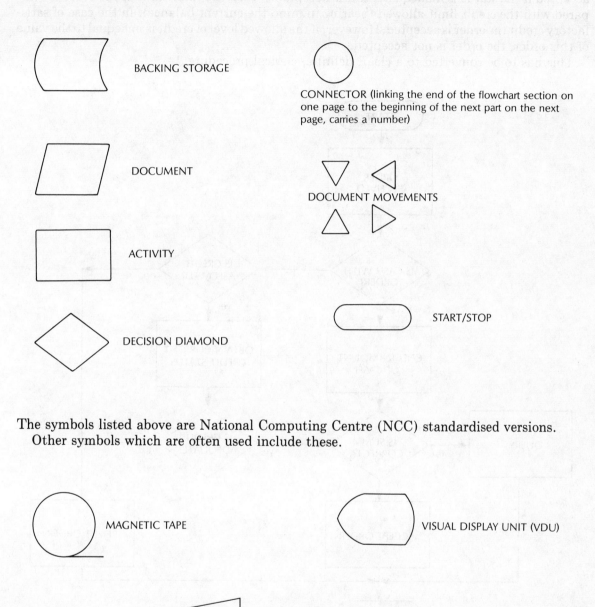

The symbols listed above are National Computing Centre (NCC) standardised versions. Other symbols which are often used include these.

Obviously, this list is far from exhaustive!

Creating flowcharts

We begin by looking at a *systems flowchart*, in fact, a clerical procedure version. Here, we simply have a description or narrative which tells us, in words, what the approach accomplishes and how it does this. Order processing is achieved in this way: an order is received and the contents checked to discover whether it is accompanied by the payment or not. If so, then the sum must

97

also be checked. If the sum is incorrect, then the customer must be advised. If the payment is not accompanying the order, then the credit status of the customer is checked. The order is not accepted if the status is inadequate. If it is acceptable, then the total value of the order is compared with the credit limit allowed (bearing in mind the current balance). In the case of satisfactory credit the order is accepted. However, if the allowed level of credit is not equal to the value of this order, the order is not accepted.

This has to be converted to a clear, definite, clerical procedure.

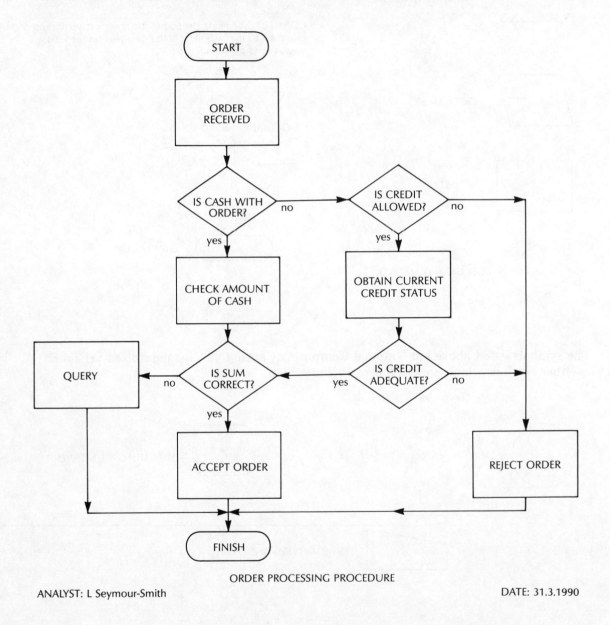

ORDER PROCESSING PROCEDURE

ANALYST: L Seymour-Smith   DATE: 31.3.1990

Suppose we have a computer system to flowchart, as opposed to a clerical version?

XYZ, plc, has a sales ledger file held on disk (in customer number sequence). There is also a warehouse (stock) disk file in inventory number order. Customer orders are prepared for input by the punched card method, with verification.

Suppose we need a flowchart now which shows the *runs* required in order to update the warehouse file and the customer file, resulting in the production of customer invoices. The flowchart could look like the one on the opposite page.

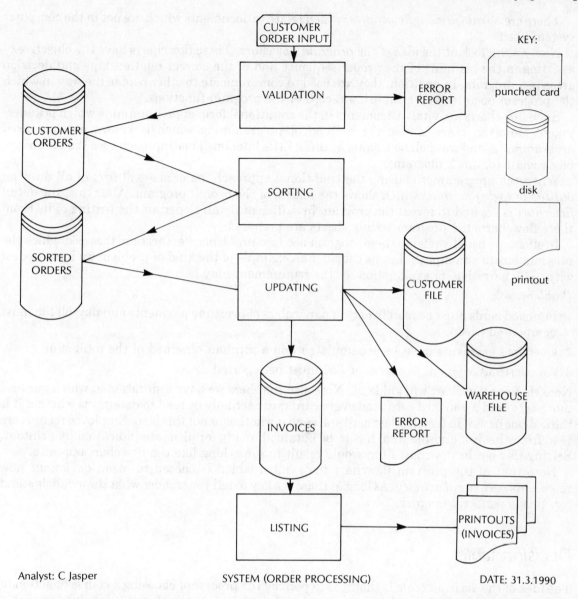

KEY:

punched card

disk

printout

Analyst: C Jasper   SYSTEM (ORDER PROCESSING)   DATE: 31.3.1990

In this example of a flowchart we have used disks both to receive sorted orders and to act as temporary storage for listing prior to printing. It is also probable that magnetic tape could be used for these purposes, depending upon the system used.

Remember that the system flowchart is intended to show how a system operates and so will usually relate to the whole system. However, we can also have a flowchart which is only concerned with part of a system. Basically, flowcharts of this type are used to:

- act as a record of the actual system adopted
- communicate the system operation to other persons
- seek improvements in the existing system
- analyse the system's working.

Remember that these charts consist of two sub-categories: for clerical (manual) systems and for computer systems.

The system flowchart will show each input, each activity involved in processing and every input and file used. The extent of the detail will differ in accordance with the complexity of the system being described. The clerical procedure flowchart represents the activities carried out in relation to a selection of documents used in connection with a particular section, department or clerical procedure.

There are also *document flowcharts,* which relate to documents which are not in the computer system itself.

Now we will look at the idea of the *program flowchart.* These flowcharts have the objective of assisting in the planning of the proper sequence and of the correct relationships and decision areas in a program. In addition, they are used to communicate to other people the way in which the program operates and establish a record of the program functions.

Such flowcharts are vital instruments in the traditional form of programming which is undertaken. However, there is also the method of programming which is known as *structured programming,* and we shall be looking at this a little later on. This approach uses the idea of the block chart (or block diagram).

When the programmer is using the traditional approach, he or she will first of all draw an *outline* or *logic flowchart* which shows the nature of the overall program. After this, the *detail flowchart* is created to reveal the program in sufficient detail to permit the writing of it. From these flowcharts the program coding sheets are prepared.

In effect, we usually refer to these program needs as *problems,* i.e. these are the tasks which the program has to accomplish. Let us consider an example of the kind of problem we have to deal with. The narrative, or explanation, of the requirement may be:

Problem:

1 Punched cards must be read to obtain particulars of overtime payments and payroll file must be updated (disk).

2 Overtime payments must be accumulated and a printout obtained of the total sum.

3 An overtime payment in excess of £50 must be reported.

Note that our flowchart will guide us. Note also that here we have a situation in which our first move is to read a punched card, and every card must actually be read to determine whether it is the last one or not. In fact, the last card states on it whether or not this is so. Employee records are read from the disk and the total has to be obtained, ready for ultimate indication by printout. Setting this out in flowchart form would result in something like the flowchart opposite.

Note that in the program flowchart the symbol which is chosen to mean *document* now represents *peripheral activity.* As long as there is a key to tell your reader what the symbols stand for, this is perfectly in order.

Decision tables

The idea of the *decision table* is that it is to portray the process of choosing a course of action in the form of a table. Perhaps the best method of demonstrating the elements involved in such a table is by means of the diagram below.

TITLE	RULE NUMBER
CONDITION STUB	CONDITION ENTRY
ACTION STUB	ACTION ENTRY

- The *condition stub* is concerned with the aspects involved.
- The *condition entry* deals with the 'yes' or 'no' status.
- The *action stub* relates to the result of a condition.
- The *action entry* tells us whether the result does, or does not, arise.

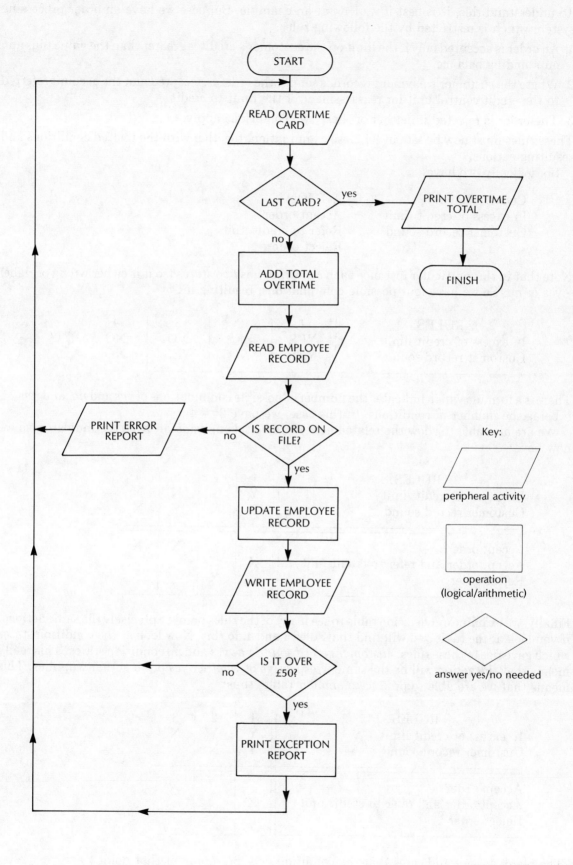

START

READ OVERTIME CARD

LAST CARD? — yes → PRINT OVERTIME TOTAL → FINISH

no

ADD TOTAL OVERTIME

READ EMPLOYEE RECORD

IS RECORD ON FILE? — no → PRINT ERROR REPORT

yes

UPDATE EMPLOYEE RECORD

WRITE EMPLOYEE RECORD

IS IT OVER £50? — no

yes

PRINT EXCEPTION REPORT

Key:

peripheral activity

operation (logical/arithmetic)

answer yes/no needed

To understand this, it is best if we look at an example. Suppose we have an order processing system which is restricted by the following rules.

1 An order is accepted only if the limit on the customer's credit is greater than the value plus any outstanding balance.

2 Where the customer's payment record is sound, the order is accepted and the account referred to the credit control unit for reassessment of the limit to credit.

3 The order is rejected if neither of these two conditions apply.

These rules must now be set out for close examination, together with the related conditions and resulting actions.

So, logically, we have:

CONDITIONS	ACTION
In excess of credit limit	Accept order
Customer record sound	Refer to credit unit
	Reject order

Note that in this particular instance each *condition* has *two states* (so it is either wrong or right) – *yes* or *no*. So we have four possible combinations, resulting in:

RULES:	1	2	3	4
In excess of credit limit	YES	YES	NO	NO
Customer record sound	YES	NO	YES	NO

There is a formula which indicates the number of possible combinations of *yes* and *no*, and it is 2^n, n being the number of conditions. In this case, we have $2^2 = 4$.

We are also able to show the related actions to be taken, using an X as the indicator, so we now have:

RULES:	1	2	3	4
In excess of credit limit	Y	Y	N	N
Customer record sound	Y	N	Y	N
Accept order			X	X
Accept order and refer to credit unit	X			
Reject order		X		

Finally, we examine our decision table to see if any of the rules point to precisely the same actions. If you look at the table you will find that rules 3 and 4 do this. Now look at the condition states which gave rise to these rules: *customer record sound* has *yes* and *no* condition states. This really means that the action will be the same irrespective of whether *yes* or *no* actually applies. This means that we are able to produce a smaller table, thus:

RULES:	1	2	3
In excess of credit limit	Y	Y	N
Customer record sound	Y	N	–
Accept order			X
Accept order and refer to credit unit	X		
Reject order		X	

(The blank space – indicates that the condition does not apply at that point.)

The decision table is a good way of determining the logic of a procedure, and it greatly assists comprehension of the rules because of the simple layout. The problem is expressed in the simplest way and it throws up any unnecessary elements, together with any elements which are somehow excluded.

What we are saying here is that a data processing problem really needs the determination of given actions which themselves relate to the responses provided to questions. For this reason, flowcharts can be less effective, especially for complex matters. The whole point of this kind of approach is simply that all the relevant conditions have to be accounted for before a definite conclusion is reached and action is taken.

The decision table we produced in this chapter concerned conditions which only have two states each. This is known as a *limited entry table*.

There is also the *extended entry table* and this has conditions entered which have more than two states, e.g. warehouse stock items could be available (on shelf), out-of-stock but on order, or out-of-stock and not on order.

A *mixed entry table* has conditions which may relate to two or more states.

The major difference between the flowchart and the decision table lies in the fact that the latter is simply problem-orientated, whilst the former is solution-orientated. The manner in which the decision table is designed gives the systems analyst the chance to establish the problem properly in his or her mind before seeking the solution. Note also that flowcharts themselves are far less standardised than decision tables, which is, of course, why the former often utilise symbols which are not standard. Decision tables must be based upon the standard format.

A note on flowcharting

For some years, flowcharting was somewhat neglected as programmers found that the task of creating them was time-consuming and laborious. Rapid system development meant that ideas needing to be incorporated into the programs developed rapidly and that new perceptions of what could be achieved by incorporating new concepts into the program occurred very frequently. This, in turn, meant that flowcharts were constantly being re-designed which resulted in much time-wasting.

The evolution of *structured programming* (see p. 107) eventually reduced the need for flowcharting as far as programs were concerned. By the end of the 1980s, however, a new flowcharting concept was introduced. This permits the interactive creation of flowcharts by using a software package known as *Interactive Easyflow*. This means that the person producing the flowchart uses keyboard and screen in much the same way as pencil and paper would be used. The boxes and the lines are created and may be rearranged in accordance with the analyst's ideas and the design may be amended as much as is needed before being printed out.

The difficulty caused by the programmers' previous attitude towards flowcharting as an activity was the resultant lack of communication by documentation, especially problematic when new programmers had to take over from previous members of the team. The interactive approach is not purely for program flowcharts but relates to any activity which can be recorded in flowchart format.

Programming

It can be seen that there are really three main job disciplines in a computer installation. These are:
- systems analysis
- programming
- operations.

We shall see in a later chapter that we have usually an *operations manager* who is assigned the responsibility of overseeing the activities of the computer operators, the staff operating the off-line devices (e.g. COM or card punches), and also the control section and the data preparation staff (who may well be allocated to user-departments). The *systems analyst* has the job of working with users and potential users of the computer systems and discovering their needs, or designing a suitable system for them and then implementing it.

The systems analyst has to have the system designed converted into instructions for the computer to understand and these take the form of the program. The analyst has to work with the *programmer* to ensure that this is carried out appropriately.

Note (and we shall discuss this later when we examine the nature of the computer staff's work) that there were, at the end of the 1980s, *programmer/analysts* or *analyst/programmers* who undertake a combination of both tasks because of the development of 4GLs, which we looked at earlier.

The task of programming

The actual work of the programmer and his or her responsibilities vary. As we saw in Chapter 8, the term *software* has various uses, but we usually adopt the title of *software programmer* for the individual programmer who creates general software. There is also often an *application programmer,* writing programs for specific computer tasks.

The exact task of the programmer differs between organisations from translating the program specification (prepared already by the analyst) step-by-step into program instructions, to the writing of the program from a basic narrative.

Sources of programs

Remember that a program is simply a group of instructions which must be carried out so that the computer is able to undertake a particular task. These programs have three major origins:
- the computer's *in-house* programmers write them for their own computer
- the computer manufacturer (supplier) provides certain specific programs which the computer has to have (e.g. sort or sort-and-merge programs)
- *software houses* – firms specialising in the writing of programs for specific tasks (e.g. database, or spreadsheets) – provide *packages* which are *ready-made.*

Program development

The stages involved in the development (writing) of the program are important:
- the program specification is devised (by the systems analyst)
- the programmer studies the specification
- the programmer draws the logic or program flowchart or adopts an alternative technique
- the programmer then codes the program (e.g. writes it in COBOL)
- the high-level language program is then prepared for compilation (i.e. translated into the appropriate language by means of a compiler program) especially for the computer being used
- if the compiler program detects syntax (i.e. specific rules for the formation of instructions) error, then this has to be corrected by the programmer
- the program then has to be tested for logic errors – should these arise, the program has to be corrected and compiled again
- program documentation is created
- the program needs maintaining, which means modifying and improving as and when necessary.

We can incorporate these stages in a useful diagram to assist the memory.

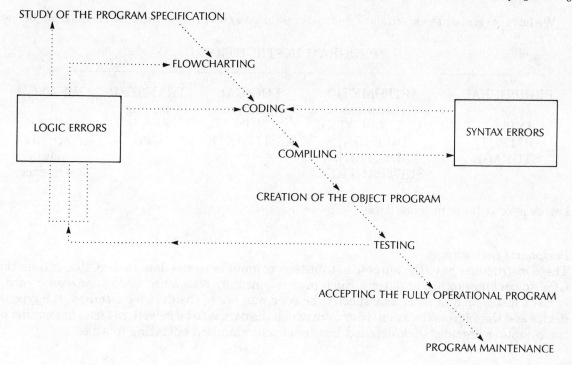

The program specification

The main features of this specification are as follows:

- the name of the job or task, its reference number, and a brief description of its objectives
- reference to the logical file specifications concerned with the job
- input media – layout of contents, including the data items, the sizes, symbols, etc., including any medium irrespective of whether it is keyed in, OCR or any other kind
- output media – contents, layout (very largely printout and display) including error messages
- checks – adopted at various processing stages, as well as to data input to the system
- processing to be undertaken including any calculations (e.g. division, updating and amendments)
- logical files – storage/access modes
- symbols and codes used for the particular task on hand e.g. dollar or sterling signs or codes indicating another processing approach
- decision tables as and when needed.

Programming principles

We know that programs are written in a programming language which permits the operator to use familiar terms to indicate and describe what is required. It is then necessary for a translating program to be used in order to convert the terminology into terms understood by the machine.

To understand the principles of programming we have to deal with a few terms. *Instructions* have two fundamental elements:

- the *operation* or *function* – what is to be undertaken by the computer
- the *operand* or *address* – the location within which the operation is to be undertaken.

The concept of *addressing* relates to the fact that computer areas which store data are segmented into locations which have their own individual numbers (i.e. a *unique address*). Any data item being processed has to have its location, or address, referred to in the program itself.

We have several different kinds of instructions and we can express these in the diagram below.

PROGRAM INSTRUCTIONS

PERIPHERAL	ARITHMETIC	LOGICAL	TRANSFER	BRANCH
for	operations	operations	moving	to
INPUT,	MULTIPLICATION	NON-	data in	undertake
OUTPUT,	DIVISION,	ARITHMETIC	CPU	activity
STORAGE	ADDITION,			out of
	SUBTRACTION			sequence

Let us look at these in more detail.

Peripheral instructions

These instructions have the purpose of transferring input or stored data to the CPU, or from the CPU to backing storage or output. Such instructions may read *write to disk,* or *read a card.*

Each instruction must clearly specify the code number of the device concerned, the type of device and the address (location) to or from which the data is to be moved. In fact, the supplier of the computer provides such detailed instructions as standard operating routines.

Arithmetic instructions

As stated in the diagram above, these instructions (again, provided by the supplier as part of the standard operating instructions) allow the fundamental arithmetic operations to be carried out.

Logical instructions

These consist of:

- *compare instructions,* which indicate the relative size of two numbers, for instance whether $D < H$
- *shift instructions* to move numbers either to the left or the right, e.g., in order to line up numbers which are to be printed out
- *zeroise instructions,* which clear the memory by substituting 0 for each number.

Transfer instructions

Whilst they do not alter data in any way at all, these instructions change the address of data within the memory, or they move data from the arithmetic logic unit (ALU) to memory or from the latter to the former.

Branch (jump) instructions

This type incorporates an address of another instruction so that the control unit is able to use this instead of taking the next instruction in the sequence of the given program it is following.

This prevents the unit from blindly pursuing the given sequence regardless. It allows the program to incorporate a decision-making function. Branch instructions may be:

- *conditional branches,* which allow control to be transferred *if* a given condition is satisfied (if it is not satisfied, then the next instruction is automatically adopted)
- *unconditional branches,* which oblige the control unit to move to the instruction in the specific address listed, e.g. as when a cycle of operations is complete and the unit is to return to the start of the program again
- *switches (indicators),* which are an element of the ALU and which indicate a calculation's result, e.g. if the result is zero a certain activity must follow, whereas if it is negative (say, debit) another activity has to be undertaken.

Techniques in programming

Here we shall be looking at a selection of techniques which are commonly used in the writing of programs.

Looping

This is a way of avoiding writing the same instruction over and over again. If the instruction is to read a punched card, for example, then after one had been read, the same instruction would usually have to be re-written for as many times as there were cards to read.

The idea is that the computer should re-read the identical instruction. This is *looping*. Every loop has to incorporate a means of *exit* so that the unit moves on to the next instruction as soon as the current one has been read as many times as necessary (i.e. after, in our example, a given number of cards have been read). Or there may be a special symbol on the last card which tells the unit it is the last one.

Modifying and demodifying

This has to be carried out where looping is introduced. It has to alter or modify the address to which the instruction refers. If this is not done, then the re-reading of the instruction would simply mean that the same data item would be processed again and again.

There also has to be a demodifying process to re-establish the address in the instruction in the original form. When the loop is commenced on another occasion it will be at the start of the sequence, and all will be well.

Using sub-routines

This allows the same sequence of instructions to be used at various stages. So, often-used sets of instructions are gathered together to constitute a sub-routine to be adopted at any location in the program. Some of these sub-routines are provided by the computer supplier but programmers will often create their own versions as needed. There are:

- *closed sub-routines,* which transfer control to the sub-routine from another segment of the program (using a branch instruction)
- *open sub-routines* to be placed in the program at the location at which they are needed.

Structured programming

The majority of computer programmers today adopt the approach known as *structured programming* to create computer programs needed by their organisations. This is an alternative to using flowcharts because these standard devices encourage branching and the division of control by means of decision diamonds.

The purpose of structured programming is to break a problem into separate functions; each logically different component is then inserted into a separate block in the *structure chart* and each function divided into parts and then subdivided again. The lowest level of this hierarchy constitutes the steps which may be expressed using a high-level language.

Generally speaking, there are only three basic constructions in the concept of structured programming. Therefore, we can say that in this approach we have:

- sequence – *do this and then that . . .*
- selection – *do this, or do that depending upon the results of a specific test*
- repetition – *continue doing this until . . .*

Actually, we can put these in flowchart format to demonstrate.

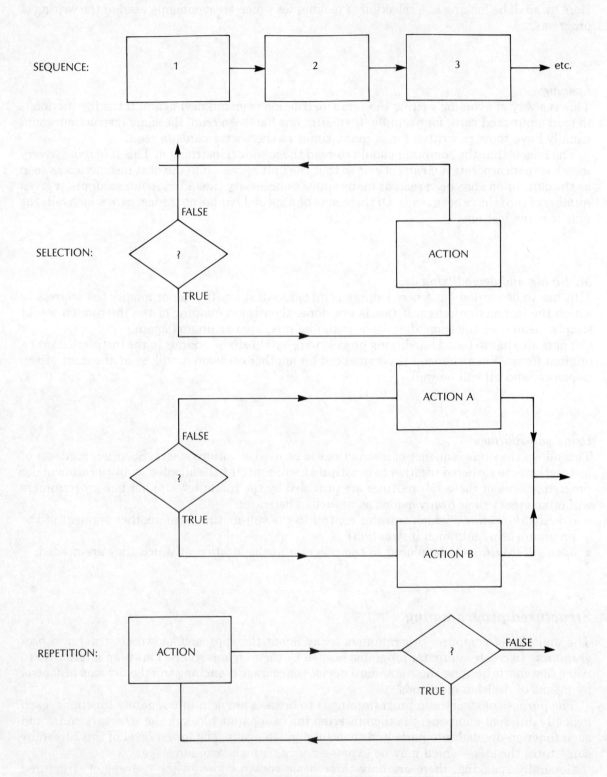

It should be noted that these three constructions may be combined to attain any result which may be achieved through a flowchart technique.

Thus, *top down* programming, as it may sometimes be called, derives a simple set of steps from a complex situation or problem. This idea maintains components of a program which are separate *in logic,* and also physically separate *in actual design.* This, in turn, also assists in testing the program and identifying the source of errors.

There is also the idea of *modular programming* which differs from the idea of structured programming in that it is specifically orientated to the independent testing – and coding – of each module on a separate and independent basis. The module may be determined in size by the amount of coding a programmer can accomplish in, say, a week, or perhaps by the amount of main storage it should occupy.

Algorithms

This term is an important one because it means a set of clear rules defining how a specific problem may be solved in a finite sequence of stages. This may sound more complicated than it is, in fact. For instance, a cookery recipe is an algorithm, and so is the set of instructions we find in a telephone kiosk on how to operate the telephone.

We can specify an algorithm in a narrative form, by charts and diagrams, or by special language (as in a knitting pattern).

Pseudocode

This is the informal language we use when we have determined our diagrammatic representation of the structure of our program. The idea is that pseudocode allows the actual coding to be created easily. Usually we use program definition language (PDL) and the intention is to reveal the logic, as opposed to the minor details of the individual processes.

Examples of pseudocode expressions for input and output instructions, referring, for example, to the fact that the contents of a given file are to be read, and data written to the file are: READ and WRITE. If a given data item is needed, we would use the term GET, and so on.

Program documentation

Documentation has to be undertaken in accordance with specific standards, and these establish the way in which the programmer has to support his or her activities in writing. There are four reasons for emphasising the need for documentation:
- it provides evidence of the work undertaken (and is thus a major costing record)
- it assists in the establishment of installation efficiency and is part of the approach to effective planning and disciplined organisation
- it removes complete dependence upon a given individual programmer, because if that member of the installation staff leaves the organisation without providing a record of the programming in question, then detailed documentation is needed to point out any program amendments and so on
- it also offers to the user(s) the opportunity of obtaining an unambiguous statement confirming what the program is to achieve.

The *documentation users* include:
- the programmers themselves (especially where a program needs to be amended by someone other than the original writer)
- managers who need general information about functions of the programs for review purposes
- operators during processing
- program users who need to familiarise themselves with the program output.

The program documentation includes a number of separate records, ranging from flowcharts (where used) to manuals. A major component of the documentation as a whole is seen in the *maintenance manual* which consists of two parts: the *operating manual* (relating to the working of the system devices) and the *programming manual* (concerning changes to the program).

The operating manual

This is the first segment of the maintenance manual and incorporates the following.

The summary which describes the program in brief, the objectives, its characteristics, the inputs and the outputs

The flowchart to indicate the basic configuration needed for the program, to show the basic functions of the program and also provide an overall idea of the general program needs

The operating instructions which have several parts:

- *the console set-up* (incorporating a list of necessary inputs and outputs, specifically referring to forms required and other necessaries, together with the set-up instructions and the sequence in which the devices are to be used)
- *take-down instructions* (relating to the removal of input and output files in correct order)
- *operator's notes* (advising as to the *normal operation* of the machine so that he or she can be aware of unusual events, also messages and halts)
- *errors and abnormal events* (when these procedures arise they are documented here).

The programming manual

This part of the maintenance manual is intended to assist in program maintenance and provide information concerning the program functions. It usually includes:

- test data used
- any special features in the program
- the detailed, standard description of the program parts or blocks, with reference to any subroutines
- tape and memory layouts.

Summary

In this chapter we have discussed:

- the concept of flowcharting: categories, flowchart users, flowchart rules, standard symbols, drawing the flowchart
- decision tables
- programming: the task, sources, development stages, program specification, programming principles, instructions, techniques
- structured programming: program documentation.

Self-test Questions

Answer these questions, then check your answers in the chapter.

1 What is a flowchart, and what is its purpose?
2 Who uses a flowchart in an organisation, and why?
3 List six standard flowchart symbols.
4 Explain the purpose of a condition stub and an action entry in a decision table.
5 What is the task of programming?
6 List the stages involved in program development.
7 What is contained in the program specification?
8 Briefly explain these terms.
    a) peripheral instructions   b) logical instructions   c) looping   d) sub-routine
9 What is meant by structured programming?
10 Explain pseudocode and algorithm.

CHAPTER 10
Organisation and control 1

Introduction

We have to remember that there are three parts to a system.

INPUT ⟶ PROCESSING ⟶ OUTPUT

At any point errors may very easily arise. The greatest source of error is, in fact, the human being – computer errors are far less commonly encountered in modern computer systems! Because of this, controls have to be adopted in order to reduce error. Complete error prevention is extremely unlikely. The purposes of *processing controls* are to:
- ensure processing of all data input
- detect and correct error
- detect and prevent fraud.

In this chapter we are concerned with the first two points.

Remember that the reason for such precautions lies in the need for correct and complete information. In ideal (theoretical!) circumstances, all data presented to the computer system will be 100 per cent accurate and complete. In reality, this objective is seldom, if ever, attained, but all computer-based systems do allow thorough checking to be carried out.

What sort of errors arise? We could have:
- data which has been duplicated
- data which is missing
- file records which are not up to date
- wrong input data.

Data controls

In the diagram overleaf we look at the typical system and its associated data control stages.

Processing controls

In the diagram on page 112, we can see the various stages undertaken by the system in question, and we can relate controls to them. We shall now look at these devices.

Pre-input controls

These are simply checks introduced before the actual input of the data to the system itself. Here, we are talking about errors which occur in *data capture* and also in *data transcription*. By *data capture* we mean the recording of the facts and figures which will ultimately be processed. But what kind of errors may be anticipated? Here we have some examples:
- written errors involving incorrect spelling of a name or designation
- errors in measurement, e.g. misreading of a dial

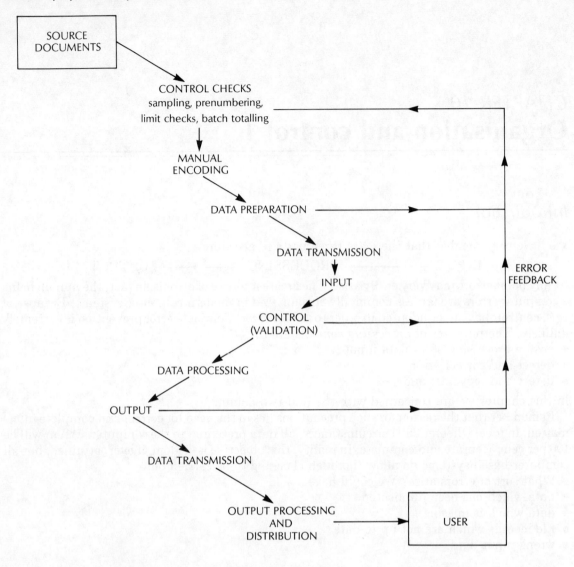

- transposition errors – putting a figure or letter in the wrong place, e.g. £7171, instead of £7117
- errors of classification, e.g. totals placed in the wrong product category.

There may also be errors in *transcribing the data*, i.e. in copying from one document to another. A typical example of this is when a message is taken on the telephone and then written out again incorrectly.

The original data – already captured in its original form – has to be converted into machine-readable format, and this could be on tape or disk. These are termed *data conversion errors* because of incorrect copying on to the machine-sensible format for input.

The *transmission* of the data to the input point where it enters the computer can, of course, be by courier, by post or often by means of a terminal within a network. Thus, there are many ways in which the data can be lost or in some way corrupted.

In view of the possibilities of error arising during these four major stages (i.e. data capture, transcription, conversion and transmission), special measures are taken.

Data capture controls
Measures adopted can include:
- an internal check, or cross-checking by two people, e.g. one will carry out the calculation of

wages on an individual basis whereas the second person will total the wage payments of the various work units

- the adoption of carefully-designed documents, which reduce the need for completion by incorporating as much pre-printing as can be adopted, and which also contain very clear instructions for completion
- restricting manual work by adopting such devices as bar-coding or optical character recognition (OCR), or in the case of the banking institutions, magnetisable ink character recognition (MICR).

Data transcription and conversion controls

For these activities, controls can include:

- proper supervision of staff who are themselves properly trained
- document design orientated to error-free completion
- data verification, which is adopted in the case of data to be converted from one medium to another one e.g. from a document to magnetic disk (see note below)
- direct keyboard input for *keying in.* The screen display is carefully designed to assist proper input (e.g. menu-driven guidance to lead the operator along the proper path of procedure), and there may be devices to assist input (e.g. a mouse – a pointing device causing movement on the screen)
- adoption of an identification coding contained in the input record, so that when data is keyed in, the program seeks the record on file and displays this so that the operator can check that the correct record is being used for processing
- in the case of *batched input,* a printout of the input may be produced in the form of a checklist for visual comparison.

However, before we continue we must take a closer look at the idea of *verification.* Data verification procedures are adopted, as are the others we have been examining in this section, in order to maintain the input's integrity. This was originally the approach in relation to punched cards (which some computer professionals regard as virtually obsolete), but the verification approach is used extensively nowadays for batch processing for which magnetic media are utilised.

Let us see where, in punched card systems, this process fits in. This data collection method has the following stages:

- manual recording of data on the source document
- transmission of documents in batches to the data preparation unit (equipped with card punches)
- punching data on to the cards (high error-rate possible)
- the data verification activity – another punch operator inputs the punched cards into a device known as a *data verifier,* and then repeats the keying-in so that the device is able to report any differences between the new punching and the input on the cards.

This procedure also applies to paper tape. However, *key-to-disk* or *key-to-tape* is the common approach as we saw in Chapter 3. Strictly speaking, we refer to this approach as *encoding.* Again, the stages are:

- keying in at the terminal and establishment of the identification code
- validation of the data (by the program which incorporates its own form of checking automatically), and subsequent screen display for operator approval for writing on to the magnetic medium
- verification undertaken by a second operator at another terminal (adopting *verifying mode*) who repeats the keying in for comparison with the data already on the medium, and undertakes necessary corrections
- ultimately, approved batches are gathered to constitute the *transaction file* (this being, as a rule, written to the final disk, or tape).

Usually, these stages are undertaken with the use of disks, the final transfer of the completed batches being written to either disk or tape. The same approach applies to cassettes or diskettes.

Note that *validation* can occur because the device concerned can use a program for this activity. In the case of *document reading* methods (e.g. OCR, MICR), the source document would actually be the input, thus eliminating the need for transcription. This means that verification would not be extensively necessary.

Data transmission controls

We can consider two different forms of transmission here:
- physical transmission (e.g. carried on a trolley by a member of staff, or sent by courier)
- input from a terminal/workstation.

Physical transmission This involves the use of identification numbers, one for each batch, and the allocation of each unique identification number by a responsible person in the user department who lists the numbers on a *batch control document* which is then sent to the computer department (a copy being retained). Checks are undertaken by the computer department's control section, using the batch control document.

Terminal input This involves a manual check by the user, comparing with a special printout listing the actual input, or a visual (screen) comparison presented on the visual display unit (VDU).

Input controls

We refer to the major kinds of input controls as *data validation* and, as we saw earlier, they may well be incorporated within a given application program (job), or in a special validation program. We saw, for example, how validation occurred during the key-to-disk activity as part of the operation.

Note that although this section is entitled *Input controls,* some of the checks are, in fact, used as monitors for the actual processing activity. What you must remember is that input controls themselves are especially orientated to:
- completeness
- accuracy
- authorisation.

Completeness

This simply refers to the objective that all the data must be processed. The usual completeness checks involve:
- assigning numbers to all documents and then carrying out a check as to their sequence
- listing the total number of documents (this applies especially to batch processing)
- adopting the *one-for-one* approach, which entails relating each input form to the processed documents for accuracy.

Accuracy

Achieving accuracy requires the input to be a reproduction of the data without any verification or difference of any kind. This is usually assisted by:
- data validation methods and routines
- thorough batch techniques
- the one-for-one method mentioned above.

Authorisation

Here we mean approval for processing and this may be one of two kinds:
- manual (the documents are checked and are officially signed or initialled to declare approval)
- computerised (as in the adoption of a special data validation program).

114

The various controls considered in the section on pre-input controls are not very likely to have highlighted mistakes in the *original source* and the same applies to any data which is missing. Because of this, the first computer run will be the *control run* and will carry out three major types of checks:
- completeness checks
- validity checks
- sequence checks.

Completeness checks

For this check a further calculation is made and compared with a listing of the count and value totals in their original form. A common method is to create a *hash total* (i.e. a total which is not itself significant, such as an aggregate of all account numbers calculated on input and then compared with the aggregate of account numbers output).

EXAMPLE

Customer number: 77747

Hash total is thus $7 + 7 + 7 + 4 + 7 = 32$

Hash totals may be aggregates of *all* code numbers, or groups of numbers, or of individual numbers. However, note that the checking of hash totals does not prevent transposition (i.e. the total of 7171 would be 16, even if it were incorrectly transcribed as 7117).

Validity checks

These are usually termed *data vet routines* and are, as a rule, built in to the system. We will look at the most commonly-encountered versions of these:
- code credibility
- range limits
- check digits.

Code credibility This seeks out a wide range of errors including use of the wrong symbols (including £ instead of $, or − instead of +), adoption of the wrong mode (e.g., numeric instead of alphabetic), or use of the wrong format.

Range limits Data fields which are outside of specific limits or ranges will cause an error report to be made as a warning of error. The limits are statements incorporated within the program to make sure that data values exist within given ranges, such as credit limits (£0 to £500), wage rates (£4 to £6.50 per hour), hours of overtime worked (0 to 10).

Check digits This is a more complicated form of check, involving self-checking numbers. A calculation founded upon the original number produces the check digit. A number of ways exist for carrying out this form of check.

Check digits are primarily applied to code numbers on the assumption that the longer the code number is, the higher the probability that an error will arise. Check digits are usually adopted for numbers consisting of five or more digits. The principle adopted here is the use of an additional digit which is produced from the code number itself by use of an algorithm (see Chapter 9, p. 109).

The approach most commonly adopted uses *modulus 11*. The stages are:
- multiply each digit in the number concerned by its weight; the least significant number, (i.e. the one at the end on the righthand side) has a weight of two, the next one to the left of this one has three and so on
- add the products (i.e. the sum of each digit times its weight)
- divide the result by 11 (the modulus in this case)
- where the remainder is 0 the check digit is also 0
- where the remainder is not 0 subtract this figure from the modulus (11) and this gives the check digit; where this figure is 10, we use X for the check digit.

EXAMPLE

Suppose our code number is 174256.

Then:

$$
\begin{array}{llllll}
\text{weighting} = & 1 & 7 & 4 & 2 & 5 & 6 \\
& 7 & 6 & 5 & 4 & 3 & 2
\end{array}
$$

$$
\begin{array}{ll}
\text{products} = & 7 \quad 42 \quad 20 \quad 8 \quad 15 \quad 12 \\
\text{total} = & 104 \\
\dfrac{\text{total}}{11} = & 9 \text{ remainder } 5 \\
\text{check digit} = & 11 - 5 = 6.
\end{array}
$$

The new code number is therefore 1742566.

To check the accuracy of the code number, we now allocate a weight of 1 to the check digit (6) and carry out exactly the same process as we did before. If the remainder this time is 0, then the code number is correct.

In fact, various devices used in data preparation are able to create and monitor check digits, usually incorporating modulus 11. A key-to-disk system, for instance, will be able to create or check the check digits, or they may well be copied manually from existing documents (or perhaps keyed in). Whenever the code number is input to the computer, then the check digit is automatically checked, the required sub-routines being always available.

Sequence checks

It can happen that data files are not sequenced properly (in accordance with the needs of the computer application) and that this occurs at a point between data preparation and actual input. A specific run carries out an examination of all sequences prior to the commencement of actual processing.

Controls used during actual processing

By this we mean controls which are adopted after input and until production of the result of the processing (output). There are often various hardware controls established which are automatic in operation, the aim of which is to restrict malfunctions. These include:
- parity bits (see Chapter 2, p. 18) used to monitor the CPU's immediate access storage (IAS)
- parity bits used in conjunction with paper tape
- punched card readers which read input twice and then read what has been input and processed.

The operation of the system has also to be monitored, which involves two approaches to checking:
- processing security
- file security.

Processing security

For this purpose we have such checks as:
- counts (block records)
- operator intervention (restart)
- balance control totals
- suspense files.

Counts These relate to a file which is serially organised (see Chapter 5, p. 55, if you are in doubt about this important category!). Usually such files are founded on *blocks* and the end record in each block can contain a control total of the number of records in the block concerned. This can then be compared with an aggregated record count which has been processed. This idea makes certain that the processing is complete.

Restart check At times the computer operator has to cause an intervention and then restart, so this may make dumping of the entire contents in the memory (IAS) to the backing storage necessary. This is the occasion for a check to be carried out in order to determine any loss of data during the dumping process.

Balance control totals The idea here is the concept that:

$$\text{NEW BALANCE} = \text{OLD BALANCE} + \text{AMENDMENTS}.$$

Totals are obtained for specific records in a file segment (area) for old balances, amendments and newly-created balances so that correct processing is obtained.

Suspense files When, for any reason at all, data is not immediately processed, it is held in a special *suspense file*. In such cases, this must be taken into account in using the balance control totals. Usually, there is also a printout of such contents.

File security

The results from the processing (i.e. output) stem from input, programs or files (but usually a combination of these three). Therefore, in addition to all the other vital controls which have to be used, we also have file controls. Security against file error is of great importance. Usual checks are:

- file labels
- procedures for direct access
- audit checks
- file content checking.

File labels The first record on file (or the first block) contains the name of the file and any other formal identification. The program relating to file handling will carry out an automatic check to see that the correct file is being used and that current data is not overwritten.

Direct access procedures All direct access files (refer to Chapter 5 if you have forgotten this one!) are updated, as a general rule, by overlay, which means that the new versions of the records are written on top of the old ones. Thus, there must be dumping to magnetic tape or, as an alternative, printout of the file contents as a precaution against the incorrect elimination of records.

Audit checks These are spot checks undertaken by routines which are written into programs and may either print out files (or information from files) or produce screen displays, or both.

File content checks Again, this is undertaken by printout and then by manual check, for instance, to monitor the use of credit limits.

We also have specific controls relating to *master files.* You will recall that these files are what may be termed *look-up files,* holding all the standing data (not likely to alter a great deal over a short period of time, if at all) and also the transaction data (current, and very likely to alter, e.g. invoice sums). Such files must be properly and appropriately set up and must obviously be up-to-date.

It therefore follows that there must be effective controls on such aspects as the procedure for updating, for deletion of items, and also for insertion. These master file controls usually include:

- manual verification by regular printout
- file balance checks, carried out on a computer or manually and similar in approach to the balance control totals discussed above. Here, the totals indicate the brought forward situation + or − the transaction (or update), to provide the carried forward position
- updating authorisation, which must be obtained before any modification of any record is undertaken.

Output controls

When the results of the processing are deemed to be accurate and valid, then the user department receives the output in the required format and medium. That output must be checked to confirm its completeness and accuracy. To do this means to undertake these procedures:

- carry out a count of pages and the control totals on output reports
- identify the data on printout by adopting page numbers
- use range limit and credibility checks
- provide subtotals for checking each page printed out
- inform the user that the document is complete by indicating the end by the statement END OF REPORT after the final line.

Note that careful and effective distribution of output to the authorised user(s) must also be arranged.

Database control

In Chapter 5, p. 61, we discussed databases. Because this is such a widespread facility offered by computer systems we will now look at it from the control aspect.

The larger databases all have comprehensive control and monitoring systems simply because it is not impossible that a specific logical combination has not been accounted for in the program (DBMS) and that the result may well be misinformation.

The key to efficient and effective databases lies in the data-structure and some kind of centralised control is essential. The larger systems are in the charge of a database administrator, or controller (DBA). The DBA has the responsibility for the monitoring of the database operations and also for making certain that all updating is undertaken with due regard to the established and formal procedures.

A database is generally operated in *on-line* mode, although some are capable of being operated in batch mode.

What is important to remember is that the sophisticated database is equally in need of control and does not offer any magic solution to provide error-free operation! The controller of the database must also be in charge of the password or *lockword* system used by authorised users of the system. A special code has to be keyed in in order to obtain access.

The real-time MIS – a practical illustration of control

Having looked at various types of control applied to systems, we now look at a specific MIS in the form of the real-time system (see Chapter 2, p. 21 to refresh your memory!) and the approach adopted for controlling this.

Controls applied to a two-directional information flow do pose special difficulties which did not exist in relation to batch processing systems. Consider, for example:

- what happens to data inside this system when the computer is being repaired or in some way modified
- how we can ensure accuracy in this kind of ultra-rapid processing.

On-line processing controls

Messages may be confused and/or missing. This may well be due to a malfunction of the terminal(s). This means we need protection from the use of wrong data and this is provided by program routines:

- message identification allows each message received by the computer to be recognised for what it actually is (using a code number per message, indication of the terminal transmitting, the date and time of transmission and a special message code)

- message parity check, to verify message accuracy. This approach adds a check digit (as explained earlier in this chapter) at the despatching terminal, to represent the bits contained in the message. The reception terminal will calculate a check digit based on the message received and a comparison is then made. When the two check digits are identical an automatic message is sent to the device which transmitted the message to signify correct receipt. If the two check digits are *not* identical, then retransmission is requested
- message transmission control ensures that *all* messages have been received and consists of a periodic check of the message identification numbers (seeking lack of sequence or missing numbers), or an automatic request for confirmation of the arrival of each message.

Message numbers not accounted for are printed out for investigation.

Diagnostic controls

The system could also suffer badly from some programming error and/or hardware malfunction, and this could occur during operations. To deal with this situation, we have *diagnostic programs* which detect and isolate such error conditions. Once indicated, such error conditions can be dealt with. Any necessary modifications are subsequently carried out by the *executive* (see Chapter 8, p. 83) or *supervisory* program, such as transferring to *error routine,* halting the system completely, or restarting the program involved.

Note that *halting,* and also *closing down,* relate to hardware problems.

The diagnostic program checks the complete network to discover the existence of a problem, and another will check each individual linkage to track down the terminal(s) involved. After the diagnosis has been carried out, then the executive program takes charge and may shut the line(s) down and re-allocate a route using an alternative terminal.

In the case of a total shutdown, emergency procedures come into force to deal with operations during the time of repair. Some media (tape or disk) will retain messages and also the data processed so far (this is a *checkpoint record*). At the restart of the system, this record is able to allow it to pick up from the point at which it was halted.

Controls for the protection of data

Such controls deal with problems such as:
- the accidental overwriting of data in internal memory by programs brought in by the computer to its memory from backing storage
- amendment of the same record by two separate transactions at the same time (thus causing a clash).

To assist in the protection of data we have programs which undertake:
- prevention of *unauthorised access,* by introducing *passwords* and *authority listings* – the former allowing general access and the latter restricting that access to the kind of information listed under the respective password
- prevention of *data-loss due to simultaneous amendment of a record.* This is achieved by an *executive protection program* which allows one data transmission for updating/amending a given record on-line at one time. Given the availability of the record, the required machine-instructions are issued, but no other access is permitted during the updating or amending process
- restriction of *the number of attempts to transmit a message.* Another approach is for the number of attempts from a terminal to send a message (e.g. to make a request for information) to be limited. In other words, the attempts are counted and if they exceed, for example, three, the computer issues a warning that some person who is either unauthorised or inexperienced (or both) is trying to use the terminal.

The virus

We cannot consider aspects of control and monitoring operations without reference to the virus. This term relates to computer program code which can automatically repeat and duplicate itself in other machines (either through a network or any other type of communication link, or even through magnetic storage media such as tape or disk).

We also have *Trojan code* which is a special part of a computer program code which can be attached to a genuine program so that the code is not detected easily. Implanted program code can cause damage or permit fraud to be undertaken. Examples in the past have been of unhappy employees who have secretly implanted code in order to damage and confuse data processing operations. Trojan code has latterly arisen in programs as a result of external interference through WANs, but the virus is relatively new in concept.

A classic example of a virus coding activity occurred in 1989 when an employee of an American insurance company deliberately created a code which resulted in the destruction of over 160 000 customer records.

The virus is not *necessarily* a deliberate act of confusion or damage. It has been associated with IBM PC compatibles, and a good deal of research has gone into data protection from virus presence.

One popular approach to protection is to obtain a strictly accurate copy of all files at present held and maintain regular checks as to their integrity or check on operator instruction. But it must be added that virus detection is by no means a simple matter.

Control and the personal computer

The proliferation of personal computers is so great that you should know the various aspects of controls applied to PC systems, many of which exist in small and medium-sized organisations.

First of all, let us look at the advantages attributed to PCs generally:
- simplicity in operation
- simplicity in programming
- data entry and operation are interactive (i.e. the operation and entry mode permits the operator-user and the computer to communicate with each other)
- the PC accepts a normal environment
- files used by the PC are direct access versions
- software packages are easily and relatively cheaply obtained.

So, what problems arise in PC systems? They include:
- simplicity in operation frequently induces inexperienced and careless handling
- inexperienced and unauthorised amendment of programs can lead to unsatisfactory operation
- the interactive approach often results in unofficial, informal operation of the machine with the result that the monitoring and checking procedures become difficult to follow
- the PCs acceptance of normal environmental conditions allows it to be sited in the office and it is thus more accessible to dishonest practices and damage
- if copies of files are not regularly produced, there is the danger of data corruption
- software packages may require considerable amendments if they are to be used to advantage.

But there are other controls which are used in respect of the PC. These are:
- the regular printing out of major (master) files in order to carry out internal audit
- manually produced logs
- restriction of access by passwords (lockwords)
- keyboard entry of data can be traced back through source data clerical controls
- for bigger PCs (and for minicomputers) there is a log file maintained by the machine to maintain the audit trail
- back-up files (copies of existing files) are stored in another location and/or in a fireproof facility
- visual monitoring (on-screen) of data entries.

It is also claimed for the PC that it only requires one part-time operator, but this does not really add to its advantages in terms of control. It is possible that lack of supervision in this case may permit abuse of the system by the part-time operator. Also, there can be no specialisation by subdivision of the operator's duties.

Summary

In this chapter we have discussed:
- the stages relating to data control
- pre-input controls at data capture and data transcription, and data capture controls including: internal check, document design, limiting manual effort; data transcription and conversion controls including: supervision, document design, screen assistance for direct input, identification coding, batch printout
- the concept of verification
- data transmission controls
- input controls: objectives, checks used; completeness, validity, sequence
- controls while actual processing is undertaken; processing security and file security
- database controls
- real-time MIS controls
- the virus
- control and the personal computer.

Self-test Questions

Now tackle the following questions and check your answers in the chapter.

1 Explain the nature of processing controls in a computer system. What kind of errors are likely to arise in processing?
2 List the stages involved in data control.
3 Describe two types of checks undertaken in each of these processes: data capture and data transcription/conversion.
4 What is *data validation*?
5 Give an example of the working of each of these: hash total, check digits and code credibility.
6 Describe the purpose and nature of hardware controls.
7 What would you expect to find under the heading of 'file security controls'?
8 What procedures would you suggest to carry out adequate output control?
9 Explain what diagnostic controls are.
10 What problems arise in the control of a PC system?

CHAPTER 11
Organisation and control 2

Introduction

In this chapter, we are dealing with the most vital resource linked to any computer system – human beings!

We begin by looking at the EDP Department and its structure, and then we look at what is known in the USA as the *people factor,* and the effect which systems have upon humans.

The EDP Department

This unit may be called various things, ranging from 'the EDP Department' (i.e. Electronic Data Processing Department), or the 'DP Department' (Data Processing Department) to 'Computer Department' or 'IT Department'.

There is no standard structure or format for it. Very large organisations will have very large computer units and the computer system itself, as you know, may well be centralised or distributed. On the other hand, it could be decentralised. In any case, such organisations will have some form of computer unit with full-time staff.

A couple of decades ago, the computer was largely used for routine and tedious financial activities (e.g. production of the weekly payroll) and because of this the head of the computer unit was directly responsible to the Director of Finance or Chief Accountant. This is rarely the case today, although we do tend to find this in computer units based in local government. But for the most part the unit is not solely responsible for a given, specialist organisational function, that is, in commercial and industrial bodies.

Instead the unit is generally responsible to the Head of Management Services (which provides all services, for instance, organisation and methods).

There are also computer units which are directly responsible to the Administration Department.

Computer unit structure

The general organisation and the structure of the computer unit or department may be readily compared with that of a small workshop or factory. As far as the computer unit is concerned we have data input processed by the system and, of course, the output is information. The data input constitutes the raw material. Following this analogy, we can say we recognise two aspects in the computer organisation: *production* and *maintenance.*

The production staff have the task of preparing data for input, of operating the machine and of making certain that the output (results of the processing) are appropriately allocated to the users (i.e. distribution). The maintenance aspect refers to the work involved in keeping the system quality at the desired level, thus we have development of programs, upgrading the configuration and peripherals, and so on.

We will take this opportunity of reviewing the various activities involved in running the computer so that we can then look at the tasks allocated to the computer staff. The basic major task is to make sure that the computer system actually carries out the tasks (the *workload*) allocated to do it in the most efficient and effective manner possible. The system must be cost-effective. The individual work areas to accomplish this are:

- data preparation
- computer operation
- output monitoring
- task scheduling
- maintaining the library.

The tasks involved in these jobs are listed below.

Data preparation
Here we have the familiar idea of converting data into a form suitable for input to the computer, and, of course, the task of verification.

Computer operation
This consists of physical activity and security maintenance. The former includes preparing the computer for an application by providing (*setting up*) the required files and necessary paper for printout.

Output monitoring
This is undertaken by computer staff initially and then by the users.

Task scheduling
This involves putting the computer tasks into an acceptable sequence and also includes ensuring appropriate deadlines for each task.

Maintaining the library
This includes cataloguing, physical security of files and recording usage and updates.

So far we have really been looking at the production element but it follows that there are many other activities apart from the actual computer operation. These come under the broad heading of *systems development,* or, as we expressed it earlier, *maintenance.* This incorporates designing and creating new computer systems, and altering, upgrading and extending programs and systems which already exist.

In all computer units it is essential to organise in such a way that the varying demands on it are met (similar to the need to arrange for production to meet product demand from customers). To do this, the unit must be:

- able to accept and undertake new projects
- staffed by individuals who are aware of current programs and who are thus able to maintain these as necessary
- flexible to allow rapid transfer from one given project to another.

What we have said so far indicates that in the computer unit, as in most other units within a given organisation, we necessarily have to contend with several categories of activity, which relate to each other in terms of data processing. Here is an example of a general structure.

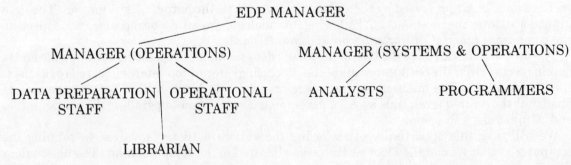

In fact, we have a number of different ways in which the actual systems and programming sub-units may be arranged. These are:
- by function
- by project
- by application.

By function
We put this one first of all because it is the most widely adopted. The principle involved is that the specialist activities are easily grouped into identifiable categories, e.g. programming, systems analysis. Thus we could have this format.

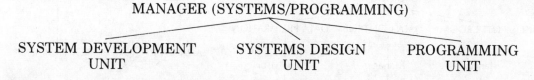

The major need here is to ensure the maximum degree of interactive cooperation between the units, or groups, and this includes the task of providing each unit with adequate briefing as to the tasks undertaken by the others.

By project
Below we have an example of this approach.

The project teams are individually organised as independent units but these have to be altered each time we have a new project or one is completed.

The gain from this approach is that staff most suited to specific projects are able to take part in a given project.

By application
This is achieved by dividing the two units, programming and systems, into groups, each of which is dealing with a given category of applications related to each other. Thus we could have this format.

MANAGER
(SYSTEMS/PROGRAMMING)

MARKETING/SALES   PRODUCTION   PERSONNEL   FINANCE
                         INCLUDING   INCLUDING
                         WAREHOUSING   PAYROLL

This particular structure is reasonably flexible, and yet there is a high degree of cooperation between, for example, the programmers and the systems analysts.

Overall structure

Overall, the general organisational structure of a large computer unit operating within a large firm or other body would usually look like this.

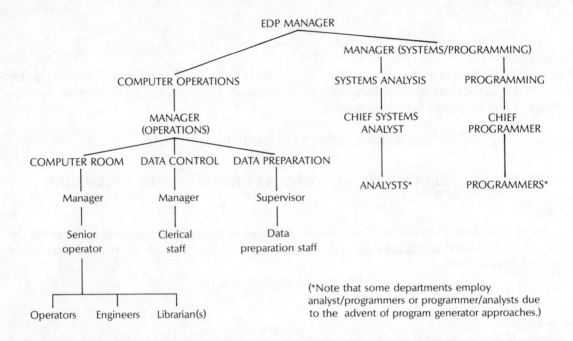

(*Note that some departments employ analyst/programmers or programmer/analysts due to the advent of program generator approaches.)

Staff duties

We must now look at the various duties of specific posts held in the computer department, commencing with the most senior person.

The EDP (or DP) Manager

Sometimes, in extremely large organisations, his or her title is *Director of Computing,* or perhaps *Head of Computer Department.* In any case, he or she is responsible for the work of the computer unit. We would expect this manager to have a very good knowledge of computing generally, coupled with an awareness of contemporary system development in the computer areas, plus the ability to control the administration.

For the organisation as a whole, the EDP Manager would need the ability to liaise extensively and obtain cooperation. The duties include:

- preparation of capital and expenditure budgets for the department
- planning of a tactical and operational nature to incorporate major decisions, all relating to the objectives of the department (in line with corporate strategic objectives)
- monitoring the services offered by the department and relating these to departmental expenditure budgets
- accepting responsibility for the department's security (e.g. file security, hardware security)
- controlling the acceptance and maintenance of work standards
- supervision of staff selection, welfare and education and training plans
- reporting to the appropriate authority concerning departmental results and future development plans
- being responsible for the interaction of specialist staff and line management.

The kind of decisions which must be taken by the department (and, therefore, for which this manager is responsible) include:

- purchasing ex-house software (i.e. written by a software house) or to develop in-house originated software

- seeking external support for a project to supplement the work of existing staff, or not
- recommending specific developments in user systems, or not.

What the manager has to do will, to some extent, depend upon the nature of the policy relating to computers.

It could be that the organisation has a very large central computer unit or there could be extensive networking with the use of distributed computing, each function within the organisation (e.g. marketing) using its own locally-sited PCs. In the latter case, some EDP staff could be working in those independent functions, as, in fact, is the case when data preparation section staff are dispersed to operate, say, card punches or input terminals.

Contemporary computer departments sometimes regard this as a reduction in their own specialist authority over organisational computing.

Manager (operations)

As we can see from our overall chart we looked at earlier, this grade as a rule has control over three major activity groupings:

- the computer room itself
- data control section
- data preparation section.

Note that when we refer to *operations staff* we are really discussing persons working with a large computer (or more than one!) in what is usually called an *operations centre*. Duties involved are:

- the provision of an efficient service for users, including appropriate data preparation, ensuring the security of data files, proper distribution of output to user(s) and the return of the input documentation
- operations planning, which involves maintaining adequate resources (including trained staff) to satisfy the tasks to be accomplished
- dealing with dissatisfaction expressed by users (where operations staff are concerned), e.g. file corruption
- ensuring adoption of established task procedures
- maintaining computer security standards
- organising regular maintenance of computer hardware
- cooperating and coordinating with analysts and programmers with reference to implementing and testing system modifications and upgrading.

Computer room manager (supervisor)

The grade of manager or supervisor will depend upon the size of the computer room in question, but, in any case, if the computer is operated in, say, eight-hour shifts, each shift will have a supervisor or chief operator. The duties of the manager/supervisor are:

- organising daily and shift work schedules, and operator duties
- undertaking tasks (usually received from 'data control')
- ensuring adequate provision of hardware devices needed for a specific task (e.g. input, output) and an adequate supply of appropriate stationery
- loading appropriate files (input and output)
- monitoring repair requirements (arranging repairs with engineers) and ensuring proper hardware maintenance
- maintaining an operations log of activities and machine use
- coordinating computer room tasks with the tasks of other sections, and with programmers as necessary.

Data control manager (supervisor)

Note that the data control or *job control* section is less specialist than clerical in nature. Its staff carry out the majority of the clerical activities which we usually link with computer processing

127

work. Incidentally, sometimes the *file librarian* is part of this section, whereas in other organisations he or she will be part of the computer room staff. The duties are:

- ensuring that data for processing is punctual
- logging the reception of input data and checking this prior to passing it to data preparation section
- undertaking controls relating to data processing
- answering queries, and rectifying errors which occur in data processing
- output checking and distributing
- providing the relevant files for a given application (note that these are then loaded as part of the responsibility of the computer room staff)
- undertaking responsibility for advising users of any major errors or difficulties such as major delay due to breakdowns on the part of devices.

Data preparation supervisor

As you will know by now, the objective of this section is to get data ready for processing by the computer. This means that data is converted into machine-comprehensible format and so it will only be discovered as a specific activity where and when batch processing is carried out (whether large volumes are input in batches by being punched on to paper tape or cards, or encoded on tape or disk prior to input).

Duties involve responsibility for:

- allocating input batches to operators to encode/punch
- allocating data encoded to operators (other than those who undertook the encoding originally) for verifying
- undertaking supervision of operator efficiency (encoding rate, error rate)
- ensuring equitable workloads so that data preparation activity is completed in accordance with the schedule arranged.

Systems and programming manager

Broadly speaking, the area of responsibility here lies in systems and program development, testing, implementing results and then continuing maintenance (i.e. of quality, efficiency and effectiveness by undertaking any subsequent modifications). Duties thus involve:

- the planning and organising of development projects handed down from the EDP manager
- ensuring adequacy of specialists to carry out the projects
- coordinating activities of systems analysis and programming units
- ensuring timely commencement and completion of projects for development and a satisfactory level of efficiency and effectiveness.

Systems manager

Sometimes called *the Chief Systems Analyst,* this manager has to:

- allocate tasks to the analyst team
- monitor progress of systems staff and arrange task schedules
- act as project leader, unless an external consultant is used or a senior systems analyst is allocated, depending upon the nature and size of the project
- act as adviser on systems analysis and design to the EDP Manager and the organisation generally
- organise training
- consult with other departmental specialists (e.g. the Operations Manager) as necessary
- be aware of contemporary computer systems developments.

Programming manager

Again, the title could be *Chief Programmer,* the tasks involved being similar in context:

- allocate tasks to the programming team
- monitor progress of programming staff and task schedules
- organise training

- consult with other departmental specialists as necessary
- be aware of contemporary developments in software and programming techniques (e.g. 5GLs).

We have now looked at the work of the managerial grades within the computer department. We will go on to look at the tasks of specific kinds of specialists within that structure.

Librarian

Often referred to as the *File Librarian* since he or she has custody of the physical files (tapes, disks), the key issues here are *organisation* and *security*. The records must be maintained in order to indicate unambiguously what each file contains, with reference to:

- which programs are on which files
- which files may be overwritten, either because they currently contain data which is no longer needed, or because they are blank files
- which files are *master* or *reference files* and which are *transaction files* (see Chapter 5, p. 52)
- which files are used as duplicates of important files (as a security measure).

Files must also be securely kept from damage (fire, water, magnetic effects and so on) and also unauthorised access and deliberate maltreatment. So the tasks further include:

- adhering to procedures whereby files may only be provided at the request of data control and collected by duly authorised persons
- requiring files to be returned within a given period of time, in accordance with the operations work schedule
- maintaining secure storage facilities
- ensuring that adequate labelling identifies the files in both human- and computer-comprehensible language.

Computer operator

The operators must be aware of a range of factors which can affect their machines' performance:

- the activity and operation of each element of the CPU
- the detailed aspects of the internal memory
- the control function of each device linked to the control console and on the console itself
- the available software utilised.

The duties are:

- operation of the computer control console
- receiving computer input
- removal of processing results (output) from the computer
- operating, as required, devices which handle stationery (e.g. guillotines)
- peripheral loading (e.g. printers, disk drives).

As we saw above, there is also a *shift leader,* a senior operator who takes responsibility for the work undertaken in a given shift. Whilst he or she would carry out the general duties of computer operators, the additional duties would include organising the workflow to the machine, maintaining the logs, and taking decisions in the event of a program/hardware failure.

Systems analysts

Basically, the work of systems analysts may be expressed as:

- carrying out investigations of existing systems
- designing and installing systems
- maintaining their design efficiency.

In other words, the job is to design a system which will carry out the tasks required by the user in accordance with the user's specification. The systems analyst must determine the nature of the hardware needed, the programs which are necessary, and also the files required.

The analyst specifies the need for the program(s) and the programmer will then write the program(s) thus set out. The analyst also assists in *system changeover* (i.e. adoption of the new system by the user) and in training staff in certain aspects of the new procedures.

There is also the responsibility, together with programmers, for documenting the system. In larger installations, the senior systems analyst is usually a project leader functioning as an analyst but having extra responsibilities of allocating duties, coordination of efforts and monitoring progress.

Programmer

The general title of *programmer* signifies that the holder has to:
- plan, write (and then test) and document programs
- maintain existing programs
- undertake the correction of program errors (often during the undertaking by the computer of an actual application), a process known as *debugging*.

In writing the program (program development) the tasks involve:
- comprehending the program specification (provided by the systems analyst)
- establishing the processing problem in detail
- using a programming language to write the program
- establishing testing
- debugging as needed
- advising the systems analyst of the completion.

We can distinguish three categories of programmers, i.e., three specialist programming areas:
- development programmers, who write new programs
- maintenance programmers, who make amendment to current programs
- software programmers, who are familiar with programs supplied externally, and their capabilities.

A senior programmer, as well as programming, also undertakes leadership of programmers working with analysts on a systems project, assigns tasks, monitors progress and standards adopted, assists in training and advises on development.

Engineer

We cannot consider this list complete without mentioning the engineer. As a rule, the engineer is an employee of either a maintenance organisation or a computer supplier. This specialist is concerned with regular maintenance of the computer hardware and/or undertaking any repairs needed.

The role of the analyst/programmer (or programmer/analyst)

The traditional roles of systems analysts and programmers evolved steadily during the 1960s in a computing environment which was completely unlike that of today. In particular, in those days systems development was very expensive, took much longer and the *single user system* which existed operated always in batch mode.

The analyst/programmer differs in role from the earlier analyst or programmer in that, today, the role is arguably more demanding (i.e. in overall responsibility and also in the techniques to be adopted in the role). With 4GLs in mind, the end-users commence the project by defining the functional requirements and then, working with the analyst/programmers, they develop these. The analyst/programmer's role is to:
- help the user with detailing functions needed for the system
- undertake data analysis to achieve file-design
- break down the activities so that the necessary transactions and physical files may be designed
- develop and test transactions undertaken by the system
- manage projects
- render assistance to the user in further development
- document the technical areas.

A 4GL is really a complete collection of tools for system development, going well beyond simply being a language. It is thus claimed that using a 4GL approach takes one fifth as long as using COBOL as the language for development. Adopting this approach, we find changes arising in traditional computer staff roles, the emergence of the analyst/programmer, for instance, and also the diminishing number of traditional analysts and programmers. The idea is that the analyst/programmers will create, as complete professionals, computerised answers to organisational difficulties.

The information centre

The information centre is a small unit which has the purpose of giving advice and help (so it is a support function) to system-users in the organisation. This centre exists mostly in organisations in which the computer-users frequently acquire and use computer equipment from their own budgets. This means that there is a high degree of decentralisation.

There may also be an EDP department, however, in which case the centre will act as a link between this and the users. Where there is no computer unit, as such, the centre acts as a link between users and computer suppliers and/or software houses.

Objectives and role

The centres have two major objectives:
- the encouragement of users to develop their own software to satisfy their requirements
- provision of technical support/training to users of the programs and software packages already in existence.

To achieve these objectives, the role of the centre is:
- encouragement of self-developed applications
- advising the various departments and sections in the organisation of successful self-development to encourage the adoption of these in units other than those originating them
- making sure of the adoption of requisite controls in the variously developed applications
- ensuring the acceptance of and conformation to organisational standards (e.g. compatibility of PCs).

A large proportion of users have had very little experience or training in programming. The assistance offered by the centre is intended to avoid error and make sure that programs used are as efficient as possible.

Encouragement in the use of 4GL approaches is today a common centre activity. The information centre will also advise concerning operating the system (e.g. file organisation), or using PCs in a network (e.g. to access the central mainframe), and so on.

It is also worth noting that in most organisations there are many *local systems* (obtained and operated by the users themselves). These include:
- word-processors
- workstations
- file storage and access systems
- copiers
- facsimile devices
- specialist database.

131

The impact of information technology

The rapid development and availability of IT devices for the use of organisations is creating a definite impact upon the organisation's internal environment. Obviously IT exists in all types of businesses (commercial and industrial), government bodies (central and local government) and in public corporations. However, we can say that all applications consist of three fundamental parts:
- specific functions (activity areas), such as production or personnel
- the human resources of all grades and responsibility
- the technology used.

Control in the organisation

The IT approach to information systems within the organisation does develop a more positive form of control over activities.

This is due to the fact that IT summarises, processes and transmits information very rapidly. This, in turn, means that the number of subordinates who can be controlled by one superior is increased (i.e. the span of control becomes greater).

IT therefore permits a more effective degree of performance monitoring.

Users and the EDP department

Some computer professionals describe the relationship between EDP staff and the system-users which they seek to achieve as *mature*. This term really means the acceptance of the fact that the complete system (i.e., software, hardware, human beings, policies and procedures) should be both efficient and effective – not simply one or two aspects of the system! The mature user, for instance, is well aware that attention to only one aspect would merely detract from any sound usage of the others. The ideal mature users:
- try to use computer devices to augment human effort, initially directing their usage to the area of highest productivity
- do not adopt the computerised system to acquire status
- expect high-level performance from the system and so they participate with specialists to achieve this
- are thoroughly well aware of the system capability
- avoid inefficiency and utilise all resources at optimum level.

The mature EDP department:
- will interact and communicate with the users appropriately (frequently, punctually, honestly)
- makes a relevant charge for services against the user-budget
- is always prepared to hear complaints, requests for assistance and suggestions for improvements and to take the appropriate action
- encourages users to select their own applications after considering advice offered, to operate their own devices, to write their own programs and to use the maximum capability of their systems.

System charging

Reference was made earlier to the concept of charging the users. The idea here is that the system is regarded by the EDP department and by the users as having value. The psychology behind this idea is that a charge for using the system renders that system *valuable,* in contrast to the situation where charges do not arise and the user considers the free system to be of inferior value. Also, payment for usage, however notional, is equivalent to and part of the philosophy of allocating resources at optimum level.

Again, it is believed in some organisations that the EDP department will tend to increase responsiveness where its income relates to the quality of service it offers.

Benefits of office automation

We have tended to use the term *information technology* so far, but there is also the alternative (and widely used) term *office automation*. The latter tends to be adopted to indicate the use of *devices* in the place of human effort, whereas the former stresses the transmission and accessibility of needed facts and figures.

A major aspect of the total benefit achieved from the introduction of the devices is, of course, the increase in *worker productivity*. It has been noted that there are several areas in which this arises:

- optimisation of human resources, by producing the same results with fewer staff, or more results with the same number of staff (so, higher output per head)
- greater efficiency, i.e. less time taken to perform tasks
- higher quality of work performed, of services and products, and also of decisions taken (due to better information handling throughout the organisation).

We can divide actual benefits into those which economise in effort and time (*tangible* benefits) and those which exist but which are not really quantifiable as such (*intangible*).

Effort and time economies

These are brought about through:

- reduced need for meetings and for journeys because of *tele-conferencing* (the adoption of television transmissions to link individuals) and/or *computer-conferencing* (the linking of individuals through PCs and/or terminals, using LANs or WANs)
- adoption of various devices to eliminate or reduce human effort
- reduction or elimination of unpredictable events which hinder productivity (e.g. hunting for a file, or misdialling a telephone number)
- increased output.

Non-quantifiable economies

These are brought about through:

- improved information (e.g. promptly supplied)
- improved service and, therefore, greater customer satisfaction
- greater control by management
- greater independence for functions and departments in the organisation (e.g. less reliance placed upon availability of typing-pool staff)
- decision-making is quicker and more appropriate (e.g. due to the decision support system or DSS)
- higher level of work quality (e.g. due to the simplicity of document revision in desk-top publishing)
- more rapid and effective communication.

What most organisations *expect* from office automation is, in general:
- an increase in the contribution of individual managers and staff
- individual accessibility (e.g. due to Email systems which store and transmit at an appropriate time, any messages)
- accessibility of information (through the computerised MIS)
- control over individual tasks (i.e. control by the individual who is able to concentrate on, for example, the reading of messages using a lap-portable unit, and who can undertake this in a remote location free of interruption).

As we have stated, these are the anticipated or expected advantages. To achieve this target, however, requires training, motivation and what was described earlier in this chapter as a 'mature' approach!

Summary

In this chapter, we have discussed:
- the nature and structure of the EDP department to carry out its tasks of data preparation, computer operation, output monitoring, task scheduling, maintaining the library
- the manner in which the typical large computer unit is organised into computer operations management and systems and programming management
- the various staff duties involved:
  EDP manager
  manager (operations)
  computer room manager
  data control manager
  data preparation supervisor
  systems and programming manager
  systems manager
  programming manager
  librarian
  computer operator
  systems analysts
  programmers
  engineer
  programmer/analyst
- the nature and role of the information centre
- the impact of IT on organisational control, the users and the EDP Department, 'maturity', system charging, office automation benefits.

Self-test Questions

Answer the following questions and then check your answers.

1 What activities are undertaken by the EDP Department?
2 Construct a typical organisation chart indicating the EDP Department's general outline.
3 Describe the duties connected with the following posts:
   a) operations manager   b) computer operator.
4 How does the task of the programmer differ from that of the analyst/programmer, and why?
5 What effect has the arrival of the 4GL had upon the EDP Department?
6 Explain the function of the information centre.
7 Explain the meaning of these terms.
   a) local systems   b) systems development.
8 What sort of relationship is desired between the EDP Department and users? Why?
9 Explain system charging.
10 Indicate the benefits expected from office automation.

CHAPTER 12
Organisation and control 3

Introduction

In this chapter, we are going to look at computer security, controls and techniques. In Chapter 10 we considered the idea and the application of processing controls and, of course, these are an important part of the overall extent of system controls in general. We are now going to examine the idea of types of controls which deal with the vexed question of the security of the computer system.

To be quite clear about these controls, we will list the major functions of the information system in general. It has to be able to:
- undertake processing as required and with the maximum degree of accuracy
- provide security at the level needed
- surmount any difficulties caused by lack of continuity (i.e. disruption as the result of absence of staff who have specific system functions)
- comply with audit requirements.

All controls must be *necessary* (if the answer to the question, 'Would it *really* matter if this control did not exist?' is 'No!' then it *ought not to exist!*). Again, all controls must have *sufficiently rapid feedback* to allow corrective action to be taken. The controls also have to be relevant, i.e. linked to a specific aspect of the system.

Simplicity is another essential characteristic of control – the approach must not require complicated procedures which detract from system performance. A control system itself is technically referred to as a *cybernetic system,* cybernetics being the science of communication and control (the idea being that communication cannot exist without control, and vice versa!).

Computer security

The computer system is especially vulnerable to security breaches of various kinds. The British Computer Society (BCS) has defined security in this way:

> . . . the establishment and application of safeguards to protect data, software and computer hardware from accidental or malicious modification, destruction or disclosure.

The *accidental* aspects relate to errors, and they range from the virus (which, remember, can also be deliberate) to serious damage caused by accidental explosions, fire and flooding. At times, error can be caused by damaged hardware which, in turn, misreads files or affects programs.

The *malicious* events include sabotage of some kind, unauthorised disclosure of information, computer fraud, and industrial espionage.

Control categories

Conventionally, computer system controls are listed as:
- administrative controls
- processing controls
- systems development controls.

We will look at each of these categories in turn (remembering that we discussed most of the important issues concerning the processing controls category earlier).

Administrative controls

These are sometimes referred to as *management controls* and they originate from management, as a function, in order to ensure that the tasks undertaken by the system are correctly carried out.

Basically, we have certain general controls which are established to create a proper environment for EDP activity. Typical rules are:

- computer installation unit staff should *not* be given any responsibility for tasks within a user department – division of responsibility must be ensured, as between the user and the EDP unit
- staff performance should be monitored through appropriate supervision
- training of staff is essential, with continuous education and training programmes to ensure they are up to date in terms of latest developments in computing areas
- users should not have access to control records kept by EDP staff, and the reverse applies too
- coordination should develop from work schedules and the monitoring of project progress
- staff should have a suitable ergonomic environment (i.e. the physiological and psychological working conditions should be such that they encourage effort)
- documentation relating to all EDP activities should be maintained efficiently and be updated
- programmers should not be permitted to carry out testing of their own programs
- no computer operator should write programs or modify existing ones
- measures should be adopted to protect confidential data from any form of corruption or unauthorised access and to ensure compliance with the Data Protection Act, 1984
- there must be appropriate and relevant protection for hardware against any form of damage (deliberate or accidental).

Looking at these controls more closely, we are able to distinguish two major kinds, those relating to the *organisation* of the EDP Department, and those relating to *operations*.

Organisation controls

Controls of this kind are vitally necessary in the case of the establishment of a new organisational unit such as an Information Centre. Again, the form which is taken by these controls will depend greatly upon the topology of the system and whether it is a distributed version, perhaps using a large number of PCs covering a wide area. However, if we assume that there is an EDP Department with the usual functions within the organisation, then we have two important considerations evolving:

- there should be a separation of the EDP department and/or the Information Centre
- there should be allocation of sub-functions within the unit concerned, each sub-unit being separate from the others (as we saw in our sections on the EDP Department in Chapter 11).

We also established procedures which are usually adopted to give control over the computer system in general. They are:

- the EDP manager is directly responsible to the *Head of Management Services* (or, in some cases to the *Board of Directors*)
- user and auditor participation is insisted upon in projects for systems development of any kind
- thorough performance reviews and post-implementation analyses are undertaken in relation to the system
- standards are established and documentation required (see Chapter 13).

All organisation controls arise because of the *ordered, organised nature of the job structures within the EDP Department* in the sense that the work is divided and sub-divided into tasks undertaken by systems analysts, programmers and staff responsible for operations. So, the control objectives of the organisation structure are to:

- prevent error which is deliberate (division of the work renders fraud, for example, less easy, since a conspiracy would have to be undertaken to include a number of people who would have to be involved)
- assign the responsibility for specific work to specific persons and jobs (indicated in the relevant job descriptions).

The actual division of work within the unit is, as we saw earlier:
- data capture/authorisation for processing to be undertaken (user department responsibility here)
- actual operations (computer activity)
- systems analysis/programming.

What this really means is that individual members of the staff who have tasks concerned with data capture/entry do not become involved in actual computer operations. Also, they are not involved in systems analysis or programming. In the same way, neither may operations staff or analysts or programmers become involved in work outside their specific areas.

These controls are termed *organisation controls* but they also deal with:
- *cost control* (procedures are introduced to oblige managers to consider the cost-justification of any acquisition of additional or replacement hardware or software)
- *personnel recruitment and selection,* because of the urgent need for established policies to obtain trustworthy staff for both the EDP Department and the users.

Note that there are two categories of post which are intended to provide support to overall administrative organisation control: librarian and data control clerk(s). These are listed under *operational controls.*

Operations controls librarian Somebody must carry out these duties, even in the case of a small organisation which does not require someone to occupy the post on a full-time basis. Duties are:
- computer files are to be stored so that they are secure physically, free from damage, deliberate or accidental and not available to unauthorised users
- back-up files are provided as needed
- file contents are retained until *purging* or clearing is properly authorised
- an index is retained of all file contents and there are up-to-date external labels on all files
- a complete record is maintained of the whereabouts of each and every file in the library
- the appropriate file version is provided for specific processing.

This presupposes that there is an established set of library procedures which must be adopted for every issue and return of each file, and also definite safety standards for file preservation.

Data control clerk(s) These are members of the staff of the *control section.* Their duties are:
- ensuring all data is processed accurately, using control registers
- undertaking *job assembly* (preparing the work for operations) and also *job scheduling* (arranging the sequence and timing of jobs)
- maintaining job records
- making sure of the return of all source documents from data preparation
- ensuring the return of all library files at the proper time
- checking on all rejected data items (because of the presence of error) and ensuring correction where applicable and resubmission to processing
- liaising with the user department with reference to any difficulties encountered
- distributing output appropriately.

These two posts looked at above are closely linked to administrative control, but, as you see, they lie within the category we are now discussing. Other important operations control areas are:
Data preparation staff They must adopt correct procedures to ensure that:
- all data is prepared (e.g. punched) and verified *independently*
- there is no duplication of processing, by officially cancelling each document upon completion of the conversion process
- records of work carried out are made.

Computer operator The important issue to consider here is that the operator is in complete

charge of the processing and so the control he or she exercises is of paramount significance. For this reason, their work is controlled by:
- adoption of standards laid down in the *Installation Standards Manual*
- specific operating instructions being issued
- rotation of shift duties, i.e. no individual is allowed to undertake the same duties for a prolonged period of time before the task is taken over by someone else, and this applies to attendance on a particular shift
- the rule that there must be at least two operators per shift
- the *machine usage log* prepared by the operators on shift-duty is compared with the automatic computer-compiled log held in the control console, the *console log*.

Note that the Control Section's preparation of the issued job assembly and the job schedule is also a major control device for operators. In addition, control is assisted by adequate monitoring of each shift undertaken, and by forbidding operators to carry out any amendment to any input data irrespective of the reason.

It is worth noting also that the small computer unit would usually entrust the duties of librarian, operator and probably control clerk to one individual.

Data processing controls

Chapter 10 dealt with this category of control in some detail. They are established at a number of checkpoint areas within the system in order to make certain that staff and the computer are carrying out their tasks in the required manner.

Remember, the idea here is the detection and correction of errors, and that these errors may arise from several sources:
- programs and operations (human error)
- the electronic circuitry (ranging from CPU failure to electric power variation or failure)
- file media (e.g. the effects of humidity)
- peripheral units.

Systems development control

This relates literally to the monitoring of the development of (i.e. creation of, amendment to and maintenance of) systems.

There are special procedures which relate to these activities, and these are not really the concern of this study. But it has to be said that you should know the very broad outline of any development project. The stages of such a project are, in general:
- the project is selected
- a preliminary investigation is undertaken to discover its feasibility
- detailed analysis and design is carried out
- the system specification is drawn up
- necessary activities such as programming or conversion of files from manual versions to computer media is undertaken
- the new system is tested and implemented.

Irrespective of whether the system is being developed as completely new or as a simple modification or amendment to programs, there are necessary controls over actual design and actual implementation. The important aspect here is that *system development* is expensive as far as the organisation is concerned in terms of specialist effort, money and time consumed. For these reasons we have to maintain a high standard of control. What objectives exist for systems development control? They should be able:
- to ensure that each system being developed has definite, stated objectives
- to ensure the incorporation of administrative and operational controls within the new system design
- to ensure appropriate system documentation

- to introduce a procedure for review of the system by those responsible for it
- to allow for future maintenance of the system and its programs
- to make sure that systems are developed only if and when they are advantageous to the organisation as a whole
- to ensure adequate system-testing activity, adequate control and attainment of predetermined objectives
- to provide sound user-comprehension of the system.

The major controls are listed below.

Official control

In the case of extensive development of a system (e.g. replacement), a *Steering* or *Project Committee* is usually established. This authorises the development and monitors its progress. Its members consist of senior management, specialists involved and also representative users.

Improvements and error-correction (debugging)

Here, there are controls to ensure that the change is duly authorised, tested and documented.

Training of users

Responsibility for the usage of the system on the part of users must be fully accepted and understood, and so various training activities are adopted to ensure this.

System testing

This is undertaken as a specific procedure in order to support user acceptability of the system results (output). The testing is followed by a formal report stating the nature of the test and also the results.

Standards and documentation

The *standards* or measures of expected performance are presented to the individuals concerned for the undertaking of control of input and output, data control activities, data preparation, console operating, file provision and recording and terminal operation. Documentation is provided to give complete details concerning the system from all aspects.

Security of files

Here, we have to deal with a specific security area which has become exceedingly important over the past few years. It is, as a general rule, an installation-staff responsibility. Loss of data from files can (and will!) cause total chaos for an organisation.

What dangers emerge concerning physical aspects of computer files? Most commonly encountered ones appear to be:

- hardware malfunctioning (e.g. damage due to the fact that the component which reads, records or erases data on the storage device, the head, has collided with the surface of the medium causing a head crash)
- inadequate environmental conditions (e.g. the presence of dust particles or moisture in the air)
- fire
- mishandling by the operator (e.g. scratches on the surface of a disk)
- theft.

Of course, there is also the danger of unauthorised access to confidential information on file, and we shall also be dealing with that aspect.

Precautions against physical dangers

There are various conventional measures taken against these, including:
- standby facilities permitting use of an alternative hardware device
- proper controls over the physical environment, e.g. air-conditioning, double-glazing, de-humidifiers
- halogen gas sprinklers (not water!)
- specific procedure standards for operators and others who handle files as part of their duties
- access restricted to the EDP department, and burglar alarms.

The conventional approach to cope with the possible destruction of a file is the provision of *back-up*. This refers to the practice of maintaining copies of files in a special unit and also any update transactions. This means that the missing file can be reconstituted.

There are two approaches to the question of back-up.

For disks

Back-up could be:
- full-copy which means *dumping* or placing contents on to a second disk after each updating procedure has been carried out
- after-state copy, which is retaining all updating material and using this to reconstitute the full-copy file.

For tapes

The grandfather-father-son or *three generation* method, which is illustrated here, can be used.

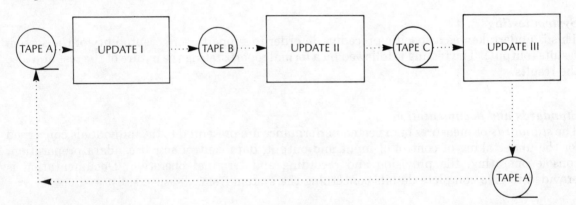

The stages are:
- UPDATE PROGRAM I reads data from TAPE FILE A, and then writes the new file to TAPE FILE B
- UPDATE PROGRAM II reads data from TAPE FILE B, and then writes the new file to TAPE FILE C
- UPDATE PROGRAM III reads data from TAPE FILE C, and then writes the new file to TAPE FILE A (i.e. it overwrites the original file)

Note that only two generations are on the computer at any one time, so the file can still be reconstituted from the third version if necessary.

General physical security

We are now looking at the broad outlines of data security in the office generally. There are some general rules for good security practice:

a) Fireproof units should be used as media storage (safes in the case of confidential material).

b) Any computer printout carrying confidential data should be shredded.

c) Unauthorised data access should be rendered very difficult.

d) Disks should always be in use or in storage; if they are left in the office they could be damaged (e.g. by spilt coffee).
e) The computer environment must be carefully monitored.
f) Computer files should receive regular back-up as a procedure.
g) A specialist should be appointed in the office who has the task of learning as much as possible about, for example, PCs and their problems.
h) Some form of standby system should be available so that there is no interruption of the continuous service offered by the existing system.

Contingency planning

Suppose the overall computer broke down for a period of time for any reason. With the complete reliance placed upon their systems by organisations it is suggested that firms could become bankrupt within a very short time if this occurred.

In fact, some organisations could be very severely disrupted by the collapse of their computer. For this reason, *contingency planning* has become a major issue. Contingency services are sometimes referred to as *disaster recovery* (e.g. as provided by Datasolve's *Datashield* service).

For contingency planning, the firm has four fundamental options which we shall now look at.

The fortress approach
This means the setting up of a top-security installation to protect the system from damage, accidental or malicious. This approach is very expensive and does not, of course, offer any protection against internally organised sabotage (which has been experienced in a number of countries).

Hot and cold centres
The *cold centre* is an alternative location which is able to accept equipment (which must be provided). It will have space, power cables, and telecommunication linkages as a rule. Some centres are mobile and may be driven to the scene.

The *hot* version is the cold one *plus* all the equipment already installed. It is possible that the hot centre may be already in use as a computer unit which sells temporary services to other organisations in order to offset its costs.

Mutual support
Some organisations have mutual agreements to assist each other by providing computer services in an emergency. However, this could result in great inconvenience if the disaster occurred at the wrong time, and there have been some cases in which disputes have arisen over the period of time in which the services were available.

Contingency services bureaux
In the event of a computer disaster, a firm subscribing to the computer bureau's services has the right of access to the alternative system available to it for a given period of time. This allows arrangements to be made for replacement of the original system.

The problem of unauthorised access

This, largely due to the creation of the Data Protection Act of 1984, is another vital issue in security terms. A major aspect of this is the acceptance of the PC as an individual device which allows computing to be undertaken by individual members of the office staff. Bear in mind that this actually puts computing power on the desk of the manager and it allows a person who is *not* a computer specialist to put together – and, of course, use – corporate facts and figures at his or her own work location. No reference need be made to the EDP staff. However, the arrival of the PC

141

has tended to decrease the level of confidence in the extent of organisational security. This is because the hard disk currently in common usage (this is a disk store using a rigid base, normally sealed into the drive mechanism), unlike the floppy disk, cannot be physically locked away from the PC itself. Furthermore, the major usage of data communications allows messages to be intercepted during transmission between devices and today, a large number of users are able to access the same files.

As far as computers are concerned, there are two kinds of security risk:

- unauthorised data access
- data interception.

Unauthorised access

We are talking about people accessing data when they have no right to do so. Access of this kind can cause many problems (e.g. where a member of staff gains access to, say, payroll data relating to themselves or colleagues).

Obviously, the simplest approach is for the contents of certain files to be locked away in a filing cabinet. This is a sound idea for manual versions, of course, but the need to lock up disk packs or tapes in this manner does detract somewhat from the idea of computer access!

So, for the on-line system, files are able to be inspected via terminals. In this case, we have several security measures:

- there must be adequate physical security – that is, the terminal itself must be located in a locked room and/or must have its own lock. Access to terminals must be recorded and monitored
- the operating system should not permit access unless an individual password or *lockword* is keyed in prior to access. The password itself would be linked to a particular list of files which the user is permitted to use and so access is restricted to this list. Where the user tries to access files *not* authorised, then the operating system will not allow this and a report will be made to the central computer. This means that the user (say, an invoice clerk) would be able to access files directly relevant to his or her task, but not, say, a personnel file
- random checks may also be made by the central computer to determine who is using the system and why
- encryption is adopted as a security measure; we will be discussing this a little later on.

Data interception

This is different from our previous topic. A message being transmitted from computer (or terminal) to computer (or terminal) may be received by an individual who in some way taps into the transmission. In fact, this can be done by the *hacker* who links his or her microcomputer to the cable (or telephone line) being used for the transmission, or by simply tuning in a radio receiver to receive messages which are transmitted via satellite (remember the gateway network?).

This means that the advantages of being able to send data to and receive data from a computer installed in a different part of the world, and the ability to send Email messages to any suitably equipped location, or use fax facilities, are somewhat clouded by the fact that there is a major security threat.

The only possible answer to this threat seems to be the adoption of *encryption*. Note these two terms:

- *cryptography,* which is the art of communicating in, and in deciphering, codes
- *encryption,* which is transforming and masking text/messages by adopting a cipher or code.

In encryption, the text transmitted is in code. If it were intercepted in some way, then it would not make sense to the individual concerned. However, the difficulty here is that a *cipher algorithm* – in other words the key to the code – has to be known by both the sender of the message and the receiver. This means that the actual code itself is a vulnerable item and therefore a security risk.

One answer is that each individual using the network could possess a specific code. Thus, a thousand users – not at all unlikely in a multinational corporation – would have a thousand different codes and these would have to be maintained on file. This, in itself, provides a security risk! The only alternative to this is that the same code would have to be adopted by all users (providing an obvious security risk).

There is also the introduction of *dual or public key encryption.* There is one key for encoding and another one for decoding. The former key is commonly understood (i.e. is *public*) and the latter is withheld privately.

For microcomputers it is advisable to provide an additional device which is purely useed for encryption, and an example of this advanced idea is British Simulations' FAP4 which is a rapid arithmetic processor.

We have been looking at encryption largely as a device to provide security against interception but, as we said earlier, it may be used for unauthorised access. In this event, the file of text in storage is encrypted. Examples of packages which carry this idea out are File Lock (produced by Inmac) and Padlock (produced by Janus Sovereign Ent).

The techniques listed above are not infallible. Disencryption of coded messages has been carried out by experts in mathematics. The Audit Commission for Local Authorities, for example, reported in 1987 that, despite security measures in the authorities, 32 reported cases included unauthorised access to payroll and personnel systems, word and text processing, and that the persons involved were usually computer enthusiasts motivated by curiosity. There were, incidentally, also 13 reported cases of unauthorised private work being undertaken unacceptably!

Computer audit

The increasing degree of dependency of organisations of all kinds on computer systems, plus the fact that access and control to and of these systems tend to be decentralised, lead to the establishment of a new set of disciplines and the introduction of the *computer auditor.* Computer auditors are particularly effective when the design stage of the computer system is being undertaken. They are called in to offer advice on computer security and control at a very early stage. Computer auditing is now a vital set of techniques.

Structured evaluation technique for computer controls

Research on an international basis in the early 1980s resulted in the introduction of this technique (abbreviated to *SECCONS*). The approach is very analytical and objective in assessing the controls in a business system which are computer orientated.

The functions in the system, which are effectively controlled only if and when controls within the computer system operate correctly, are designated. These are *computer dependent* controls. Other functions, *not* dependent, can be checked independently by manual controls.

The evaluation undertaken by SECCONS uses two basic criteria: that only authorised access is carried out, and that operation, and development, of the computer system are effective. Five questions are asked relating to access restriction, indicating the names of individuals having unauthorised access. Four other questions are raised concerning system effectiveness. Negative responses suggest system errors.

Corporate security policy

Ultimate responsibility for the security of computer systems inevitably rests with the higher echelons of the organisation. In fact, only the Board of Directors is able to establish guidelines to be adopted by system users to ensure proper security measures are undertaken.

Security education programmes

In efficient organisations staff are provided with security-orientated education programmes. But the overall approach to security at corporate planning and organisation level involves computer policy which embraces:

- security education
- physical security
- financial security
- privacy
- contingency planning
- confidentially.

The Data Protection Act, 1984

This is a very significant Act, which was introduced in the mid-1980s in the UK to comply with the agreement resulting from the Council of Europe Data Protection Convention.

It was also motivated by the great increase in the number of computer systems which are now used to store, process and transfer personal data and which can constitute a threat to privacy.

The scope and principles involved in the Act

The Act relates to *personal data,* concerning the *data subjects* which are involved in processing for use of *data users.*

Personal data are facts concerning a living person who is able to be identified from those facts. It does *not* include persons who are no longer living, and it does *not* relate to organisations as entities.

Data subjects are the persons to whom the data refers.

Data users hold the data, that is to say:

- the user controls the use and the contents of the record(s) constituted by the data
- the user is the individual requiring the processing resulting in the data
- the data is in the format for processing.

Note that the user could actually use a computer bureau to process the data, and also that intention is important here. Mere possession of a disk of data does not in reality legally constitute actual intent to use it.

Also note that the term *data* itself means facts and figures which are stored so that they may be processed by some kind of automatic operating device(s). The term *computer* is avoided in the Act.

The Act's principles generally state that personal data must:

- be collected and processed equitably and lawfully
- only be held for specific or lawful reasons
- be used or disclosed in a manner which is compatible with the specific reasons for holding the data
- be held in extent and form which is relevant and adequate to and for the specific reason for holding it
- be updated and accurate
- not be held for longer than is necessary to accomplish the stated purpose
- be revealed to the data subject and be erased and/or corrected as necessary
- be protected by adequate security safeguards.

If the user does not comply with these principles, then there is a penalty in the form of an unlimited fine, and confiscation of the data.

Data Protection Registrar

The Registrar was first appointed in 1984. Data users have to register and provide broad details concerning the personal data held and the purpose in holding it. A major task of the Registrar is to uphold the responsibility of data users to protect personal data and also to investigate complaints made against users.

The Registrar has the power to issue:
- a notice of enforcement requiring the user to comply
- a notice prohibiting transfer of specific data from the UK
- a notice of deregistration indicating that the user will be excluded from the registration list – an event which could close a business down.

The Registrar also issues guidelines intended to assist management concerned with the application of the Act.

Exemptions

Certain records are not the concern of the Act:
- those which are *not* held in computer storage but in manual files
- those not identifying a person who is alive now
- external data i.e. not processed in the UK, and not intended for use in the UK
- records for text preparation, in the author's name, unless held for a further reason
- records relating to clubs (e.g. golf club members)
- distribution lists
- criminal taxation and national security records.

Organisational implications of the Act

How does the operation of the Act affect organisations, then? Apart from having to comply with the Act's requirements, there are the following aspects to take into account:
- someone is usually appointed to bear responsibility for organising the protection of data
- regular and random security checks are introduced, with special reference to PC and end users
- examination of data held has to be undertaken regularly with a view to considering the justification for storing it
- staff training must also consider the Act's implications, especially in relation to individuals concerned with handling the data
- it must be emphasised to staff that data subjects have the legal right to receive information concerning their records.

Summary

In this chapter we have discussed:
- a review of the information system and its functions
- concepts of computer security
- control categories: administrative controls, processing controls, system development controls
- administrative controls (management controls), basic rules relating to organisation and operations controls
- processing controls (error detection and correction)
- system development controls, including official control, also training, testing, standards and documentation
- file security: dangers and precautions, back-up for disk and tape
- general physical security
- contingency planning: fortress approach, hot/cold centres, mutual support, bureaux

- unauthorised access: data interception
- computer audit
- computer security policy
- The Data Protection Act, 1984: scope and principles, the Data Protection Registrar, exemptions, organisational implications.

Self-test Questions

Answer the following questions and then check your answers from the text.

1 List the qualities required of an effective control approach.
2 Explain the nature of two categories of computer system controls and give examples of each.
3 List the main duties of the librarian. What are the control implications of these?
4 How is the work of the computer operator controlled?
5 List precautions taken against physical dangers to files.
6 Describe the *three generation* method of tape file back-up.
7 What impact has the arrival of the PC had as far as organisational information security is concerned?
8 Explain the role of encryption in data interception security.
9 Outline the technique of SECCONS.
10 What principles are established by the Data Protection Act?

CHAPTER 13
Organisation and control 4

Introduction

In this chapter we shall be looking at two important topics: standards and documentation.

Although these appear as two separate terms, they are closely linked. We may define *standards* as guidelines which relate to the expected performance of given tasks. In this subject we are specifically relating these to EDP, and so we have the concept of EDP or DP standards.

Documentation is the collection of information which is needed in order to assist in undertaking a given activity. In the organisation this documentation includes diverse versions such as job descriptions and listed procedures for activities including invoicing. As far as EDP is concerned there are various manuals which refer to system activities.

Standards

Standards, as defined above, may be applied to any kind of assessable and measurable activity. Since they relate to every aspect of control, to procedures and also to documentation itself, we are able to make references to *the standard procedure* or *the standard performance*. Note that the former refers to *how* an activity is undertaken, whereas the latter relates to the expected result(s) or what is accomplished.

Origins

The actual sources of the standards are as follows.

Recognised standards bodies
The major ones are, in relation to the UK:
- International Standards Organisation (ISO) which provides a framework within which member organisations are able democratically to evolve standards. It does not draft standards itself, as a general rule, but distributes and publishes them. A working committee always meets periodically and puts forward ideas concerning standards. They correspond and, where a concept has majority approval, it is accepted for publication. The ISO derives members and funds from national standard bodies and acts as a coordinating unit. Members include representatives from the International Telegraph and Telephone Consultative Committee (CCITT) and also the United Nations Economic Commission for Europe (UN/ECE)
- British Standards Institute (BSI) which has technical committees (also linked to ISO committees), with user representation possible through trade associations and other kinds of representative and other bodies
- National Computing Centre (NCC)
- established in 1984, the Information Technology Users' Standards Association (ITUSA), launched with the assistance of the Department of Trade and Industry and the NCC, and including the support of large firms such as British Petroleum, and many different

organisations such as Barclays Bank, ICI and Reuters News Agency. It has the major task of providing members with information on current and expected standards developments, and also of indicating to what extent these are actually being incorporated into products.

The bodies discussed above are very largely concerned with hardware and software standards. They do not have any legal power to establish standards, although certain governments may insist on compliance for their purchases. Users themselves are usually not aware of standards which apply to specific devices and computer suppliers often do not see much point in complying with those standards because of this.

User groups
These are firms using the same type of devices, grouped together as a unit or forum to exchange views and experiences. The supplier generally forms the groups from customers, and thus it is a useful body to put forward ideas concerning standards.

Staff
EDP and other members of the staff may well submit ideas relating to standards, based upon their practical experience.

Manufacturers of computer devices
Apart from establishing user groups, suppliers can give much practical information if their advice is sought, or in manuals which they issue.

The need for standards

Management needs standards to:
- enable actual performance to be assessed and monitored
- assign responsibility for given elements of the system
- establish procedures which may be undertaken by replacement staff when individuals are absent from work, thus minimising disruption and allowing continuity, and also reducing dependency.

Communication requires standards so that:
- information required is clearly understood
- the required format is explained, e.g. so that programmers, system analysts, operators and end users can interact with a minimum of difficulty.

Standards are needed for documentation in order that:
- the need to document a system is emphasised
- a system may be clearly understood and used effectively and efficiently
- everything is incorporated in the documentation or manual which is needed for explanation.

Standards form an important aspect of staff training in systems.

The EDP manual of standards

Where the organisation has its own individual EDP department we would expect to discover such a manual, a copy of which ought to be available in every section using the computer system. There is no recognised format, but a typical version of its structure would be as follows.

PREFACE
Comment concerning the adoption and maintenance of organisational EDP standards.
Index of contents.

STANDARDS FOR MANAGEMENT
Procedures for
- budgeting and costing
- computer performance standards
- management reports

- systems development (including project plans and controls)
- the feasibility report (submitting proposal for development, complete with analysis of costs and benefits)
- system design
- new system specification (including program)
- acquisition of hardware and/or software
- proposed amendments to programs.

STANDARDS FOR PROCEDURES

Standards to be adopted for:
- systems analysis and design
- programming (working standards, flowcharting, coding, testing)
- operating (e.g. security, procedure in the event of a breakdown).

HARDWARE STANDARDS

Specifications provided relating to:
- processor(s), peripherals, etc.

DOCUMENTATION

The system must be documented in an agreed manner and:
- standardised to state specific information
- recorded in a specific manner
- presented in a given format, to include program specifications, instruction manuals and so on.

An example of an EDP input standard

Here, we have an illustration of the standard format for the system analyst's program specification which is provided to the programmer. This particular version is orientated to input and constitutes an EDP standard for this approach:
- name clearly and definitely stated (also for the input file, the system and the program concerned)
- document sample (in the case of input to be adopted by disk or tape medium)
- declaration of variable or fixed length of record
- declaration as to variability of input record format
- maximum size of record specified
- declaration of nature of fields constituting the record and the appropriate lengths
- ranges of value per field stated
- statement of field relationships
- validation check specification
- action to be taken in the event of error discovery
- any manual procedures.

Adopting standards

The standards adopted can have been determined by undertaking the scientific approach (measurement using random sampling, or timings), by carrying out a subjective assessment (rule-of-thumb approach) or by studying existing records of past performance.

We also have three kinds of individual assessment:
- listing activities in some order of priority (setting a priority standard)
- determining the quantity of output during a specific period of time (quantity standard)
- ascertaining the acceptability of results (quality standard).

Of course, by the successful adoption of standards, we derive certain advantages. These are:
- higher levels of efficiency and effectiveness
- simplification of procedures
- less complex resource-planning (correct requirements are determined by the use of standards)

- closer monitoring
- greater comprehension of their work by staff
- minimisation of staff dependency upon specific individuals.

Methods or procedural standards

As we indicated earlier, these standards show *how* things should be carried out. Documentation of such standards adds definitely to the understanding of staff concerning their tasks.

As a general rule, we relate methods standards to three major areas relating to computer systems:

- systems analysis (not a detailed part of your present study, but you need to know its output line)
- programming
- system operations.

Systems analysis

Here, standards refer to recording facts for an existing system and then using such information in order to design a replacement or else a modification of some kind. For this purpose, standards are needed for:

- the terms (*jargon*) adopted, which may differ between organisations and which could cause confusion
- the use of documents (*forms*) to record the facts, e.g. noting information during interviews
- the use of flowcharts, decision tables, coding
- establishing input/output format, printout (hard copy)
- problem definition (mathematical or other techniques)
- system specification
- obtaining user and other approval.

Programming

Standards are established for:

- the way in which the program specification (drawn up by the analyst, you will recall) is utilised – according to whether structured or traditional methods are to be adopted
- use of symbols, coding, rules (to minimise possibility of error in programming)
- control measures (e.g. audit procedures)
- the approach to testing, in relation to desk checking, test data creation, conversion, complete testing of programs.

Note that there are also specific standard routines, especially where a 4GL is used, which assist programming activity.

Systems operation

As we saw from our look at control as a special topic in previous chapters, there are particular EDP department functions which must embrace standards. These standards include:

- those relating to general order and neatness in the department's rooms (i.e. 'general house-keeping' rules)
- those concerning the general operation of machines (including, of course, peripherals) and, in particular, the control console activity undertaken by operators
- those for the attention of the librarian, including procedures for issuing files and programs, and security measures
- those relating to recording of machine-usage, to allow for performance evaluation (operator and machine), and also cost-allocation in relation to time taken.

Note that there must also be standards which refer to general activities and to departmental control (such as scheduling and routing of input).

Documentation

The documentation of the system must be performed carefully and be extremely effective. This means that certain criteria (standards!) must be adopted. These criteria are that each document should:

- be based upon fact, not theory
- be self-contained, not dependent upon other documents, e.g. a glossary of terms relating to the specific area should be incorporated
- be retained in a collection, or set, of documents which cannot be taken from the library section without specific authority
- contain a single topic only, permitting easier text alterations
- be headed by the title, author's name and issue date.

Typical documents produced as a result of a system's existence would be:

- routines with an explanation of their purpose and individual flowcharts
- source data, procedures for input to the system
- processing runs with specifications
- processing and operating instructions
- output formatting
- procedures for system amendment
- program specifications.

Note that various documents will be generated through the system's cycle of development, i.e. by the initial investigation, the analysis of needs, the system design, programming, testing the completed system and the operating activities themselves.

Manuals

In addition to all the other documents, we have the manuals which are written for definite specialist groups. The basic ones are the user manual, and the operations manual.

It has to be said that there is a good deal of current criticism about the manner in which these manuals are sometimes produced. A major problem is that a single manual usually has to be consulted by three quite different kinds of user: complete newcomers who know nothing of the system at all, individuals who are investigating difficulties, and specialists who are developing (*enhancing* is the usual term here) the system. How do the needs of these three groups differ? Look at each one:

- newcomers seek a general outline of the system initially and find it hard to comprehend details at this stage
- investigators seek documentation which offers rapid referencing, since they need to identify reasons for the problem relatively quickly
- system developers are usually systems analysts or programmers, or a programmer/analyst, and they need an overview together with information about a specific part of the system which is considered for improvement.

It is also a fact that the most commonly accessed part of any manual is the index, and so this must be efficiently put together. The efficient index is not simply a list of words and their page numbers, but is an important cross-reference, placing terms in their proper context and indicating links.

The user manual

This manual is orientated to the users of the system, who are not computer specialists, so it must be free of jargon. The objective is to provide instructions for user staff in relation to the clerical (manual) procedures and also as far as the system as a whole is concerned.

It covers such important aspects as error correction and action in the event of system failure.

151

Despite the views of some EDP specialists to the contrary, this manual is not intended to be used for training purposes. A master copy will be retained in the EDP department, with copies in the user department. It is a reference work. A typical outline of the contents is as follows.

PREFACE

Official title, author's name, date of origin and of last update, list of individuals (and telephone numbers) able to assist in case of system difficulties, list of contents – headings and page numbers

BRIEF SYSTEM SUMMARY (in non-technical language)

INPUT PROCEDURES

- system description – narrative with system flowchart
- sectional description with procedure flowcharts as appropriate
- batching (where appropriate) description, error procedures (detection and correction), controls
- appropriate timings

COMPUTER INPUT

- document/display samples accompanied by narrative
- error handling and correction activity
- tables of coding/conversion

OUTPUT

- narrative description and samples of output
- output distribution list
- error reports
- error handling

LISTING AND DETAILS OF AMENDMENTS TO SYSTEM

GLOSSARY OF TERMINOLOGY

Note that the sections of the manual listed above would also contain relevant information concerning performance needs, such as response times, equipment/software environment, volumes of data, frequencies, files accessed, control needs and dialogue.

Operating manual

This particular manual has the objective of assisting specialist computer staff by acting as the authoritative document describing the routine work of the system, any special features and so on.

The manual is usually divided into specific areas or sections relating to data capture, data control checks, operations, etc. It consists eventually of the whole set of applications undertaken on the computer and there is thus a particular description of and information for, each one. As in the case of the user manual, the master copy is usually held in the files of the EDP department, and copies are also held in the operations area.

Typical structure would be as follows.

PREFACE

As for the user manual.

APPLICATION DETAILS

General description of the specific application concerned, alternatives and options and exceptional events.

SYSTEM LOCATION IN ORGANISATION

The inter-relationship of this system and the type of interfacing with other systems in the same organisation.

OPERATIONS SUMMARY

- outline of system
- system flowchart

- computer run chart
- listing of programs and files

SYSTEM TIMINGS
- frequency of all runs
- duration (minimum, maximum)
- priority order
- date of implementation (planned and actual)

SYSTEM (COMPUTER) NEEDS
- input/output, support
- size of storage needed
- peripheral devices

INPUTS
- input document source
- samples
- quantities involved (minimum, maximum)
- controls
- arrival, data preparation timings
- procedure flowchart
- individual responsible for dealing with queries and undertaking checks

OUTPUTS
- samples, output media
- any off-line requirements
- procedure flowchart
- specification of any documents
- listing of other needs (e.g. guillotining)

FILES
- listing of files needed; number of disk-packs, reels
- nature of individual files
- retention periods
- links with other systems
- file security requirements
- library location (e.g. shelf number)

PROCEDURES FOR OPERATING
Normal
- listing of events per run, in sequence
- computer operator activities needed, controls
- reports and dialogue
- activities in loading/unloading peripheral devices

Abnormal
- listing of failure reports and necessary action

Restart
- actions to be adopted to restart (i.e. after some kind of system failure)

SYSTEM PROGRAMS
- listing of programs involved (packages included)
- programmers involved
- individual responsible for fault-correction
- dates of programs' origination
- listing of amendments and dates undertaken

LISTING AND DETAILS OF AMENDMENTS TO SYSTEM

Summary

In this chapter, we have discussed:
- the nature of standards: their origins, the need for them, the EDP manual of standards, adopting standards, methods (procedural standards) with reference to systems analysis, programming and systems operation
- documentation: criteria adopted for effective documentation; user and operating manuals.

Note

We have now completed this particular study of *Elements of Information Systems*. At this point you should realise that all the topics fit into each other, rather like a jigsaw puzzle. Remember the terms used – in the examination these have to be defined properly! Whilst this text gives you the basic relationships, for example, the configuration, the peripheral devices, the network used, and so on, you should make a special point of becoming aware of new ideas and computing approaches by regular reading of the 'serious' newspapers. The business sections of these newspapers (and journals) will often provide you with valuable insights into the use of computing in organisations.

Self-test Questions

Answer the following questions, then check your answers in this chapter.

1 Define standards and documentation.
2 Discuss the origins of standards relating to computer systems. In your answer make reference to ITUSA.
3 Why are standards necessary in an organisation?
4 List the contents of a typical standards manual.
5 What standard would you suggest for EDP input specification?
6 What advantages are gained by the adoption of standards for EDP in an organisation?
7 What standards will usually be adopted for programming?
8 List criteria relating to documentation to ensure its effectiveness in use.
9 For whom are manuals provided concerning EDP?
10 List typical contents of a user manual.

CHAPTER 14
Twenty questions and answers

(These questions are all of AAT standard and deal with areas contained in the EIS syllabus.)

1. An MIS may be described as a complex, deterministic system. What exactly does this mean, and what are the functions of an MIS?
2. Explain how we are able to categorise information within an organisation. Explain the nature of the categories.
3. What individual and organisational problems arise in communication?
4. Give a brief explanation of the following terms.
   a) information overload   b) information environment
   c) information channel   d) vertical information flow
5. What is meant by the information processing cycle? Briefly discuss the nature of each stage in this cycle.
6. Contrast the processing mode categories of batch processing and on-line processing.
7. Describe the procedure for the input of data to a computer using
   a) magnetic tape encoding   b) the key-to-disk approach.
   Refer to any advantages and disadvantages involved.
8. What aspects would you expect a firm to consider in making a decision to acquire
   a) a printer   b) a VDU
   for their new computer system?
9. Briefly discuss the nature of IT in the office, and indicate the function of
   a) DTP   b) Email   c) Fax.
10. Provide a list of the different categories of files in the contemporary office. Give an indication of the function of each one.
11. Explain the construction of computer files. What kind of computer operations involve files?
12. A direct access device extends the choice of file organisation. Explain why this should be so, and outline the factors affecting this choice.
13. Give an account of the nature of magnetic storage media, and suggest the advantages and disadvantages of using magnetic tape.
14. Discuss the nature of:
   a) full-duplex transmission mode   b) synchronous transmission
   c) the front-end processor   d) polling.
15. A computer network is comprised of the host computer, the communication interface devices, and the communication processor.
   What are these units? Give three examples of network architecture, illustrating by use of diagrams.
16. What problems are the following approaches intended to overcome, and how do they undertake this task?
   a) multiprogramming   b) simultaneity
   c) buffering   d) spooling
17. Explain the use of spreadsheets and give examples of these uses.
18. The PC offers great advantages to user departments. What are these, and what difficulties does the PC present from the viewpoint of efficiency and effectiveness?
19. What basic controls are established to create a proper EDP activity environment?
20. Give an outline of the typical contents of *either* a) a user manual *or* b) an operations manual.

Suggested answers

1 Firstly, define the term *system*. This is a collection of elements, components or parts which interact in an organised manner in order to achieve a predetermined objective. The MIS, or management information system is regarded as complex since it incorporates various functions, such as marketing and production, within the organisation. It is *deterministic* because the output, in this case information or processed facts and figures, is reasonably predictable as it is the result of a series of logical procedures and rules by which the processing is carried out. It must be noted that a precise forecast of the result is not possible, and that predictability here only refers to the knowledge that the system *will* produce, say, a set of totals or a percentage change.

If the results were not predictable in any way at all, then the system would be referred to as *probabilistic*.

Ths MIS itself may be defined as an approach to the collection, processing and communication of data in the format appropriate to assist those concerned with utilisation of resources.

In fact, the integrated management information system (IMIS) is commonly encountered and consists of various coordinated information subsystems on a centralised basis.

Irrespective of the extent of integration, the MIS consists of a set of techniques – more sophisticated ones including simulation and modelling to assist management decisions – processing means (large quantities of data to be processed) and also routine-undertaking subsystems (e.g. invoicing).

The efficient and effective MIS will incorporate all types of facts and figures connected with the organisation and its management, and has internal and external information aspects.

2 There are three major ways of categorising information, according to the need. By information, we mean processed facts and figures (unprocessed, they remain data).

One approach is to identify internally generated or externally generated information. The former is generated by the actual activities of the organisation itself, e.g. relating to sales or number of personnel. The latter is of direct interest to the organisation because it is generated by the external environment – as opposed to the internal environment – and consists of information relating to the economy, population, legal aspects and so on.

However, the other approach relates to the grading of information according to usage within the organisation. Thus, we have three general levels of information:

Strategic used by senior functional management (e.g. Director of Production). This is usually to determine corporate strategy (long-term courses of action to achieve corporate objectives). It originates internally and externally, and is broad and general in nature, also relating to a long timespan in terms of long-range forecasting.

Tactical used by line managers to monitor the work activities and thus achieve optimum resource usage. It is largely accounting-based and generally from internal sources. The broad outline information is provided by the line managers' superiors (strategic management) and tactical managers use this as an indicator to orient their activities. Typical examples of tactical information include costings and availability of resources.

Operational used at supervisor (or foreman) level – information which is basic, detailed and dealing with the relatively short-period, largely originating from the internal environment.

A third approach is to provide groups of information users, according to the nature of their use:
- group A consists of the public in general, official users (e.g. central government) and shareholders
- group B consists of the Board of Directors, strategic and tactical management
- group C is comprised of employees, union representatives.

The point here is that group A can influence the organisation somehow and provision of information is largely statutory. Group B needs information to carry out their activities. Group C – especially in a participatory management firm – require motivational information as well as statutory provision to enable negotiations to be undertaken with management.

3 By *communication* we mean the transmission of a message in some form understood by the recipient. To carry this out we need a transmitter, a recipient, a channel and a message. However, problems can arise and barriers have to be overcome. The two major problem areas are organisational and individual in nature. If you now re-read Chapter 1, p. 9, you will find the complete lists there. They apply directly to this question.

4 a) Information overload arises where the source of the information using a channel is greater than the capacity of that channel. Thus, the input of information to the channel exceeds the processing system itself. This condition causes stress and tension and is a major source of error. It requires complete reorganisation. The opposite condition is known as *information underload.*

b) The information environment is the term adopted to indicate the complete, overall view of how the total organisation (everyone working in it) perceives the corporate objectives, the products, performance, culture and so on. The internal aspects are linked to the external in terms of information and communication to constitute the complete version.

c) An information channel is the medium through which a message is despatched. There are various channels of this kind in existence within the organisation with different capacities and physical constraints (e.g. distance).

d) Vertical information flow is the direction of communication between superior and subordinate(s), upwards being *feedback* or reporting and downwards being transmission of ideas and instructions. This is in contrast to *lateral* flow between staff or managers of the same grading, and *diagonal,* usually an informal approach, where a superior contacts another's subordinate or vice versa.

5 Look at Chapter 2, page 13, and you will see this answer virtually laid out for you!

You should begin your answer by explaining what the term means. It is the specific activities involved in the creation of information (output) – facts and figures in meaningful format – by manipulation of the data input, including storage and control. After this, the items from page 14, from 'origination' to 'control', are exactly what is needed.

6 The *processing mode* is the way in which a computer system deals with input in order to transform it into information (meaningful facts and figures). *Batch processing mode* is not confined to computer systems, and is usually found in many commercial applications.

This mode is one in which the data to be input is gathered into a group, or batch, and then processed as that group at one time. Typically, this could be related documents gathered together over the period of a week. The classic example here is that of the payroll, using timecards or sheets.

Each batch has an individual batch control slip which lists the number of the batch, identification code and the batch control totals, including *hash totals* which are the simple totals of invoice numbers, dates and so forth to be used as a computer check, and the due authorisation, consisting of the date prepared and the name of the individual responsible.

There are *advantages* to batch processing:

- very rapid processing is not required because this mode usually deals with periodic processing (e.g. as we said, payroll)
- the approach is relatively easy to construct
- the computer is able to cope with one task at a time.

Disadvantages are:

- delay arises between transaction origination and information output
- management information is not up-to-the-minute or current.

On-line processing mode involves input at the point of data origin, usually by terminal linked on-line with the computer. The data is generally collated on to some form of backing storage (tape or disk) until actually input for processing. Usually the remote terminal possesses such storage facilities thus permitting total input at a given time. This does involve batching. On-line processing can also be *demand processing.* This means that files can be accessed on demand, with updating occurring at off-peak times. Furthermore, terminals, are, of course, used to convey processing requests and for receiving responses on-line.

7 There is a straightforward answer available if you read Chapter 3, pages 30–37.

8 This answer is simply put in Chapter 4, pages 44–45.

9 An officially acceptable definition of *information technology* (IT) is: *the use of computers, microelectronics and telecommunications, to help us produce, store, obtain and send information in the form of pictures, words and numbers, more reliably, quickly and economically.*

Some people regard the terms *electronic office* and *office automation* in the same light. It must, however, be borne in mind that IT devices are not intended as substitutes for human control but to supplement and assist. One aspect of IT usage is ergonomic – the relationship of the human being to the physiological and psychological environment – and it is important that this should be catered for in the design and implementation of IT devices generally.

Three major IT devices are DTP, Email and fax. DTP is *desktop publishing,* not to be confused with WP, word-processing.

Desktop publishing (DTP) is the natural development from what is known as *wysiwyg* (what you see is what you get). Certainly this concept applies also to WPs, but in the case of DTP, the use of what is called a *machine-independent page description language* (pdl) allows the idea to apply to page printers linked to the DTP device, and thus to produce high-quality printing of the formalised pages. It conveys requirements to the print-control unit.

DTP is able to mix both text and graphics on screen and on the printed page and is thus aimed at creating more effective communication. An example of DTP is seen in the Macintosh PageMaker desktop publishing system which allows the user to design and lay out a publication on the microcomputer's screen, amend the text, add graphics and mix typestyles and typefaces without difficulty. Standard items of text can, if required, be inserted on each individual page, or on selected pages.

Email is an abbreviation of 'electronic mail' and the device of the future in Email terms is probably 'supertelex', transmitting at a rate of one page per ten seconds.

The complete set of transmissible characters has 300 members, including capital letters, accents and non-English characters (although they must be based on the Latin format, so Russian and Greek transmissions in those languages are not yet possible).

It is also suggested that a *gateway* (i.e. a link between two dissimilar systems) could now be established between teletex and fax.

The approach to Email is sometimes called *mailboxing,* i.e. at some point or other in the system, the subscriber has a *mailbox* to which all other subscribers are able to despatch mail (letters, notes, etc.) which is only accessible to the individual supervising that mailbox. The large mailbox systems in the UK include British Telecom Gold. This is an electronic mail system linking telex with a text editor, a noticeboard (drawing attention to important issues) and a device to check spelling. There is also Istel's Comet which is a privately-operated bureau service.

Fax is an abbreviation for *facsimile.*

This approach has been called *photocopying down the telephone.* The typical late 1980s version (no bigger than the office typewriter) was able to transmit any page of text to any remote location which has a telephone linkage and a compatible machine. This includes diagrams, signatures, rough sketches, handwritten messages and so on. The more advanced versions link the fax to computers and to electronic document storage.

It is also possible to transmit hard copy images (including graphics) of text from a fax device to a microcomputer. The latter stores the text received and it can thus be displayed on-screen, merged with WP documents, amended and edited, and then returned to the fax unit for distribution. The material can also be stored on the micro's disk memory, sent to other computers and/or printed out (using any kind of printer).

10 The list you need for this question is found in Chapter 5, pages 52–53. Remember that you need an explanation for each category.

11 Chapter 5, pages 53–54 are needed here. The diagram is a very useful mark-earning device! Also, if you have the time, reference to the *fixed variable length* is a sound idea.

12 The concept of direct access refers to the method chosen to approach information on file by proceeding immediately to the correct location, even though some minor adjustment to the position has probably to be made.

A good example of direct access is seen in the human being's approach to looking up a word in a dictionary – not beginning at page 1, item one and reading each successive definition until the correct one has been discovered.

There are different methods of file organisation (i.e. the order in which records are placed on file) and there is a clear relationship between the organisation and the method of access. In direct access, records not immediately needed for reference are ignored and records may be processed in any order.

Serial access, on the other hand, means that the records are stored in a single strip (as in the case of tape or punched cards) so to process the file all records pass under the reading head. Unwanted records cannot be omitted and they have to be processed in the manner in which they are stored.

In direct access, any record may be accessed irrespective of its location, or address. Disks used for storage and for direct access may have records organised serially, sequentially, indexed-sequentially, or randomly.

An outline of the factors affecting the choice of file organisation is given below:
- file activity (number of accessed records on a run, divided by the total number of records on file; hit rate)
- file volatility (extent of deletion from or addition to the file)
- file size
- data format (including packing density)
- blocks (groupings of records adopted)
- file density (% of space utilised for records)
- file maintenance (number of updates).

13 Read Chapter 6, pages 66–68 for the answer to this question.

14 You can see the explanations of these four terms in Chapter 7, pages 73–77. Did you know them?

15 The components of the computer network (which is an interlinking of the devices involved over a short or – frequently – a long distance) are:
- the host computer (which is the executive device and the central unit dealing with the major processing activities)
- the communication interface devices (modems, multiplexers)
- the communications processor or front-end processor which is often a microcomputer linking the mux with the host computer.

There are three major examples of network architecture.

Ring
Each unit (node) can communicate directly with two others. Where one node is *down* (fails) then the ring has to be disconnected until repairs are undertaken.

Star

The failure of the central unit would cause a breakdown of the whole network, but this is an efficient way of direct communication using the central controller. It does utilise more cable than either the ring or the bus.

Bus

This type uses less cable than the other two and can be added to easily.

There is also the more complex and expensive version known as the *fully connected network* in which the nodes are so arranged that any transmitted message never has to pass through more than one component to reach its intended destination.

16 Reading Chapter 8, pages 83–87, will give you the answer. It is very true that this common kind of question does indicate the vital importance of gathering your EIS vocabulary together!

17 Chapter 8, pages 89–90, provides the answer here. Note the updating comment about dedicated financial modelling software packages which you should mention in your answer – best used as a disadvantage of spreadsheeting.

18 Look at Chapter 10, pages 120–121, to see the kind of points to be raised here. Remember that this is an *end 1980s* problem, and this is the kind of thing which invites questions!

19 This question refers to the administrative or management controls indicated in Chapter 12, pages 136–138. This is a largish section, but your answer should consist of the statement relating to the more general type of controls, with reference to the two types, organisation and operation, with some examples.

20 Look at the listings in Chapter 13 for the obvious answer here. Whichever one you tackle, do explain what the purpose of the specific manual *is*!

Abbreviations used in this book

3GL	Third generation language
4GL	Fourth generation language
5GL	Fifth generation language
AI	Artificial intelligence
ALU	Arithmetic logic unit
ASCII	American Standard Code for Information Interchange
BA	British Airways
BABS	British Airways Booking System
BASIC	Beginners All-purpose Symbolic Instruction Code
BCS	British Computer Society
BP	British Petroleum
BSI	British Standards Institution
CAD	Computer aided (or assisted) design
CAR	Computer assisted retrieval
CBA	Cost benefit analysis
CCITT	International Telegraph and Telephone Consultative Committee
CD-ROM	Compact disk – read only memory
COBOL	Common Business Oriented Language
COM	Computer output in microform
CPS	Characters per second
CPU	Central processing unit
DBA	Database administrator
DBMS	Database management system
DBS	Database system
DOR	Digital optical recording
DP	Data processing
DSS	Decision support system
DTI	Department of Trade and Industry
DTP	Desktop publishing
EDP	Electronic data processing
Email	Electronic mail
EPROM	Erasable programmable read only memory
ESS	Executive support system
Fax	Facsimile
Fortran	Formula translation language
GIGO	Garbage in, garbage out
IAS	Immediate access storage
ibg	Inter-block gap
IBM	International Business Machines
ICL	International Computers Ltd

IE	Information environment
IMIS	Integrated management information system
IT	Information technology
ITT	International Telephones and Telegraph
ITUSA	Information Technology Users' Standards Association
k	Kilo (1000)
K	Kilo (1024)
LAN	Local area network
Mb	Megabytes
MFLOPS	Millions of floating point instructions per second
MICR	Magnetic ink character recognition
MIPS	Millions of instructions per second
MIS	Management information system
Mux	Multiplexor
NCC	National Computing Centre
OA	Office automation
OCR	Optical character recognition
OLRT	On-line real-time
OMR	Optical mark reader
OPD	One per desk
OS	Operating system
PABX	Private automatic branch exchange
PAYE	Pay as you earn
PC	Personal computer
PDL	Machine independent page description language
PDL	Program definition language
PERT	Program evaluation and review technique
PL/1	Programming language one
PoS	Point of sale
PROM	Programmable read only memory
PSE	Packet switching exchange
PSS	Packet switching system
PSTN	Public switched telephone network
RAM	Random access memory
ROM	Read only memory
SECCONS	Structured evaluation technique for computer controls
UN/ECE	United Nations Economic Commission for Europe
VANS	Value added and data network services
VCR	Video cassette recorder
VDU	Visual display unit
VRC	Visible record computer
WAN	Wide area network
WORM	Write once read many
WP	Word-processor, word-processing

Bibliography

Business Systems & Information Technology, R. Anderson (Paradigm), 1988.
Data Processing, Volumes 1 & 2, R.G. Anderson (M & E Handbooks).
This Is IT, (2nd Edition), Eaton & Smithers (Philip Alan), 1988.
Computer Studies, (2nd Edition), Carl French (DP Publications), 1986.
Computing in a Small Business, (2nd Edition), Horner & Shipley (Century Hutchinson), 1988.
Computers & Common Sense, (4th Edition), Hunt & Shelley (Prentice Hall), 1988.
Data Processing, Volume 1, (3rd Edition), G.C. Lester (Polytech Publishers), 1988.

Index

3GL   92
3.5″ disk   67
3-in-1 system   15
4GL   90, 92, 131
5GL   129
abnormal events   110
access   140
   mode   60
   time   60, 61, 70
accidental damage   135
accountants   90
accounting   87
accounting board   15
accounting machine   15, 33
accumulator   27
accuracy   114
acoustic coupler   29, 74
action   102
   entry   100
   stub   100
active file   59
activity   95
ad hoc reports   6
Ada   92
adding machine   15
address   58, 105
   header   76
addressable locations   28
administration department   122
administrative controls   135, 136
adopting standards   149
after-state copy   140
Agfa   69
aggregate record count   117
AI – see artificial intelligence
air-conditioning   140
algorithm   109
allocating resources   132
all-digital cellular radio   80
all-digital technology   73
alternative approaches to information processing   14
ALU – see arithmetic logic unit
American Standard Code for Information
   Interchange   40
analogue computers   27
analogue form   74
analysis   95
analyst   92, 124, 131
analyst/programmer   104, 131

application
   generator   92
   package   29, 86, 87
   program   84
   programmer   104
   software   86, 87, 88
archive   66, 68
arithmetic
   instructions   106
   logic unit   25, 26, 27, 106
Arrow Computer Systems   29
artificial intelligence   87
ASCII – see American Standard Code for Information
   Interchange
assembler program   86, 91
Astron IC   70
asynchronous transmission   74
audio
   output   44
   response   39
audit   87
   checks   117
   trail   120
Audit Commission for Local Authorities   143
auditor   96, 136
   participation   136
authorisation   20, 114
authority listings   119
automated
   cash book   90
   on-board system for navigation   68
automatic feed   15

BA – see British Airways
BABS – see British Airways Booking System   21
background task   85
backing storage   21, 25, 27, 32
back-up   55, 68, 120, 140
badge reader   34
balance control totals   116, 117
bar coding   30, 34, 113
Barclays Bank   148
barrel printer   42, 43
base two system   17
BASIC – see Beginners' All-purpose Symbolic
   Instruction Code
basic configuration   110
batch
   control book   20

control data	20
control document	114
control slip	20
mode	118, 130
number	20
processing	21, 77, 78, 113
batched input	113
batching	21
baud	74
BCS – *see* British Computer Society	
Beginners' All-purpose Symbolic Instruction Code	92
benefits of office automation	132
binary	17, 26, 68, 74, 90
coded decimal	18
digits	17, 22
n-cube	29
bits	17, 66, 74
bits per second	74
blind user	44
block	
diagram	100
number	58
records	116
size	59, 60
blocking	60
blocks	57, 58, 59, 60
board of directors	136, 143
book-keeping transactions	15
BP – *see* British Petroleum	
branch instruction	106, 107
branches	61
British Airways	48
British Airways Booking System	21
British Computer Society	135
British Petroleum	146
British Simulation FAP4	143
British Standards Institute	146
British Telecom	30, 47, 74, 81
British Telecom Gold	47
broadcast network	79
brokers	81
Brother	42
brought-forward	
file	67
record	67
BSI – *see* British Standards Institution	
bubble	
memory	68
printer	41
storage	66
buckets	58
budgets	73
buffer	77
store	76
buffering	84
building societies	87
burglar alarms	140
Burroughs	40
bus	80
network	79
business	1
business graphics	88
byte	17, 74
by-product	30
techniques	33
CAD – *see* computer aided design	
calculator	15, 16
Canon BJ-130	41
capacity	67, 70
capital and expenditure budget	126
capital investment	88
CAR – *see* computer assisted retrieval	
Card Devices Ltd	70
card	
punch	16, 104
punching	30
reader	30
storage	69, 70
carried-forward	
file	67
record	67
cartridges	66, 67
cash register	30, 33
cashflow	90
cash dispensers	21
cassette	113
tape	66
cataloguing	124
categories of file	52
CBA – *see* cost benefit analysis	
CCITT – *see* International Telegraph and Telephone Consultative Committee	74, 146
CD-ROM – *see* compact disk – read only memory	
Ceefax	47
cell	89
central computer	76
central computer unit	127
central controller	79
central filing	51
central mainframe computer	77, 131
central processing unit	25, 26, 27, 28, 83, 84, 106, 116, 129
centralised disk	79
centralised system	77, 78
cents per bit	70
chain printer	42, 43
chained organisation	55
channel	10, 12, 30, 75
character	17, 40
attributes	42
printer	40, 41
characteristics of information	12
characters per second	32, 33, 65
check digit	115, 116
checkpoint	
areas	138
record	119
chief accountant	122
chief programmer	128
chief systems analyst	128
chip	68
Citycall	81

clerical
  procedure flowchart   95, 97, 99
  procedures   98, 151
  system   95, 99
closed sub-routine   107
COBOL – *see* Common Business Oriented Language
code credibility   115
cold centre   141
collator   16
colour
  displays   88
  matrix printer   42
column   89
COM – *see* computer output in microform
commercial/financial application   92
common business oriented language   92, 104, 131
communicating information   9
communication   78, 83, 84
  interface devices   78
  link   120
  load   10
  network   78
  problems   12
  processor   78
  program   89
communications   73–82
  linkages   73
  protocol   76
compact disk – read only memory   68, 69
compare instructions   106
compatibility   30
competitive environment   8
compiler program   86, 92, 104
compiling   92
completeness   114
  checks   115
components   73
computer
  activities, functionally oriented 77
  activities, specialist   77
  activity   137
  audit   143
  auditor   143
  bureau   144
  communication network   78
  communications   73
  conferencing   30, 132
  configuration   25
  database   69
  definition of   25
  department   122
  failure   78
  file   53
  fraud   135
  hardware   25–50
  installation   103
  manufacturer   104
  memory   65
  network   76
  operation   17, 124
  operator   104, 129, 138
  output in microform   39, 40, 60, 104

register   17
room   127
room supervisor   127
room tasks   127
scientist   91
security   135
security standards   127
sizes   28
supplier   130, 131
system   16, 27, 83, 85, 98, 99, 111, 143
unit   122, 131
unit structure   122
computer aided design   88
computer aided retrieval   40, 69
computer assisted retrieval   40
computer-comprehensible language   129
computer dependent controls   143
computer room manager (supervisor)   127
computerised system   19
concentrator   76
conception of the cycle   14
condition   102, 103
  entry   100
  stub   100
conditional branch   106
confidentiality   144
configuration   27
console
  log   138
  set-up   110
  terminal   84
contention   79
contingency planning   141, 144
contingency services bureaux   141
control   14, 19, 111–16, 123–34, 135–46, 147–54
  block   57
  categories   135
  clerk   20, 138
  console   25, 26, 129
  data   68, 76
  of organisational data   73
  operations   120
  program   84
  run   115
  section   104, 137, 138
  total   20, 57
  unit   25, 26, 27
controls   135
conversion   112
  control   113
copier   131
copy-producer   34
core resident   83
core storage   26
corporate planning   144
  model   88
corporate security policy   143
cost
  control   137
  justification   137
  of storage   70, 78
  per stored unit of data   70

costing activity	90
cost-benefit analysis	22
Council of Europe Data Protection Convention	144
counts	116
CPS – *see* characters per second	
CPU – *see* central processing unit	
creating flowchart	97
credit card	70
credit limit	98
credit status	98
critical path analysis	3
cryptography	142
Cullinet's ADS	92
customer	
invoice	98
payment record	102
cybernetic system	135
cylinder	
concept	58
number	58
cypher algorithm	142
daily work schedules	127
daisywheel printer	40, 42, 44
damage	135
data	1, 77
analysis	131
bit	74
block	56
capture	30, 111, 112, 137
capture controls	112
collection	30
communications	30, 73, 76, 80, 142
control	111, 129
control clerk	137
control manager	127
control section	127
control supervisor	127
conversion error	112
input: off-line	30
input: on-line	30
interception	142
loss	119
preparation	104, 124
preparation section	127
preparation staff	104, 124, 137
preparation supervisor	128
processing	13, 83
processing controls	138
processing department	122
Protection Act 1984	136, 141, 144
Protection Registrar	145
security	65
storage density	67
structure	118
subjects	144
switching	76
traffic	73
transcription	111
transcription control	113
transfer rates	32
transmission	73, 74
control	114
devices	73
system	75
users	144, 145
validation	114
verification	113
verifier	113
vet routines	115
databank	61
database	61, 69, 74, 104, 131
administrator	118
controls	118
language	92
management system	61, 87, 118
program	89
structures: relational, hierarchical, network	61
system	61
dataplexor	76
Datasolve Datashield Service	141
data-only mobile communications	80
DBA – *see* database administrator	
DBMS – *see* database management system	
DBS – *see* database system	
debugging	86, 130, 139
DEC minicomputer	69
decentralised system	77
decimal system	17
decision support system	87, 88, 89, 132
decision tables	95, 100, 103, 105
decision making	90
dedicated financial modelling software package	90
dedicated line	75
dedicated terminal	47
demand processing	21
demodifying	107
demodulator	74
demultiplexing	75
Department of Trade and Industry	45, 81, 146
departmental computing	77
desktop	65
publishing	46, 132, 143
detail flowchart	100
deterministic system	4
development programmer	130
diagnostic	
controls	119
program	119
dialogue	22, 39, 84
Diconix (Kodak) Model 150	41
dictionary	46
digital computer	27
digital format	74
digital mode	74
digital optical recording	68
direct access	57
devices	56
mass storage	70
procedures	117
direct keyboard input	113
director of computing	126

director of finance	77, 132
disabled user	44
disaster recovery	141
discrete items	27
disencryption	143
disk	60, 68, 85, 91, 99, 119, 140
access time	70
capacity	70
file label	86
pack	58, 84
spindle	70
storage	32
surface	58
diskettes – *see* floppy disks	
distributed system	77, 78
division of responsibility	136
document	
count	20
design	113
entry station	69
flowchart	100
printing system	69
processors	36
reading	114
scanning system	36
documentation	103, 139, 146, 149, 151
standards	151
DOR – *see* digital optical recording	
dot matrix printer	42, 45
DP – *see* data processing	
DP department – *see* data processing department	
DP manager	126
DP standards	146
draft mode	42
drive mechanism	58, 66
driver	68
drug clinical trials	81
Drugwatch	81
drum	
printer	42, 43
storage	66
DSS – *see* decision support system	
DTI – *see* Department of Trade and Industry	
DTP – *see* desktop publishing	
dual key encryption	143
dump	
file	53
point	85
dumping	85, 140
duplex	73
dynamic environment	8
dynamic file	52
econometric model	88
edit	86
EDP – *see also* electronic data processing	
activity	136
department – *see* electronic data processing department	
input standard	149
management	77
manager	124, 126, 128, 136

manual of standards	148
staff	141
standards	146
electronic cash register	34
electronic data processing	16, 77, 152
department	122, 131, 136, 137, 140, 148, 152
electronic data transmission	73
electronic mail	46, 47, 73, 74, 132
electronic switches	17
electronic typewriter	41
electrostatic devices	42
electrostatic printer	42, 43
electro-mechanical device	15
electro-thermal printer	41
Email – *see* electronic mail	
employee record	100
emulator	86
encoded data	27
encoder	32, 33
encoding	113
encoding rate	128
encryption	142, 143
encryption unit	47
end-user	131
engineer	130
entity model	88
environmental	
conditions	139
constraints	10
EPROM cards	70
erasable disks	69
erase	66
ergonomics	45, 48
error	
checking	84
correction	81, 139, 151
handling	78
routine	119
errors	110
ESS – *see* executive support system	
ETA-10	28
even-parity	30
ex-house	87
exception reports	6
exchangeable reel	66
execution time	18
executive	83, 119
protection program	119
support system	87
exemptions	145
exit	107
expansion space	59
external backing store	83
external storage	26
eyes and hands busy	37
facsimile	46, 47, 73, 142
device	131
father tape	67
fax – *see* facsimile	

fiche 40
field 54
fifth generation language 92
file
  access 91
  access time 60
  activity 59
  content checks 117
  conversion 85
  copying 85
  density 59, 60
  dumping 85
  enquiry 54
  format 59
  labels 117
  librarian 128, 129, 137
  lock 143
  maintenance 54, 59, 60, 85
  media 14
  organisation 54, 58, 61
  preservation 137
  processing: serial, sequential, selective-
    sequential, random 55
  reorganisation 85
  security 116, 117, 139
  size 59, 60
  storage 131
  structure 53
  update 54, 67
  volatility 59
Filenet Document Image Processor 69
files 51–63, 95
filing 51
film 40, 89
film storage cabinet 69
financial
  data 77
  information 2
  security 144
fire-proof facility 120
firmware 28
fixed length 54
  block 58, 60
floating point operations 28
floppies – *see* floppy disk
floppy disk 33, 67, 113, 142
flowchart 95, 98, 99, 103, 107, 108, 109
  user 96
flowcharting 95–100
flows 95
fly printing 43
formula translation 92
Fortran 92
fortress approach 141
fourth generation language 28, 90, 92
front-end processor 76, 78
fully connected network 80
full-copy 140
full-duplex 73
function 92, 105
functional managers 73
functionally-orientated computer activities 77

garbage in: garbage out 14
gateway 47
generating 92
generator 86, 92
gigastore 66
GIGO – *see* garbage in: garbage out
golfball printer 42
government bodies 132
grading of information 4
grandfather, father, son updating technique 66, 67, 140
graph plotter 42
graphic decision support system 88
graphic
  format 89
  information 89
graphics 87, 88
graphs 88

hacker 142
half duplex 73
halogen gas 140
handwritten methods 15
hard copy 34
hard disk 67, 69, 142
hardcopy printer 69
hardware iv, 25, 83, 84, 130
  malfunction 139
  standards 149
hash total 20, 115
head 66
  crash 139
head of computer department 126
head of management services 122, 136
Hewlett-Packard Thinkjet 41
hierarchical database 61
hierarchical system 78
hierarchy 78
high level language 90, 91, 107
  program 86
high resolution printing 43
histograms 88
hit rate 59, 61, 67
Hitachi 68
holiday tour operator 81
Hollerith punched card 15, 16
home computer 28
Honeywell 4/66 42
Honeywell Easicoder 91
hopper 16, 30
host computer 75, 76, 78
hot centre 141
housekeeping routines 86
human comprehensible 39
human operator 83
hybrid 4GL 92
hybrid computer 27
hypercube 29

IAS – *see* immediate access storage
ibg – *see* inter block gap
IBM 81
  laboratory 67

IBM PC   70
  AT   65, 67, 69
    compatible   120
ICL   30, 40, 81, 148
  System 4 Usercode   91
identification coding   113
IE – *see* information environment
IMIS – *see* integrated management information system
immediate access storage   17, 25, 26, 27, 28, 83, 116, 117
impact of information technology   132
impact printer   40, 41, 42, 45
in-house   87
inactive file   59
index system   55
indexed-sequential organisation   54, 55
index-sequential data   58
indicator   106
industrial espionage   135
information   iv, 1–12
  centre   131, 136
  characteristics   10
  communication   88
  environment   8, 12
  flows, diagonal, horizontal, vertical   7, 12
  grade   12
  handling   7, 12
  handling capability   10
  overload   10
information systems   73
information technology   45, 48, 80, 88, 132
  definition of   45
information underload   10
information value   11
information processing   13–24
  cycle: input, origination, output, preparation
    processing   13, 22
  cycle: storage and control   22
  methods   14, 18
  methods: accounting machines, computer
    systems   22
  methods: handwritten (manual), punched card
    systems, VRCs   22
Information Technology Users' Standards
  Association   146
initial program instruction   27
ink-jet printer   41
Inmac   143
input   14, 95, 111
  controls   114
  data   77
  file   52
  media   44, 155
  methods   44
  unit   25, 26, 27
  workstation   69
inputting   85
installation standards manual   138
instruction   17
  time   18
instructions   95, 104, 105
insurance companies   81
integrated circuits   70

integrated management information system   3
integrated packages   89
intelligent character reader   36
intelligent character recognition   36
intelligent terminal   78
inter-block gap   57
interactive Easyflow   103
interactive terminal   77, 78
interchangeability   70
interface   45
  devices   78
intermediate access store   28
intermediate storage unit   27
internal computer memory   17
internal memory   66
international carriers   74
International Standards Organisation   146
International Telegraph and Telephone
  Consultative Committee   146
interpreter   92
interrupts   84
inventory control   2
invoicing machines   33
in-house programmer   104
ion deposition   43
Istel's Comet   47
IT – *see* information technology
IT department   122
IT devices   45
ITT 3536   47
ITUSA – *see* Information Technology Users'
  Standards Association

Janus Sovereign Ent   143
job   26
  assembly   137
  control section   127
  descriptions   146
  discipline   103
  schedule   138
  structures   136

K – *see* kilobyte
key   55
  depression per hour   16
  field sequence   85
  fields   54
keyboard   30, 32, 34, 69
keystation   33
key-punch   33
  operator   16
key-to-disk   32, 114
  system   116
key-to-tape   32, 113
kilobyte   28, 65
kimball tags   30, 34
knowledge processing   13
Kurzweil K5000 document scanning system   36

LAN – *see* local area network
laptop computer   29
laser beam   43

Laser Optic 1000 Filing System 69
laser printer 43, 69
laser storage 68
laser technology 68
Late Availability Service 81
lateral system 78
leader 56
letter quality 42, 45
levels of information 5
librarian 124, 125, 128, 137, 138
library
   file 53
   maintenance 124
   procedures 137
light amplification by stimulated emission of
   radiation – *see* laser technology
light pen 34
limited entry file 103
line management 5
line printer 40, 42, 43
lines per minute 42
listed procedures 146
loading the channel 10
local area network 73, 79, 80, 132
local authority 87
local system 131
location 9
lockword 118, 120, 142
log 84
   file 120
logic
   area 104
   flowchart 100
   hierarchy 90
logical file 105
   specification 105
logical instructions 106
long-term information 8
look-up files 117
looping 107
Lotus 1-2-3 89
low activity file 67
low level language 86, 90, 91
low volatility 60

machine code 86, 90, 91, 92
   instructions 91
machine dependent 91
machine independent page description language 46
machine language 90, 91, 92
machine usage log 138
machine-comprehensible
   coding 90
   format 128
machine-readable input 34
machine-understandable instruction 91
Macintosh Page Maker 46
macro 91
   instruction 90, 92
magnetic character sorter/readers 36
magnetic disk 26, 30, 32, 33, 57, 66, 67
magnetic ink

character recognition 30, 33, 36, 113, 114
   readers 36
magnetic media 32, 39, 66
magnetic particles 66
magnetic storage 70
   media 120
magnetic stripe card 15
magnetic tape 20, 26, 30, 32, 34, 56, 60, 66, 84, 99
   deck 66
   drive 32, 66
   encoding 32
   transport 66
   unit 33, 66
magnetisable ink 36
magnetography 43
mailbox 47
mailboxing 47
mail-merging 46
main storage 25, 85, 86, 109
mainframe computer 28, 29, 30, 77, 78, 88, 89
maintenance 124
   manual 109, 110
   organisation 130
   programmer 130
malicious events 135
malicious damage 135
management
   control 136
   information 1, 87
   information system 3, 12, 90, 118, 132
manager 96
   (operations) 124, 127
   (systems and operations) 124
   (systems/programmer) 125
manual 109
manual standards 151
manual system 18
manuals 151
marker 57
marketing information 2
marketing model 88
mass storage device 68
master file 52, 54, 67, 85, 117, 129
matrix printer 40, 42
mature EDP department 132
mature user 132
Mb – *see* megabytes
mechanised system 19
media 119
   conversion 85
megabytes 65
memory dumping 85
Mercury 74
merge program 104
merging 85
message
   identification 118
   parity check 119
   transmission control 119
methods procedural standards 150
MFLOPS 28
MICR – *see* magnetic ink character recognition

Micro Focus Source Writer   92
microcomputer   3, 28, 29, 30, 47, 65, 73, 76, 77,
                                         78, 79, 89, 90
    graphics   88
    network   84
microfiche   40
microfilm   40, 69
    printer   69
    reader   69
    reader/printer   69
    reference   69
Microsoft Excel   89
micro-mainframe linkage   77, 89
micro-Winchester disk   67
middle management   5
millions of instructions per second   28
minicomputer   29, 30, 34, 40, 69, 75, 76, 77, 78
MIPS – *see* millions of instructions per second
MIS – *see* management information system
mixed entry table   103
mnemonic coding   91
mobile data communications   80
mobile data systems   80
mobile radio technology   80
mobile terminals   80
model   87, 88, 90
modem   47, 73, 74, 75, 78, 81
modifying   107
modular programming   109
modulator   74
module   109
modulus   115
modulus 11   115, 116
monitoring
    operations   120
    peripherals   83
motor vehicle industry   88
Multi Plan   89
multifunction colour matrix printer   42
multiplexing device   75
multiplexor   73, 75, 76
multiprogramming   83, 84
multi-user
    approach   78
    system   65, 78, 79
mutual support   141
mux – *see* multiplexor   75, 78

nanoseconds   28
National Computing Centre   45, 97, 146
NCC – *see* National Computing Centre   45
NCube/10   29
need for standards   148
need (information requirements)   10
network   30, 69, 78, 89, 120
    analysis   87
    architecture   79
    database   61
    management   80
networking   73, 78
node   80
noise   9

non-impact printer   40, 41, 42, 43, 44, 45
non-procedural language   92
notice of deregistration   145
notice of enforcement   145
notice prohibiting transfer of data   145

OA – *see* office automation   45, 47, 48
object-oriented development   92
Object-Pascal   92
OCR – *see also* optical character recognition
    documents   36
    fonts   34
    readers   34
OCR-A   34
OCR-B   34
office automation   45, 132
    systems   47
official control   139
off-line   19, 34
    data input   30
    devices   104
    mode   36
Olivetti   69
OLRT – *see* on-line real-time
OMR – *see* optical mark reading
one per desk   30
on-demand reports   6
on-line
    computer device   34
    data input   30
    enquiry system   67
    input   34
    mode   118
    processing control   118
    processing mode   34
    real-time   21
    system   56, 142
OPD – *see* one per desk
open subroutine   107
operand   105
operating
    instructions   110
    manual   109, 152
    system   83, 84
operation   105
operational information   5, 12
operational management   5
operational staff   124
operations   104, 136
    centre   127
    controls librarian   137
    log   127
    manager   104, 128
    manual   151
    planning   127
    staff   127
    work schedule   129
operator   30, 138
    intervention   116
    notes   110
optical character recognition   30, 34, 44, 105, 113, 114
optical disk   69, 70

filing system 69
storage 69
optical mark
reading 30, 34, 36
recognition 34
optical media 39, 66
optical printer 43
optical readers 36
optical storage 68
Oracle 47
order processing 97
system 100
organisation 111–22, 123–34, 135–46, 147–54
organisation and control iv
organisation controls 136, 137
organisational communication problems 9
organisational implications of the Data
Protection Act 145
organisational levels 9
organisation-wide network 80
origination 14
OS – *see* operating system
outline flowchart 100
output 14, 39, 77, 95, 111
controls 118
file 52
media 44, 105
methods 39, 44
monitoring 124
on-line 36
unit 25, 27
overall size 9
overflow 59, 60, 85
overhead projector transparencies 89
overtime payment 100

PABX – *see* private automatic branch exchanges
package 104
packet switching 76, 79
exchange 76
system 65, 77
packets of data 76, 77
packing density 59, 60
Padlock 143
page 40
page printer 40, 43, 46
paging 39
paper tape 32, 33, 34, 39, 40, 57, 113, 116
punch 34
reader 34
parallel
computing 29
processing 29
system 28
parallelism 28
parity
bit 18, 30, 74, 116
channel 30
part-time operator 121
passenger reservations 48
password 118, 119, 120, 142
system 118

PAYE 86
payroll 87
file 100
PC – *see also* personal computer
adaptor card 70
compatibility 131
network 80
system 120
PDL – *see* machine-independent page description
language 46
PDL – *see* program definition language 109
people factor 122
performance
monitoring 132
reviews 136
peripheral
activity 100
control 84
instructions 106
loading 129
peripherals 27, 83
permanent transmission link 76
personal computers 14, 29, 65, 69, 78, 121, 132, 141
control 120
personal data 144, 145
personnel
information 2
recruitment 137
selection 137
PERT 87
petal printer 42
pharmaceutical firms 81
Phillips 68
photocopying down the telephone 47
physical dangers 140
physical security 124, 129, 140, 142, 144
physical transmission 114
picoseconds 28
pie charts 88
plastic
badges 34
cards 34
player 66
plotter 68
PL/1 92
pocket telex 80
point of sale 30, 32, 33, 34, 78
point to point network 79
polling 76
port 75
portable computer 29, 74
portable fax 47
PoS – *see* point of sale
post office 68
post-implementation analyses 136
preparation 14
Prestel 81
pre-input control 111
printer 26, 42, 44, 88, 89
character, line, page 40
printing 39, 40
printout 85, 89

materials	45
speed	69
privacy	144
private automatic branch exchanges	73
private circuits	74
private lines	73
private sector	1, 87
private telephone line	76
probabilistic system	4
procedure standards	140
procedures	95
processed data	39
processing	1, 14, 111
processing control	111, 116, 135, 136
processing mode	
batch, interactive, on-line, real-time	20, 22
interactive	22
on-line	34
on-line, real-time	21
processing	
security	116
speed	78
processor	14, 32
production control	2, 87
production staff	122
profit forecasting	90
program	27, 85
bar	15
coding sheets	100
definition language	109
development	86, 104, 130
documentation	109
error	86
flowchart	95, 100, 103, 104
function	100
generator	92
instructions	106
maintenance	110
segment	107
specification	104, 105, 130
programmable read only memory	28
programmer	96, 103, 104, 109, 125, 129, 130, 131
programmer/analyst	104
programming	95, 100, 103, 104, 150
aids	86
language 1	92
languages	86, 90, 105, 130
manager	128
manual	109, 110
principles	105
standards	150
team	128
techniques	107
unit	125
project	125
committee	139
leader	130
teams	125
projections	90
PROM – *see* programmable read only memory	
protocol	76
conversion	78

PSE – *see* packet switching exchange	
pseudocode	109
pseudo-mechanical device	15
Psion	30
PSS – *see* packet switching system	
PSTN – *see* Public Switched Telephone Network	
public key encryption	143
public lines	73
public sector	1, 87
Public Switched Telephone Network	74
public telephone line	76
pulse	17
punched card	16, 20, 30, 32, 34, 40, 57, 84, 98, 100
reader	116
system	15, 16, 113
punched data	34
purchasing information	2
pure binary	18
purging	137
quiet mode	45
radar transmissions	68
radio	73
link	80, 81
telephones	80
radio-teletext	80
RAM – *see* random access memory	
random checks	142
random file processing	56
random organisation	55
randomly organised data	58
random access memory	28, 65
range limits	115
Rank Xerox Virtual Micro	79
rapid retrieval	69
rapid-access filing system	69
rate of growth	59
rate of transfer	71
read only memory	28, 65, 70
reader	40
reading heads	57
read/write head	58, 66
real-time	60, 67
applications	92
mode	22
on-line system	67
system	118
receipting machines	33
recognised standards bodies	146
record	51, 54, 56
location	61
size	61
recording track	66
reel-to-reel tapes	66
reference file	52, 129
register	17
regular reports	6
relational database	61
remote job entry	78
remote terminals	21, 34, 47, 77
removable disk cartridges	67

repertoire 40
repetition 107
reports 12
reproducer 16
Research Machines Nimbus 88
resolution 41
resources, sharing 78
response-time 21
restart check 117
restricted access 140
restrictive environment 8
retransmission 76
retrieval system 61
retrieval workstation 69
Reuters News Agency 148
ribbon 41
ring network 79
role of analyst/programmer 130
role of programmer/analyst 130
ROM – *see* read only memory
row 89
rule number 100
rules 102
rules for flowcharting 96

sabotage 135
sales ledger file 98
satellite 68, 142
   communications 80
   linkages 73
   transmissions 68, 79
scanner 69
scrolling 39
SECCONS – *see* structured evaluation technique
secondary storage 26
secure storage facilities 129
security 66, 70, 129
   education programs 144
   measures 143
   of files 139
   safeguards 144
seek area 58
selection 107
selective-sequential file processing 56
semiconductor disk storage devices 70
senior operator 129
senior programmer 130
senior systems analyst 130
sensitive paper 41
sensitivity analysis 89
sequence 107
   checks 115, 116
sequential file 59
   processing 55
sequential organisation 54, 55, 60
sequentially organised data 58
serial access devices 56
serial file processing 55
serial organisation 54, 55, 59, 60
serial printer 41
serially organised data 58
service program 85

sets of instructions 95
sharing resources 78, 80
shift instructions 106
shift leader 129
shift work 127
   schedules 127
short term information 8
shredding 140
Siemans 2300 43
simplex 73
simulation model 88
simulator 86
simultaneity 84
simultaneous amendment data loss 119
simultaneous peripheral operations on-line 84
Sinclair Research 30
single processor 28
single user system 130
Smalltalk 92
software iv, 83–94, 104
   categories 83
   hierarchy 90
   house 104, 131
   monitoring 83
   package 46, 90
   programmer 104, 130
solid ink printer 41
solid state memory device 70
solid stage storage 69, 70
son tape 67
sonar transmissions 68
Sony 68
Sony OA-P5108 43
sort
   program 104
   routine 85
sorted order 99
sorter 16
sorting 85
sorting/merging 85
sort/merge program 104
source
   data 77
   documents 14, 20, 30
speaker
   dependent 37
   independent 37
special media 66
special storage category 69
specialist computer activities 77
speech
   output 43, 44
   recognition 37
spindle 58
spooling 84
spreadsheets 87, 89, 90, 104
sprinklers 140
stable environment 8
staff duties 126
standalone 29
standard letters 46
standard operating routines 106

standard performance 146
standard procedure 146
standard symbols 97
standards 14, 139, 146, 150
  for management 148
  for procedures 149
standby
  facilities 140
  system 141
standing data 54
stand-alone computers 77
star network 79
start bit 74
start routine 85
static file 59
steering committee 139
stick 16
stockbroker 87
stop and start routines 85
stop bit 74
stop routine 85
storage 14, 51
  media 54, 60, 65–72
  media characteristics 70
  mode 60
  space 16
  system 61
  unit 71
  /access mode 105
store address 27
store-and-forward computer 77
strategic information 5, 12
strategic management 5
streamer tape 66
strips 40
structure 107
structured chart 107
structured evaluation technique 143
structured programming 100, 103, 107, 109
subroutine 86, 107, 116
suite 83
super PC 67
supercomputer 28, 29, 30
supermicro 65
supermini 30
supertelex 46
supervisor program 84, 119
supervisory management 5
supervisor's console 33
supervisor's terminal 33
supportive device 15
surface 58, 66
suspense files 116, 117
switch 106
switch-on-access 47
symbol 95, 97
symbolic form 86
sync bytes 74
synchronous transmission 74
syntax 104
system 3
  changeover 129

charging 132
controls 135
development 103
flowchart 95, 99
hardware 83
operations 150
summary 152
testing 139
systems
  analysis 103, 128, 150
  analysis programming 137
  analyst 96, 103, 104, 125, 128, 129, 130
  and program development 128
  and programming manager 128
  design unit 125
  development 124
  development controls 135, 138
  development unit 125
  flowchart 97
  manager 128
  operation standards 150
tabulator 16
tactical information 5, 12
tactical planning 126
take-down instruction 110
take-up reel 66
tape 91, 119
  header label 56
  leader 56
  marker 56, 57
  records 67
  verifier 30
tapes 67, 140
task scheduling 124
tasks of OS 83
team, or group interaction 9
technical design model 88
Telecom Gold 81
telephone
  handset 74
  lines 73
  network 73
  system 74
  traffic 73
teleprocessing 77
teletex 46, 47, 73
teletype 34
telex 46
  traffic 73
tele-conferencing 132
template 92, 95
terminal input 114
terminals 30, 34, 47, 77
terminal: remote 34
The PC Market in the UK (*Wharton
  Information Services*) 45
theft 139
three generation method 140
time before failure 68
toner 43
top down programming 108

top management   5
topology   79
top-security installation   141
Toshiba T311   29
tracks   57, 58, 60
traffic flow   88
trailer label   57
training   128
    users   139
transaction file   52, 67, 129
transcribing data   112
transcription   112
    file   113
transfer file   52
transfer instructions   106
transmission   112
    device   81
    lines   73, 75, 76
    links   34
    link, permanent   76
    modes   73
    of organisational data   73
    technologies   74
transmitting data   73
transportable computer   29
transposition error   112
travel agents   47
trees   61
Trojan code   120
turnaround documents   36

UK treasury   88
ultrafiche   40
unauthorised access   119, 141, 142
unconditional branch   106
Unidex   81
unique address   105
unit record system   15, 16
United Nations Economic Commission for
    Europe   146
UN/ECE – *see* United Nations Economic
    Commission for Europe
user   44, 131
user groups   148
user manual   151
uses of spreadsheet   89
utility software   85

validation   114
    program   114
validity check   85, 115
value added and data network services   81
value of information   12
VANS – *see* value added and data network services
variable length block   58, 60
variable length record   54
Vax   30
VCR – *see* video cassette recorder
VDU – *see* visual display unit
verification   30, 98, 114
verifier   18, 32

verifying mode   113
vertical recording   66
video cassette recorder   66
video data
    cartridge   66
    cassette tape   66
video transmission   73
videotex   46, 47, 61
viewdata   30, 47, 48, 81
viewer   40
virtual storage   84
virus   120, 135
visible record computer   15, 22
Visicalc   89
Vistec XSELL   47
visual display units   32, 34, 39, 40, 45, 89, 114
visual early warning system   88
voice
    input   30, 37
    output   43, 44
    response   39
    services   81
voice-data   74
volatile file   59
volatility   60
Von Neuman architecture   28
VRC – *see* visible record computer

wages calculation   90
WAN – *see* wide area network
wand   34
warehouse control   87
warehouse file   98
warehouse stock item   103
what if?   89
wide area network   73, 79, 80, 120, 132
Winchester disks   67
wire matrix   42
word   17
word-processing   29, 45, 46, 47, 87, 89
word-processor   46, 73, 131
work file   52
work flow   129
worker productivity   132
working store address   27
workload   124
worksheet   89
workstation   30, 32, 33, 69, 87, 89, 131
WORM – *see* write once read many
WP – *see* word-processing
write   66
write head   66
write once read many   66, 68, 69
write once read mostly   69
wysiwyg   46

Xerox 4020   41
Xerox 7010   47

yes/no status   100

zeroise instructions   106